14,95

Writing:
The Nature, Development, and
Teaching of Written Communication

Volume 1
Variation in Writing:
Functional and
Linguistic-Cultural Differences

Writing:
The Nature, Development, and Teaching of Written Communication

Volume 1
Variation in Writing:
Functional and Linguistic-Cultural Differences

Edited by
MARCIA FARR WHITEMAN
National Institute of Education

LEA LAWRENCE ERLBAUM ASSOCIATES, PUBLISHERS
1981   Hillsdale, New Jersey

Lawrence Erlbaum Associates, Inc., Publishers
365 Broadway
Hillsdale, New Jersey 07642

Library of Congress Cataloging in Publication Data

Main entry under title:

Writing : the nature, development, and teaching of
    written communication.

    Bibliography: p.
    Includes index.
    Contents: v. 1. Variation in writing, functional and
linguistic-cultural differences / edited by M.F. Whiteman. -- v. 2. Writing, process, development, and communication / edited by C.H. Frederiksen, J.F. Dominic.
    1. Writing. 2. Communication. 3. Language and
languages--Variation. 4. Literacy. 5. Rhetoric.
I. Whiteman, Marcia Farr. II. Frederiksen, Carl H.
III. Dominic, Joseph F.
P211.W72   001.54'3   81-15310

ISBN 0-89859-101-5 (v. 1)   AACR2
ISBN 0-89859-158-9 (v. 2)

Contents

Preface

The theme of these two volumes, broadly defined, might best be phrased as two questions: How can we learn more about writing? and How can we learn more about the interaction between teaching to write and learning to write?

The papers in these two volumes were originally prepared in draft form for the National Institute of Education's first Conference on Writing in June, 1977. This conference was held in collaboration with SWRL Education Research and Development Laboratory in Los Alamitos, California. The primary intent in conceptualizing and implementing this conference was to encourage multidisciplinary inquiry into writing. The intent was based on the belief that only a broadly based research effort would ultimately result in improving the learning and teaching of writing. The papers consequently represent a variety of views toward writing research and instruction; these views come from such disciplines as anthropology, linguistics (particularly sociolinguistics and psycholinguistics), psychology (particularly cognitive, developmental and educational psychology), English education, English literature and rhetoric.

We believe that to this date these volumes are unique in such a breadth of viewpoints, and hope that they will be useful in promoting multidisciplinary work on writing. The ultimate goal of such work is to better inform both educators and policy makers about the nature of writing and its importance in our society. Thus the intended audiences for these two volumes are researchers, teachers (and those who are both researchers and teachers), as well as both local and national policy makers, and others interested in writing.

Each of these two volumes focuses on different aspects of writing. Using a metaphor from photography, it is as though writing is viewed through a wide angle lens in volume one, and through a telescopic lens in volume two. Volume one explores writing in its many social and cultural variations: the papers in part one show different genres of writing serving various purposes in diverse contexts. The papers in part two explore the effects of oral language differences on the learning and teaching of writing. Writing, then, is seen in volume one in its many forms rather than in its more universal aspects.

Volume two, in contrast, centers on the more universal aspects of writing as an activity of an individual. The papers investigate writing as a cognitive, linguistic and communicative process, and discuss the ways in which such processes develop, and can be nurtured.

We would like to acknowledge several persons who helped make the publication of these two volumes a reality. While editorial responsibility for the individual volumes was divided among us, Marcia Farr Whiteman took overall responsibility for bringing to completion the publication of both volumes. Thomas Sticht, Lawrence Frase and Susan Chipman contributed to the initial planning and conceptualization of the conference. The SWRL staff provided an ideal environment for the exchange of ideas and invaluable support in the preparation of draft materials for the conference. Beatrice Cooper and Diana Thomas typed manuscript revisions under difficult pressures, and Patrick Malizio worked quickly and thoroughly to produce the subject index for each volume. Finally, Renaldo Macías gave timely advice and essential administrative support to the project. We are grateful to all of these individuals.

Marcia Farr Whiteman
National Institute of Education

Carl H. Frederiksen
McGill University
Joseph F. Dominic
National Institute of Education

Introduction

Marcia Farr Whiteman
National Institute of Education

William S. Hall
Center for the Study of Reading

One does not need to look very far for evidence of a national concern about the quality of writing in the United States today. This concern seems to be twofold: first, people are concerned that students are not learning to write, and second, they are concerned that writing as used outside of school (e.g., in public documents, at the workplace, in advertising, etc.) often is incomprehensible or misleading. Education journals and the mass media are full of complaints about illiteracy in general and "the writing problem" in particular. The focus of the concern is on our schools, because this is where students are presumably not learning to write, so that in their later roles as workers they are apparently unable to express necessary information clearly in written form.

The National Institute of Education has been responding to this problem by developing a research agenda with the ultimate goal of improving the learning and teaching of writing in this country. Writing has been selected as a major program area because of the national concern and as an outgrowth of NIE's equity concerns. The students for whom educational achievement in general and writing achievement in particular has been most elusive in this country are primarily poor, speakers of non-mainstream dialects, and members of minority groups—that is, those who are least powerful and participate least in our society. Writing can be an important tool for increasing the educational achievement of such people since writing is a central aspect of real learning, or education in its truest sense.

When the furor "functional illiteracy" is closely examined, it becomes apparent that almost the entire focus is on reading rather than writing (e.g., functional literacy tests don't test writing, even though they often test math and consumer skills). We lose sight of the lack of writing abilities as a central part of the "illiteracy problem." Some would say that it is more important to teach reading first, that it is of higher priority for surviving and succeeding in a technological society. Some would even argue that writing is becoming unnecessary because of advances in technology, but current research on industrial literacy is indicating that this is not so. The importance of reading abilities is not questioned here; what is questioned is the assumption that improvements in reading will be enough to help increase the educational achievement and societal participation of non-mainstream groups.

When people read and listen, they take in and process information. When they write, they must analyze and synthesize information (Graves, 1978). In this way, writing is an important tool of real learning—that which includes critical thinking and discovery of what we know and believe. It can be argued that skilled reading also uses critical thinking, that it is not an entirely passive process. This is true, but because writing well *requires* such critical thinking, it contributes not only to increased learning, but to increased critical reading skills as well. If we only taught minimal reading skills, we would be training a society of "receivers" rather than "senders." When carried to an extreme, this would result in a society of people who could read minimally, and thus follow orders, rather than one in which people could also write, and thus express opinions, desires and information which could influence the course of a democracy.

PART ONE: SOCIO-CULTURAL FUNCTIONS
OF WRITING

A concern for writing in society unites all the chapters in this volume. The chapters in the first part work toward defining what writing is in various socio-cultural contexts - writing, in fact, is not defined as a singular entity, but rather as a plurality. There are different *kinds* of writing which serve different functions for different groups of people at different times. In a sense, then, writing is viewed here as though through a wide angle lens—different kinds of writing are defined in and by varying contexts. Volume two in this series, in contrast, views writing as though through a telescopic lens: writing is examined as an activity of an individual, and attention is given to the development within the individual of the ability to perform this activity.

The notion of a plurality of literacies is developed in several chapters in this volume. Szwed, Heath and Scribner and Cole all tie the variety in kinds of writing to the social organization of a culture, and see different types of writing as reflecting different social practices. Szwed's starting point is the social meaning of literacy. He introduces the term "plurality of literacies", and sees five elements which combine to create this plurality: the text itself, the social context in which writing occurs, the participants (the writer and intended readers), the function the writing serves, and the motivation for the writing.

Swzed argues against absolutes in questions of literacy, both in terms of single standards and in terms of narrow school-based definitions of reading and writing. Both Szwed and Heath challenge the notion of a single standard of literacy. Heath points out that the notion of correctness in the use of English arose only in the mid to late 19th century among the upwardly mobile middle classes. Such normative judgements about standards are not intrinsic to the linguistic code, but to the language users, whose rising class consciousness was reflected in language attitudes. For Szwed, as well as for others in this volume, definitions of and standards for writing should not follow class boundaries. For the study of writing, he advocates ethnography as the only valid method, focusing as it does on the real life activities of ordinary people.

Heath also refers to a plurality of literacies by differentiating kinds of writing in society. Using data from contemporary ethnographic research and data from social history, she begins a description of writing in different communities of the United States across history: an "ethnohistory of writing." Underlying the variety of kinds of writing across communities and through history are the different functions of writing, the varying "goals of community members for learning, maintaining and improving their writing." She sees an educational problem in the lack of fit between the functions of writing outside of school and the in-school norms and methods of writing instruction. Finally, she provides a careful example of how ethnographic research has been used to define real functions of writing outside of school and how the results of this research were used to develop an effective program of writing instruction for adolescents.

Scribner and Cole reinforce the notion of a plurality of literacies by reporting a program of research completed among the Vai people of West Africa. The Vai, a "non-literate" traditional people in Liberia, invented their own form of writing approximately 135 years ago. Ethnographic studies in this research program show the importance of function in differentiating kinds of writing, including both genre (e.g., letters, personal journals, farm and trade records) and script (two alphabetic scripts, Roman and Arabic, co-exist with the indigenous Vai script). Psychological studies in this research program go further: they link literacy activities on the part of individuals with specific intellectual skills. Whereas the results of this research demonstrate that "literacy without schooling is associated with improved performance on certain cognitive tasks," it is associated in very specific ways. A key word here is specific; apparently specific kinds of reading and writing promote specific language processing and cognitive skills, but do not necessarily promote improved *general* mental abilities.

These results seem to conflict with the concept of writing as an important tool of learning. We have made the argument above that writing well requires analysis and synthesis of information, i.e., critical thinking, and as such promotes learning. What Scribner and Cole's work with the Vai seems to indicate, on the other hand, is that specific kinds of writing promote specific kinds of cognitive skills, but do not seem to promote other kinds of cognitive skills. On closer inspection, these two views about the effect of writing on cognition don't seem as contradictory. In both cases the *function* of the kind of writing referred to is crucial.

If it is the function of a piece of writing to question an idea or explore an issue, it is reasonable to assume that this kind of writing would promote the kind of cognitive activity required for critical questioning. If, on the other hand, the writing of a religious passage functions to commit the passage to memory, then it is reasonable to assume that such writing would promote cognitive capacities for memory. It may be the case, then, that the kinds of writing used in our society promote the kinds of cognitive skills needed to survive and succeed in our society. This is, at least, a question for further study.

The Cook-Gumperz and Gumperz chapter also supports the plurality of literacies concept. The first part of their chapter provides an historical framework for the development of different kinds of literacy and discusses "preliterate" and literate cultures. While cautioning against too simplistic an application of historical development to individual development, they draw some interesting parallels between the development of literacy historically and the transition to literacy which every child who learns to read and write experiences. On this latter point they stress that the notion of cultural and linguistic "mismatches" between home and school contexts is not a complete explanation for the educational difficulties experienced by many linguistic minority students. They argue that the notion of a mismatch must go beyond differences between standard and nonstandard grammar and phonology; that is, nonstandard grammar and phonology alone cannot explain the language learning problems of linguistic minorities. Rather, these ethnic differences must be understood within a broader context of historical and cultural processes in the transition to literacy. Specifically, they see ethnic distinctions as interacting with "the more basic changes in social goals and motives which accompany the transition from oral to written culture everywhere." They conclude that all children learning to read and write must learn new communicative strategies, and that this may be more difficult for those children whose home culture primarily transmits knowledge orally than for those children whose home culture traditionally transmits knowledge in written form.

All four of the chapters discussed so far discuss the kinds and functions of writing in society from a social science, and primarily ethnographic, perspective. The other three chapters in the first part of this volume (Corbett, Hendrix and Traugott) also discuss the nature of writing in society, but from different perspectives. The Corbett and Hendrix chapters focus more on policy issues than on research, discussing the social and (particularly Hendrix) political meaning of writing. The Traugott chapter focuses on fiction and also illuminates the social and political meaning of writing.

Corbett presents convincing evidence of a considerable demand and market for writing in our own society. His examples from business and industry clearly attest to a great amount and a remarkable variety of writing, rather than to a decreasing use of it in an electronic age. Specifically, he cites examples from occupational contexts and from a flourishing publishing industry. All this evidence, he feels, justifies the teaching of writing in schools. The problem, however, is that schools generally do not teach the *kind* of writing that is needed and used outside of school. He agrees strongly that although there is considerable value in reading and writing about literary texts, we must also teach students how to generate the kinds of writing that are in reality in much demand in our society.

Hendrix, like Corbett, views writing in the context of our present-day society. His focus is on writing improvement efforts within postsecondary education, and he explores problems in these improvement efforts by discussing six questions: Whose writing needs improvement? Who is responsible for improving writing? What does testing have to do with writing improvement? What kind of writing should be taught? Writing for what purpose? and, finally, What is good writing? Several of these questions are particularly difficult ones, and Hendrix argues that they cannot be answered if writing is viewed in a vacuum, outside of its social context. Furthermore, answers to them will involve educational policy as much as research and pedagogy.

Hendrix states that "writing ability is unevenly distributed in our society along class lines," and sees writing improvement efforts as efforts toward democratization and equal educational opportunity. However, for improvements to be meaningful, he argues that the personal and social purposes of writing must be taken into account. He, like Corbett, and Heath, urge that writing instruction be tied to real uses of writing outside of school, as well as to student motivations and needs. That is, students must have something meaningful to say, for their own purposes, in order to learn to write well. In this sense, learning to write is closely linked to personal growth and to the traditional goals of a liberal education. While allowing for the usefulness of the more mechanical approaches to writing instruction (e.g., autotutorial and computer based approaches) Hendrix cautions that ultimately writing cannot be divorced from personal, social or political meaning, and that the best improvement efforts will be those which stress "human validity" as well as correctness and clarity.

Traugott's chapter differs from other chapters in this section in that it does not discuss the many kinds of writing in a broad social context, but focuses instead on one kind of writing (fictional narrative) and the way in which social and ethnic language varieties are reflected in that genre. While Traugott uses methods of literary analysis, she also relies on a careful linguistic description of ethnic dialects. She discusses the use of these dialects in fiction: for "color," for comic effect (which is sometimes sympathetic and sometimes hostile), for building character (e.g., *Huck Finn*), and to represent social, ethnic and cultural differences. This latter use of dialects in fiction varies according to whether or not the author is a member of the cultural group being depicted. For outside-the-group writers (whom Traugott refers to as "Anglo" writers, like Joel Chandler Harris), the purpose may be simply to represent cultural differences. For "non-Anglo" writers, however, Traugott believes that "the function of the literary work may often itself be political and social," that is, to create a new value system about the language variety used. Like Hendrix, then, Traugott considers the political context an essential part of the meaning of a piece of writing.

PART TWO: LANGUAGE DIFFERENCES AND WRITING

The chapters in the second part of this volume focus on the teaching of writing to persons who do not come from standard-English speaking backgrounds— speakers of Black English Vernacular, Spanish-English bilinguals, and the deaf. They examine the problems inherent in teaching writing in this situation, and make a number of specific and practical suggestions.

A theme common to all these chapters is the role of the child's first language in the process of learning to write standard English. All the authors accept as a goal for the student competence in writing standard English (or a variety of standard English, for example, Black Standard English, which has SE grammar but Black rhetorical style and certain vocabulary items from Black culture). The focus in these chapters, however, is on the role that the child's first language (whether it is a nonstandard dialect or another language entirely) plays in attaining this competence. On the one hand, the fact that this language is different from standard English is a source of difficulty. On the other hand, all the authors share the view that the teacher must understand and respect the child's dialect or language, recognizing it as a rule-governed linguistic system in its own right, which the child must maintain for communication within his/her own community.

The authors in this volume agree that it is necessary for teachers of composition to learn about the nature of language variation—both to recognize the dialects of their students as rule-governed linguistic systems in their own right, and to acquire specific and detailed knowledge about these dialects. The teachers are also to pass this information on to their students to enable them to cope—in terms of both attitudes and knowledge of grammar—with the way that their dialect or language differs from standard English. The chapters themselves also include concrete examples of specific ways in which nonstandard dialects differ from Standard English, and the types of effects that this can have on the students' writing.

An interesting parallel can be drawn (although it is not made explicitly in these articles) between the situation of deaf children and ASL and minority children who are speakers of non-standard dialects of English. In the past it was the practice of educators to forbid any use of sign language in schools for the deaf. This policy was based on the idea that sign language would interfere with the child's acquisition of English, being very different from English in structure; it was perhaps also based on the idea that the child has only "so much room" for linguistic development, so that any use of or progress in sign language would be to the detriment of competence in English. As it turns out, schools permitting signing, and using some form of sign language in the classroom, produce more successful students who perform better in written English as well as in other areas.

In the first part of her paper, Reed focuses on the responsibility of the teacher to learn to appreciate, and gain concrete knowledge about, the nonstandard dialects spoken by his/her students. Such knowledge is a crucial component of the teacher's ability to help these students learn to write standard English. Two basic points made are first, that nonstandard dialects are in fact rule-governed linguistic systems in their own right, and not just a conglomeration of errors; and second, that it is possible to teach competence in a second dialect, when the right methodology and attitudes (i.e., those of second-language teaching) are adopted.

In the second half of her paper, Reed gives concrete examples to illustrate the basic ways in which nonstandard dialects can interfere with a student's writing competence in standard English. Not all errors in writing by a student from a nonstandard dialect background are simply the result of using a nonstandard form or construction instead of the standard one. The influence of the nonstandard dialect can also be seen in hypercorrections. These are cases where the student overgeneralizes a strategy intended to produce standard forms—for example, in trying to avoid the invarient *be* of Vernacular Black English, a student might delete a *be* that was actually a correct standard usage. The attempt to avoid stigmatized forms can also produce a general "linguistic insecurity" in those areas where the standard and nonstandard dialects differ. It is essential that the teacher be aware of the specific linguistic structures involved, in order to be able to help students deal with these problems.

Whiteman, like Reed, discusses the nature of dialect influence on student writing. She presents some interesting data on an analysis of nonstandard speech patterns in writing. By comparing the speech and writing of two different nonstandard dialect groups (Vernacular Black English speakers and nonstandard Southern White English speakers), she was able to explore whether or not nonstandard patterns in student writing are solely the result of influence from the speech patterns of the writer. She found that, in fact, that is not their only source. Using compositions from the National Assessment of Educational Progress, as well as other data, she found that inflectional suffixes (e.g., -s suffixes and a certain kind of -ed suffix) are the most frequent nonstandard grammatical patterns found in student writing. Interestingly enough, however, these suffixes are omitted not only in the writing of those who frequently omit them in speech (e.g., Vernacular Black English speakers), but also (although less frequently) in the writing of those who *don't* omit them regularly in speech, a clear indication that nonstandard patterns in writing are not always caused by influence from speech. Based on a quantitative sociolinguistic analysis of considerable data, she concludes that dialect influence clearly does affect the grammar in student writing, but that acquisitional factors as well cause the errors we often assume are reflections of the writer's speech.

Valadez starts by pointing out the variety of situations that can fall under the label "bilingualism." First of all, among persons who know two languages, there are various degrees and types of competence in each language. For example, there are children fluent in English who can understand but not speak Spanish, and there are children whose parents are fluent in Spanish, and can understand and not speak English; both can be called "bilingual". In addition, there is extensive regional and social variation in the Spanish and in the English spoken by U.S. Spanish-speaking bilinguals. Any bilingual education program must take such variation into account.

As for writing, Valadez suggests that the student's motivation to write must be firmly established before any teaching to improve writing in terms of rules of rhetoric or standard usage can be undertaken. This means that the teacher must respect the child's use of language, whether it is a standard dialect or not. Valadez also makes the point that learning to write carries with it a growing sense of empowerment and control over one's environment, citing Freire's work in this regard. She suggests that this growing sense of power should be nurtured carefully by teachers, and that too much critical focus on mechanics and grammar at early stages of writing development could easily overwhelm a child's tentative new sense of power.

Deaf children, according to Charrow, acquire English under conditions that are in some ways similar to, and in some ways worse than, those under which most people acquire a second language: they get a relatively late start (not until they have entered school, when normal children have already acquired substantial competence in their first language), and learn, not through normal exposure to the language and interaction, but by means of pattern practice, vocabulary lessons, and explicit rules.

Some deaf children, especially those of deaf parents, have the benefit of a first language, American Sign Language (ASL). Although ASL has a structure radically different from that of English, and thus may result in some interference where the two languages differ, children who learn ASL in infancy and are allowed to use some form of sign language in school do much better academically (including in written English) than students without this background.

Evidence is presented that there is some consistency in the errors made by the deaf in learning English, suggesting that these "errors" are systematic effects of what might be called "deaf English." While these errors have often been viewed as interference from ASL, they apparently also appear in the English of deaf persons who do not know ASL, and thus may be attributable to certain aspects of English structure—for example, the fact that many grammatically important function words *(to, in)* and suffixes (*-ed*) are not easily lip-read.

Finally, Charrow suggests that reading comprehension tests measure the language competence of the deaf only indirectly, and that writing tests will provide a more accurate picture both of their level of proficiency, and of their special problems and difficulties with English.

The last two chapters in part two (Lewis, and Hoover and Politzer) focus more on teaching than on research. Lewis details a particular instructional method, and Hoover and Politzer discuss problems of assessment.

Lewis describes the Nairobi method, a program of writing instruction for students who come from nonstandard English backgrounds and who usually have had unsuccessful experiences with school in the past. This program has been successfully implemented at Nairobi Community College in Palo Alto, California, and other places as well.

The first steps in the program are to acquaint the students with examples of written and oral communication styles from recognized Black writers and orators, and to provide them with information on the nature of language variation and the history of Vernacular Black English. These steps are aimed at giving the students an appreciation for their language, awareness of the diversity within their own linguistic and cultural background, and encouragement that they themselves can write.

The program makes much use of group work, for example in selecting topics and reviewing drafts. The first writing project is autobiographical, but the bulk of the writing work is focused on research papers. Two are written in the course of the class; the first with more substantial help and direction from the teacher, especially in providing research material, and the second more on the student's own—although group review of outlines and rough drafts are a part of both.

The course also includes instruction in both the mechanics of writing, and in points of contrast between VBE and SE grammar.

Hoover and Politzer argue for viewing writing primarily as an act of communication, avoiding two extremes: the 'anything goes' approach or unconditional acceptance of the vernacular on the one hand, and the insistence of a "superstandard" English with academic style at the expense of communicative effectiveness on the other. They give examples of how standardized composition tests tend to place much weight on stylistic factors that have more to do with cultural preferences than effective communication. For example, the accepted academic writing style puts tight restrictions on the types of metaphors and figures of speech allowed, avoiding both cliches and proverbs at one end of the scale and extreme novelty or colorfulness of metaphor at the other. Black rhetorical style, on the other hand, makes use of both proverbs and unconventional metaphors. Choices of figurative language made in line with Black rhetorical style will be counted as incorrect on standardized tests. Parallel examples are given for other aspects of style.

Hoover and Politzer conclude that at the present time, composition tests constitute an additional and arbitrary obstacle to the social mobility of minority students, and should not be used until the mechanics of writing is taught more effectively in lower grades, and until objective and unbiased scoring procedures can be achieved which allow for variety in rhetorical styles. They suggest that greater emphasis be placed on reading and writing in lower schools, and that a simple standard, rather than "superstandard" English, be used as a guideline for judging composition.

In sum, all of the chapters in this volume share an emphasis on variation. The chapters in the first part of the book explore variation in the kinds and functions of writing in social, cultural and political contexts. The chapters in the second part of the book explore variation in writing which results from the linguistic and cultural identities of different groups of writers. Variation is seen as an essential aspect in the study of writing, equally as important as studying the more universal aspects of the writing act. Both of these emphases are important; we need both to understand writing processes and their development within the individual, and we need to understand writing in its variety in society. Ultimately, combined knowledge from these two emphases can be used to improve the learning and teaching of writing in the United States and elsewhere.

Part I   SOCIO-CULTURAL FUNCTIONS OF WRITING

1 The Ethnography of Literacy

John F. Szwed
*Center for Urban Ethnography and
Department of Folklore and Folklife
University of Pennsylvania*

Literacy would appear to be one of the few elements of education that everyone agrees to be a necessity of modernity. The capacity to read and write is causally associated with earning a living, achieving expanded horizons of personal enlightenment and enjoyment, maintaining a stable and democratic society, and, historically, with the rise of civilization itself. "Underdeveloped" countries have had reading and writing touted to them as the means of a quantum leap into the future. And in the United States (especially since the 1960's) illiteracy has been singled out as a root cause of poverty.

Yet literacy as an ideal seems to be suffering a crisis. The wealthy nations of the world are now encountering rather massive failures in reading and writing among students at all levels; and it appears that despite universal schooling, a continuing percentage of the population of these nations has difficulties with these skills. In addition, there have developed "critics" of literacy, some of whom have questioned the feasibility of universal literacy as assumed in the West;[1] others now even raise questions about its ultimate relation to civilization.[2]

And behind all of this there are profound shifts appearing in the world's reading habits: in the U.S., for example, the reading (and publishing) of novels is in decline, while the reading of plays and poetry is at almost zero

---

[1]Cf. the many writings of Ivan Illich or Marshall McLuhan.

[2]Cf. Lévi-Strauss' suggestion that far from being the mainspring of civilization—i.e., the invention that allowed the rise of city states, science, etc.—the initial function of literacy was state control of the masses, taxation, military conscription, slavery, etc. (Claude Lévi-Strauss, *Tristes Tropiques,* London: Jonathan Cape, 1973, pp. 298–300.)

level. Instead, the amorphous area usually called non-fiction is on the ascendancy (though readers of an earlier generation might have difficulty in seeing the differences between the new techniques of non-fiction and fiction). The fact that many, perhaps most, English classes in the United States are geared toward fiction, drama and poetry makes this development all the more poignant.

Since professionals in the field of reading and writing instruction feel that there now exist sound, workable methods of teaching literacy, the responsibility for failure is assigned variously to poor teaching, overcrowded classes, family background (and the "culture of poverty"), the competition with the new media, or even to the directions of contemporary society itself.

But the stunning fact is that we do not fully know what literacy is. The assumption that it is simply a matter of the skills of reading and writing does not even begin to approach the fundamental problem: What are reading and writing for? Is the nature of the ability to read and write something on which there is in fact near agreement? Can these skills be satisfactorily tested? Do writing and reading always accompany each other as learned skills? Should they? Even on questions of *functional* literacy, can we agree on what the necessary minimal functions are for everyday life? It is entirely possible that teachers are able to teach reading and writing as abstract skills, but do not know what reading and writing are for in the lives and futures of their students.

I propose that we step back from the question of instruction, back to an even more basic "basic," the *social meaning of literacy:* that is, the roles these abilities play in social life; the varieties of reading and writing available for choice; the contexts for their performance; and the manner in which they are interpreted and tested, not by experts, but by ordinary people in ordinary activities. In doing this, I am following a recent trend in language studies, one which recognizes that it is not enough to know what a language looks like and to be able to describe and measure it, but one must also know what it means to its users and how it is used by them.

Literacy has typically been viewed as a yes-and-no matter, easily determined: either one reads and writes or one doesn't. And put in such terms, the goal of education is to produce a society of people who are equally competent at these skills. But the fact that no society has yet reached this state should give us pause. Historically, we know that most societies have produced specialists who have handled many of the necessities of literacy: the priest-scribe relationship, for instance, is widely remarked upon in studies of the development of civilization. In contemporary complex societies we are well aware of the negative correlation of skills in literacy with lower socioeconomic standing. But a closer look suggests that even among those of privileged background, these abilities are complexly patterned, and not at all equally distributed—the range of what is or can be "read" or "written" among, say, doctors, lawyers and teachers is often surprising. And even among those of other socioeconomic classes there is a great variety of such skills, such as can be found spread among active church members, avid followers of sports, and committed members of political parties. Consider the case of ethnic or immigrant neighborhoods, where such a distribution of abilities has a considerable historical background—that is, where certain individuals have served (and continue to serve) as interpreters of the law, citizens' benefits and rights, and the like, as well as readers and writers of letters and public documents. The distribution of these skills in bilingual and immigrant neighborhoods and communities is a complex and unexplored area. And even though the range and the number of these communities is simply not known at present, their clustering in urban areas gives the matter some urgency.

Beyond the question of who participates to what degree in reading and writing, there are even more vexing issues. Clearly, there are problems in defining the activities of reading and writing themselves. To take a simple case: what a school may define as reading may not take account of what students read in various contexts other than the classroom. A boy, otherwise labeled as retarded and unable to read assigned texts, may have considerable skill at reading and interpreting baseball record books. Or a student who shows little interest or aptitude for reading may read *Jaws* in study hall. The definitions of reading and writing, then, must include *social context* and *function* (use) as well as the reader and the text of what is being read and written.

The nexus at which reader, or writer, context, function and text join is sometimes glossed as reading *motivation*. Reading and writing skills may indeed vary according to motivation, with varying degrees of skill following differing degrees of motivation. But all of these elements form a complex whole which should not be reduced to a simple diagnosis. A reader's motivation may also vary according to context, function and text. And even motivation itself is varied: one may be moved to read by nostalgia, ambition, boredom, fear, etc.

Throughout, what one might expect to discover is that absolutes are few in questions of literacy, and that the roles of individuals and their places within social groups are preeminent in determining both what is read and written and what is necessary to reading and writing.

It should not be surprising to see differences in literacy between members of different ethnic groups, age groups, sexes, socioeconomic classes, etc.[3] Indeed, one might hypothesize the existence of *literacy-cycles,* or individual

---

[3]William Labov's work on this point is exemplary. See especially his "The Relation of Reading Failure to Peergroup Status" in his *Language in the Inner City,* Phila. University of Pennsylvania, 1972, 241–254.

variations in abilities and activities that are conditioned by one's stage and position in life. What I would expect to discover, then, is not a single-level of literacy, on a single continuum from reader to non-reader, but a variety of *configurations* of literacy, a *plurality of literacies.*

Even the everyday judgments of non-educators of what is or is not literate ability or activity is highly variable. Where for some, ability to spell is the primary marker, to others, choice of reading matter is foremost—the "classics" vs. gothic novels, the *New York Times* vs. tabloids, etc. To still others, success on standardized tests is everything. And such commonsense judgments, whether reasonable or not, help to shape the ultimate social definition of literacy.

Some words, then, about a few of these five elements of literacy—text, context, function, participants, and motivation.

TEXTS: WHAT IS IT THAT PEOPLE READ AND WRITE?

These are the primary questions, and on the surface they appear easily answered. Reading, for instance, would seem to be ascertainable by means of library circulation figures, publishers' sales figures, and questionnaires. But statistics are of limited use for a variety of reasons: first, because they have not been gathered for these purposes and thus give us only the grossest of information about texts (and none whatsoever about use). There is no agreement among publishers on what is a book, for instance. (Nor is there any among readers: magazines are often called "books" in much of the English-speaking world). What is literature? No agreement. Distinctions between genres and categories such as *functional literature* vs. *artistic literature* are of little use. Beyond the subjective judgments involved, it takes little imagination to think up artistic uses of functional literature or functional uses of artistic writing. (Can sports writing be artistic? Functional? Both?) And even seemingly well-established classes such as fiction vs. non-fiction are the basis of a very lively debate among scholars today.[4]

Circulation and sales figures tell us nothing about the informal circulation of literature, and at least among the working classes, borrowing and loaning of reading matter is common. One need only think of reading done in doctors' offices, the reading of newspapers and magazines found on public transportation, at work, etc., to sense the possibilities.

Consider also some of the reading matter that is not normally included under the category "literature:" handbills, signs, graffiti, sheet music, junk

---

[4]Robert Escarpit, *The Book Revolution.* Paris and New York: UNESCO, 1966; and *The Sociology of Literature.* Painesville, Ohio: Lake Erie College Studies, 1965, *passim.*

mail, cereal boxes, captions on television, gambling slips and racing tip sheets, juke-box labels, and pornography. (In some small towns, "Adult" bookstores are the only bookstores, and sometimes have holdings that rival, in number at least, the local library.) Victor-Levy Beaulieu, in *Manual de la petite littérature du Quebec* (1974), provides an anthology of the kind of literature which is produced and read within a rural parish in French Canada: it includes printed sermons, temperance tracts, stories of the lives of local saints and martyrs, parish monographs, and life stories used as models for improvement.

In addition, there is the question of the relation of the form of the text to other aspects of reading or writing. Consider the need for short, broken passages (such as found in mysteries and *Reader's Digest* condensations) for brief commuter trips, as opposed to longer passages for longer trips (*War and Peace* for an ocean voyage, say) or the time needed to register "raw" meaning as well as rhymes, puns, and irony in public signs in shopping centers and along roads. (The eclipse of Burma Shave signs by increased speed limits is a case in point.)[5]

Nor, incidentally, does traditional concern with literacy take account of the influence of the character of typography on readers. One small but important example is the current debate over the widespread use of Helvetic type (as used by Amtrak, Arco, Mobil and numerous other business and governmental sign and logo uses). The issue turns on whether the type's nature (presumably depersonalized, authoritative, and straightforward) brings unfair and misleading pressure to bear on its readers, as it appears to be *the* face of the largest and most powerful forces in America.

FUNCTION AND CONTEXT: WHY AND UNDER WHAT CIRCUMSTANCES IS READING AND WRITING DONE?

Available statistics tell us nothing about the variety of functions that reading and writing can serve. To consider only the use of books, in addition to providing information and pleasure—they are bought as decorations, as status symbols, gifts, investments, and for other reasons yet to be discovered.

Similarly, virtually nothing is known about the social contexts of reading and writing and how these contexts affect these skills. A quick beginning inventory of reading contexts would include bedside reading, coffee-break and lunch-time reading, vacation reading, reading to children, Sunday

---

[5]Frank Rowsome, Jr., *The Verse by the Side of the Road.* N.Y.: E. P. Dutton, 1966. Other work on signs has been done by followers of Kevin Lynch's *The Image of the City.* Cambridge, Mass.: MIT Press, 1960.

reading (perhaps the day of most intense literary activity in the United States and Europe), reading during illness, educational reading (both in institutions and informally), crisis reading (psychological, physical, spiritual), sexual reading, reading to memorize, commuter reading, reading to prevent interaction with others, etc. (In theory, at least, there is a form of reading specific to every room: books are sold for kitchens, coffeetables, desks, bedrooms *(The Bedside X)* or bathrooms. On the latter, see Alexander Kira, *The Bathroom.* N.Y.: Bantam, 1977, pp. 197–201, 287. There are also books designed for types of housing, as in English "country house" books, etc.)

Conventional thinking about reading and writing far too often uses a much out-dated model of literacy inherited from 19th century upper-class Europe. That "book culture" assumed many conventions which we can no longer assume: a small, well-educated elite; considerable spatial and temporal privacy (usually provided by large houses and the protection of wife and servants); a firm belief in the mimetic power and ultimate truthfulness of language; and possibly a belief in immortality and transcendance as mediated by books—that is, a sense that book life was somehow greater than real life.

We might here also postulate the possibility of a difference between public and private literacy, between what one reads and writes at work, at school and elsewhere. Susan U. Philips[6] has shown that at least in the case of one Native American group, there are substantial differences between these two domains, such that they may have direct and serious implications for education for literacy. For example, if children are not read to at home, and the school *assumes* that activity as part of its foundations for reading instruction, then such students are likely to encounter difficulties in learning to read. The important point to note here is not so much whether reading stories to children is or is not a proper or effective tool for preparing children to read, but that gaps between the two domains have serious consequences. And changes in home practices, even with the best intentions, are not easily accomplished and not necessarily desirable.

To cite yet another example: signs are written to be read but they are also located in certain locales and have specific designs and shapes. Thus the ability to read a public sign may take considerably more or less than the ability to read a book. For example, a sign on a building that marks a grocery store is on a building that looks like a grocery store and is located where a grocery store is likely to be. So the ability to read a sign (by definition a public event) involves at least a *different* set of skills than private reading.[7]

---

[6]Susan U. Philips, "Literacy as a Mode of Communication on the Warm Springs Indian Reservation," in *Foundations of Language Development: A Multidisciplinary Approach,* Vol. 2, Eric H. Lenneberg and Elizabeth Lenneberg, Eds. N.Y.: Academic Press and Paris; UNESCO, 1975, pp. 367–382.

[7]*Signs of Life: Symbols in the American City,* Program accompanying an exhibition at the Renwick Gallery, Washington, D.C., February 26-September 30, 1976.

Something might also be said about differing *styles* of reading and writing. For example, beyond silent reading and reading aloud, there are speed reading (with all that it implies); active, engaged, critical reading vs. that which is detached and noncommital; or the kind of reading Marcel Proust[8] was interested in: a comprehension of the text's contents, with the intention of setting off a variety of personal associations partly derived from the page and partly from the context within which it is read. Or to consider a more extreme example, Balinese Hindu priests orally read a text which, in addition to having certain standard word meanings, also has prescribed vocalizations of the words, body gestures to accompany them, and visual images to be kept in mind during the reading.[9]

I have kept most of the specifics of this discussion to reading, but the same questions can be applied to writing. We know very little about the range of uses to which writing is put, or rather, we know only just enough to put assumptions in doubt.

Educators often assume that reading and writing form a single standard set of skills to be acquired and used as a whole by individuals who acquire them in a progression of steps which cannot be varied or avoided in learning. But even preliminary thought on the problem indicates that these skills are distributed across a variety of people. For example, it is generally assumed that an author is the single master of his or her product, and that what was originally written emerges without interference as a book. But there are surely few authors who know all of the conventions and practices of editors and very few editors who know all of the practices of type setters, book designers and printers. The publication process, instead, often assumes the form of a kind of interpretation or translation of an author's original text.

The assumption of a single standard of writing is belied by even the writing habits that every one of us has. Most of us, when writing notes for ourselves, assume special conventions of spelling and even syntax and vocabulary that we would not use if we were writing for others. (Curiously, these private conventions seem to have a social character, in that we are usually able to interpret another's notes by analogy with our own procedures.)

Some variations in writing standards are even conditioned by our elaborate system of status communications. In most businesses, for example, it is a mark of success *not* to be directly responsible for one's own communications in written form—secretaries are employed to turn oral statements into acceptable written ones. (In this, the United States resembles other non-

---

[8]Marcel Proust, *On Reading.* N.Y.: Macmillan, 1971.

[9]C. Hooykaas, *Surya-Sevana, the Way to God of a Balinese Siva Priest.* Amsterdam: Noord-Hollandsche U. M., 1966. For this and the above example I am indebted to James Boon, "Further Operations of Culture in Anthropology," in *The Idea of Culture in the Social Sciences,* Louis Schneider and Charles Bonjean, Eds. Cambridge, England: Cambridge University Press, 1973, pp. 1–32.

Western cultures of the world, some of which measure the importance of messages and their senders by the number of intermediaries involved in their transmission.)

Still another example of multiple standards in writing is offered by advertising, logos and store signs, where "non-standard" spellings often communicate quite specific meanings: "quik," "rite," "nite" and the like indicate inexpensiveness or relative quality, and "kreem" and "tru-" ersatz products.

It is not only the assumption of a single standard that we must question, but also the assumption of a single, proper learning progression, such that one can only "violate" the rules when one has mastered them. Students quite properly often question this when learning the "rules" while at the same time reading works of literature which disregard them. Recently, some younger black poets (especially those published by the Broadside Press of Detroit) using unorthodox spellings and typography have been dismissed as simply semiliterate by critics not familiar with the special conventions developed to deal with black dialects and aesthetics.

Again, the point to be stressed overall is that assumptions are made in educational institutions about the literacy needs of individual students which seem not to be born out by the students' day-to-day lives. And it is this relationship between school and the outside world that I think must be observed, studied and highlighted.

One method of studying literacy—ethnography—represents a considerable break with most past research on the subject. I would contend that ethnographic methods, in fact, are the only means for finding out what literacy really is and what can be validly measured.

Questionnaires and social survey instruments on reading and writing habits do not escape the problems raised here in the study of literacy, and in fact they may compound them. An instrument sensitive enough to gather all of the needed information would have to contain all of the varieties of texts, contexts and functions we are interested in to guide informants in properly answering them. In addition, written forms would not do if for only the simple reason that they assume a certain standard of literacy in order to be completed, and it is this very standard that we wish to investigate.

More to the point, any study which attempts to cut across American society—its socioeconomic classes, age groups, ethnic groups and the like— along the lines of a skill which characterizes one social group more than others and which has been assumed to be closely associated with success and achievement, must be tempered by a considerable relativism and by the suspension of premature judgments. There is in this sort of study a need to keep literacy within the logic of the everyday lives of people; to avoid cutting these skills off from the conditions which affect them in direct and indirect ways; to shun needless abstractions and reductionist models; in short, to stay as close as possible to real cases, individual examples, in order to gain the strength of evidence that comes with being able to examine specific cases in great depth and complexity.

Another factor which makes ethnography most relevant here is that we are currently inheritors—if unwilling inheritors—of another 19th century perspective, one of distrust of mass society and culture, if not simply of the "masses" themselves. Specifically, this is the notion that "mass education," "mass literacy," etc., necessarily involves a cheapening or a debasing of culture, language and literature.[10] And though we have in this country escaped many of the elitist consequences of this position, we nonetheless suffer from its general implications. We must come to terms with the lives of people without patronizing them or falling into what can become a sociology of pathos. We need to look at reading and writing as activities having consequences in (and being affected by) family life, work patterns, economic conditions, patterns of leisure, and a complex of other factors.[11] Unlike those who often attempt to understand a class of people by a content analysis of the literature written for them by outsiders, we must take account of the readers' activities in transvaluing and reinterpreting such material.[12]

Nor can we make the easy assumption that certain media are responsible for a reduction of use of another medium. We must first be sure of the social context, function, etc., of the competing media before we assume we understand their presumed appeal. As an example, we know little more than that television sets are switched on a great deal of the time in this country; but do we know how they are socially used? We must consider the possibilities of more than simple entertainment. For example, considering only context and participants, radio listening—now a solitary activity—would seem to be competing with books more than television, still largely a group activity.

Work in the ethnography of communication has been aided immensely in recent years by the considerable accomplishments of sociolinguistics. Students of this subject have contended that in addition to close descriptions of language codes themselves we need descriptions of rules of code usage, combined with a description of the social contexts within which the various uses are activated and found appropriate. Dell Hymes has provided a framework for such studies, by isolating types of communication acts and by

---

[10]Raymond Williams, *Culture and Society*. London: Penguin, 1958.

[11]A model of this sort is Richard Hoggart, *The Uses of Literacy*. London: Chatto and Windus, 1957. (Unfortunately, there is less on the "uses" of literacy *per se* than one would wish.)

[12]For a sampling of work on writings for the working classes in Britain, see P. J. Keating, *The Working Classes in Victorian Fiction*. London: Routledge and Kegan Paul, 1971; Louis James, *Fiction for the Working Man*. London: Penguin, 1963.

analyzing them in terms of components which comprise each act, in the light of preliminary cross-cultural evidence and contrasts.[13] Such components include the participants in the act (as well as their status, role, class, etc.), the form of the message, its code, its channel of communication, its topic, its goal, its social and physical setting, and its social function. In fact, this entire preliminary discussion of questions of literacy derives from this perspective. It has put us in a position to pursue the following kinds of questions,[14] some of which were raised above.

How is the ability to read and write distributed in a community?
What is the relationship between the abilities to read and write?
How do these abilities vary with factors such as age, sex, socioeconomic class and the like?
With what kinds of activities are reading and writing associated, and in what types of settings do these activities take place?
What kinds of information are considered appropriate for transmission through written channels, and how, if at all, does this information differ from that which is passed through alternative channels such as speech?
Who sends written messages to whom, when, and for what reasons?
Is the ability to read and write a prerequisite for achieving certain social statuses, and, if so, how are these statuses elevated by other members of the community?
How do individuals acquire written codes and the ability to decode them—from whom, at what age, and under what circumstances, and for what reasons?
What are the accepted methods of instruction and of learning both in and out of school?
What kind of cognitive functions are involved?
In summary, what positions do reading and writing hold in the entire communicative economy and what is the range of their social and cultural meanings?

---

[13]See, for example, Hymes' "The Ethnography of Speaking," in *Anthropology and Human Behavior,* Thomas Gladwin and William Sturtevant, Eds., Washington, D.C.: The Anthropological Linguistic Theory," *American Anthropologist,* 66, No. 3, 1964, part 2, pp. 6–56. "The Ethnography of Communication," *American Anthropologist,* 66, No. 6, 1964, part 2, pp. 1–34; "Models of the Interaction of Language and Social Life," in *Directions in Sociolinguistics,* J. J. Gumperz and Dell Hymes, Eds. N.Y.: Holt, Rinehart and Winston, 1972, pp. 35–71. My debt to Hymes in this paper should be obvious.
[14]This list is adapted from Keith Basso, "The Ethnography of Writing," in *Explorations in the Ethnography of Speaking,* Richard Bauman and Joel Sherzer, Eds. Cambridge, England: Cambridge University Press, 1974, pp. 425–432. Basso was in turn adapting his questions from the Hymes references in footnote No. 13.

Again, many of these questions may appear to have obvious answers, and some perhaps do, but until explored systematically, we must consider every element problematic. This must especially be the case in a large, multiparted, stratified society such as ours, a society continually reshaping itself through migration, immigration and the transformation of human resources.

Among the specific methods one would use for directly observing literacy in operation within a limited setting are (1) field observations of literacy analogous to those used by linguistics: i.e., observations of writing and reading activities in natural settings (subways, schools, libraries, offices, parks, liquor stores, etc.) and elicitation of these activities; (2) obtaining "reading" and "writing autobiographies"—that is, tape recorded personal statements on the use and meaning of specific activities and genres of reading and writing to individuals at various points in their lives; ascertaining writing activities in the form of letters to friends, for business purposes and the like, invitations, condolences, local sales and advertising activities, church readings, etc.; a reconnaissance of reading materials available within public view—signs, warnings, notices, etc.; and content analysis of reading materials ostensibly aimed at communities such as the one studied—e.g., "men's" and "women's" magazines, newspapers and the like—combined with readers' reactions and interpretations.

Throughout, the focus should be on the school and its relation to the community's needs and wishes, on the school's knowledge of these needs and wishes and on the community's resources. It is possible that this may involve bilingual or multidialectal speakers, and this puts a special burden on the study: we will need to pay special attention to reading and writing in several languages, (akin to the "code-switching" of multilingual speakers) and to the consequences to readers of not having available writing in their own languages or dialects. It may become necessary to separate reading and writing as such study progresses for a variety of reasons, but at the moment this separation would not be warranted, as it would prejudge the relationship between the two, something we simply are not able to do at this time. The end product, in addition to answering many of the questions posed here, should be an inventory of at least one American sub-community's literacy needs and resources, and should provide both the model for making other similar surveys elsewhere (perhaps more quickly) and for generalizing from this one.

2 Toward an Ethnohistory of Writing in American Education

Shirley Brice Heath
School of Education
Stanford University

INTRODUCTION

Every school child is supposed to learn to write in school. This is the accepted fact about "the other half" of literacy—writing.[1] No one asks why every school child should learn to write according to the ways in which writing is taught in school. Even children rarely ask the function of their learning to write. Most are generous enough to assume that even if they do not know the reasons for their seemingly endless activity, the teacher has some purpose. The need for more writing in schools is today a frequently voiced recommendation from critics of education. They berate school personnel for the declining standards in writing, the absence of fundamental skills, and the need for a return to the basics. These criticisms rarely meet with the blunt rebuttal "Why should we teach writing?" We often ask "Why teach grammar?" "Why should kids read?", but we don't ask "What is the 'good' of writing for most of the adults in today's society?"

Educational goals and ideals, if not methods and materials, tend to be conservative. Consequently, if asked "Why teach writing?", educational personnel can provide what seem to be reasonable explanations for demanding that children write: "Writing is necessary for getting a job in

---

[1] *Writing* as defined herein refers to basic skills taught in school: the capacity to sign one's name (termed by Stone 1969 "alphabetism") and the ability to produce the written word as a means of communication in short answers and essays. This discussion does not consider writing in "creative writing" classes or in the production of the literary forms of poetry, fiction, and drama.

today's world." "Writing helps children learn to organize their ideas." "Writing is a creative outlet for children." For high-school and college students, reasons given are those which legitimate the processes of assessment and the acquisition of "cultured tastes" in higher education: written work is required as a measure of one's knowledge; only through the process of writing will students learn appreciation of literary works.

The validity of any of the above is rarely challenged. We consider that all have existed since the beginning of the education system, and that such purposes for writing are as basic as the "basics" often linked to the teaching of writing. Yet we do not know the functions of writing in American education. In histories of education, much more attention is given to the teaching of reading than to writing instruction. The general studies of writing which exist focus on writing systems (cf. Havelock 1976) and the contribution of these systems to the society-at-large, especially to traditional societies undergoing modernization (cf. Goody 1969, 1977). But what of writing in modern societies? McLuhanism notwithstanding, there has been relatively little direct attention given to the functions of writing in modern society, or more specifically, to why all individuals in a public education system should be expected to learn composition skills and the writing of essays.

It is not sufficient to ask these questions for only the present; instead they must be asked for American education in an historical perspective and for the social classes which have moved through the educational system since the early schools of the nation. How have the people of the cultures of the United States viewed the functions of writing? What roles has writing played in their communities? What writing events have they valued, and which of these have they expected schools to teach?

Such answers can come from social history which uses data left in the writings of individuals about writing—letters, diaries, comments in school texts, articles in periodicals for the general American reading public, and texts on teaching composition. Added to the data of social history must be the perspective of the ethnography of communication. Applied to writing in different communities of the United States across history, we may term this an "ethnohistory of writing."[2] Consistent with the nature and purpose of ethnohistory and social history, this approach may be conceived of as research directed toward the formulation of a descriptive theory of writing as

---

[2]Basso (1974) provides the most comprehensive summary of the study of writing systems and of the merits of the theoretical perspective of ethnography of communication for writing. Perhaps the earliest suggestion of this perspective for the study of writing was Hymes (1961). An heuristic framework of components is provided by Jakobson (1960) and in Hymes (1961, 1962, 1964, 1967) and Bauman and Sherzer (1974). Though not couched in the framework of ethnography of communication, Kochman (1974) provides an ethnographic-like analysis of "literate cultural personalities."

a part of the cultural phenomenon of literacy (including both reading and writing) and as a part of larger cultural systems (economic, religious, social). A complete description would include definitions of communities in which writing took place; the types of writing acts, events, and situations available to specific community members; norms of writing; and the methods of learning these norms and of having them reinforced. Cutting across all of these is the function of writing, the goals of community members for learning, maintaining, and improving their writing. Writing, like other systems of communication, is organized in each society in culture-specific ways and according to certain norms of interpretation which, if discovered, can provide an important perspective on modern approaches and attitudes toward writing.

In this paper, a description of selected writing events, norms of writing, and methods of learning these norms in certain writing communities of the eighteenth and nineteenth centuries will be presented to suggest how functions of writing evolved with the development of writing instruction in American education. For today's writing instruction, some suggestions will be advanced regarding the fit between the functions of writing in society and norms and methods of writing instruction. The basic purposes of this review are to prompt linguists and anthropologists to extend their theoretical frameworks to the study of writing and to assist them in this task by providing illustrative data suitable for analysis within the theoretical perspective of the ethnography of communication.

WHY LEARN TO WRITE?
THE HISTORICAL PERSPECTIVE

Long before the development of a common school system in the 1830s, individuals wrote about writing. Their definition of writing was not specialized to mean literature, as was so frequently the case after the public school system became established. On the contrary, writing as defined by the early nation was functional and even mundane. Three writing events were part of the social network of literate citizens: reports of opinion and events, how-to accounts related to nearly every imaginable aspect of daily living (from exorcising spirits to killing tobacco worms), and letters. Since most of the population had not studied English literature, they did not link the teaching of writing or the purposes of writing with literary appreciation. Instead, in the practical school of daily living, these early nationals reflected on the utility of writing events in their culture and defended the emphasis on the practical: "Utility is in every thing the truest of principles, though more intelligence and liberality than belong to a low state of civilization are necessary to its just appreciation and application."[3] Early American periodicals stressed repeatedly the preference of the reading public for an English education instead of instruction in the classical languages. Common sense, business, practical communication, and the need to acquire an education in as short a span of time as possible were reasons given for education in the English language.[4]

The writing of reports of opinion and events and how-to accounts was viewed as the responsibility of all citizens across social classes and roles. Farmers, tradesmen, ministers,and artisans wrote about what they saw, did, or believed. In the new republic, literacy was both a Christian and a patriotic responsibility. Literate men were expected to be aware of a world wider than that of their own community.[5] Their loyalties were to be stretched beyond the family and community to state and nation, as men came to see themselves as important entities in not only a political system, but also an environment which could be harnessed only through shared agricultural and scientific knowledge: "More noble employments do not engage the mind of man than when he is busy in unfolding his latent powers toward the benefit and instruction of his fellow creatures."[6] Readers of periodicals were reminded that this instruction was not the task of only the lofty; simple men had produced great inventions, ideas, and reflections on truth. Societal needs for the exchange of information on a broad range of topics were met by sending articles to periodicals, posting broadsides, and providing reports for local agrarian societies, debating groups, or literary societies. In addition, exchange of political opinions was important to the future of the democracy. During the colonial and early national periods, working-class people produced highly literate political documents and responses to political,

---

[3]Griswold 1847:50. Americans were particularly self-conscious about the practical bent of their society (Hofstadter 1963).

[4]See, for example, *Literary Miscellany* (1805):I, 12–21, (1806):II, 44–49; *Universal Asylum and Columbian Magazine* (1790):V; *American Museum or Repository* (1788):III, 538–44, (1789):V, 473–76, 524–35.

[5]Lockridge's 1974 study of literacy in colonial New England shows that between the middle of the seventeenth century and the end of the eighteenth, New England had evolved from a society no more than half-literate to a society of nearly universal male literacy. For males, writing skills were increasingly emphasized in rural and urban schools. During the eighteenth century, literacy increased sharply among back-country farmers, rural artisans, and laborers; in some areas of New England, farmer literacy surpassed 85% by 1790 (p. 21). Distinctions in occupational status were not created or supported by substantial differences in literacy. Literate farmers and artisans fared no better than did their illerate counterparts during the period studied by Lockridge. Apparently, these individuals did not wish to use their writing skills to achieve professional occupations; instead, writing was an individual benefit related to personal and societal needs for communication.

[6]"On the Converse and Communication of our ideas to the world," *The Massachusetts Magazine* (June 1796), 314–15.

social, and economic proposals of the local and national government. Moreover, these individuals read and responded in newspapers and periodicals to political and historical treatises which are rejected by college students today as too difficult and dull for reading.

A wide variety of content and form was acceptable for what may be termed "writing acts" published in the periodicals: simple questions, puzzles, math problems, word games, and anecdotes.[7] Any situation seemed appropriate to provoke a citizen to submit his thoughts in writing; the only exceptions in content were profanity, obscenity, and libel—the same restrictions repeatedly placed on oral language as well. The form of writing events—reports and instructional accounts—seemed designed to emphasize the absence of status relationships between reader and writer. Each report or account contained an introductory section in letter format: this included an opening salutation, a brief establishment of the setting or source of the following report or instruction, or a description of the usefulness of the information, and a closing politeness formula. The opening formula took such forms as "Mr. Editor," "Sir," or pseudonyms, such as "Mr. Americanus." In the late eighteenth and early nineteenth century periodicals, the closing and signature did not reveal the identity of the writer. A simple "P," "L," or a pseudonym, such as "Crito," "an American," designed to link the writer with an historical tradition or a patriotic cause, was used. In most cases, the first person was used throughout reports and instructional accounts. Individuals often identified themselves by occupation: "I am a man of business..." and sketched a setting for the event or outlined the occasion for learning the task or achievement to be shared with the reader. The writings usually presented a dyadic sender-receiver form (Hymes 1967), contributor addressing the reader as individual. Terms denoting "a readership" or a plural audience were rarely used. All writers attempted to establish a conversational mode: "I have often wondered..." "Could you tell me...?" The reader was frequently invited by the writer to respond in the next issue, and numerous periodicals contained reports and counter-reports, how-to accounts which were debunked or praised in subsequent issues, or satirical versions of "what would have happened had I followed 'P's' instructions on how to set my fence posts."

---

[7]Data for these analyses and generalizations are drawn from the American Periodical Series I and II (eighteenth and early nineteenth centuries), microfilm editions of all periodicals (publications which appeared in volumes and numbers over a period of time, excluding newspapers) published in the United States. Generalizations are supported by selections from books on language published during this period; all such publications issued in the United States from the colonial period until 1840 which could be located in major library collections of Americana have been analyzed for their perspectives on grammar, composition, and oratory. The research reported here is part of a comprehensive project to provide a social history of language in the United States.

In writing a periodical's prospectus, editors used a conversational mode to engage subscribers. Opening issues of periodicals stated the desire of the editor to "converse" with the reader, to engage him in an interaction which would be two-way. During the early national period, conversation was stressed as the most important form of communication for the advancement of both nation and individual. Periodicals contained numerous reports on how conversation should be conducted, what its merits were, and ways in which one could become a good conversant (Heath 1976). The major benefit of conversation which writing could not provide was the immediate criticism and testing of one's ideas. By urging readers to interact with each other through periodicals, editors attempted to overcome the admitted disadvantages of writing. Writing was a supreme act of ego—putting one's ideas out for public appraisal without benefit of immediate response. Within periodicals, writing was a solo and autonomous event for most contributors.

Those few individuals who did become known as writers became infamous or famous. Readers of periodicals wanted endless personal anecdotes about their lives; Tom Paine, Noah Webster, and other citizens bold enough to expose their identity openly in writing were chronicled in extreme detail in the periodicals. To be linked with a specific piece of writing was a supreme personal commitment. By the 1830's when individuals were increasingly called on to identify themselves in periodicals, they were asked to do so because of the growing nationalistic confidence in American writing. In addition, those who wanted writers identified believed that a writer's background and what might today be termed his "performance situation" were integral to evaluation of the writings: "To be able to think with him (the author) and feel with him, we must live with him; and to do this with contemporaries is sometimes to invade a privacy which is dearer than fame, though a privacy which to some extent is forfeited by the very act of publishing" (Griswold 1847:5).

Near the middle of the nineteenth century, with the increased call for identity of writers, came a change in forms of writing and definitions of writing situations. Simple writing acts submitted by readers were gradually eliminated and replaced by fillers provided by editors. Periodicals and manuals of conversation recommended correctness in conversation, and open discussions of how to talk with individuals of different social classes diminished considerably (Heath 1978). In books on language, attention to public writing increased and that formerly given to conversation, public speech, and debating—forms usually not put in writing—gradually decreased. The effect of this shift was to prescribe formal criteria for both speech and writing. An early American literary critic noted: "Formerly there was a great difference between the written language and that used in common conversation; but these styles are more nearly assimilated, and both have benefited by it" (Knapp 1829:23). Newspaper writers and authors of writing guides made clear that though they recognized "in a country like this, the views of every man on public affairs are frequently demanded because of his position as a citizen," (Haney 1867:6), they intended to be selective about the form and content of materials submitted. Individuals who wrote must learn to do so through what was considered both a laborious and an uncertain process. Even letters to the editor should be designed to appeal to a wide audience; content which would interest only a few readers could not be considered.

It is true that we have already a vast number of scribblers who, through newspapers and books inflict an astonishing amount of dullness on the community. Taking advantage of the fact that the people of the United States are a reading people and being prompted by an itch for writing, as well as a desire to see their names in print, they pour forth continually their contributions to the flood of stupidity (Haney 1867:6).

Guides to authorship, school texts, and rejection of articles and letters submitted to newspapers and periodicals signalled to the writing public that the earlier emphasis on a wide variety of content and minimal attention to form had shifted. Individuals were now told to envision their audience, to form their messages in prescribed ways which would be impersonal, and to be correct, precise, and pure in their use of language. *Eloquence* and *rhetoric,* terms which formerly applied to speech events, were redefined to refer to written materials: "Rhetoric is, therefore, the science of the laws of effective discourse, or the art of speaking and writing effectively" (Hill 1884:1).

"The eloquence of the literary department" was prescribed in terms of subject, style, "the profound thinking, the admirable reasoning, and the eloquent passages" (Grimke 1834:31) it contained. Would-be writers were warned that before they wrote, they must learn to think; descriptions and narratives could take the place of the earlier instructional accounts and reports of events or opinions, but they must embody a "power for good over all intelligent beings" (Parker 1838:iii; Hill 1884:3). One orator reflecting on the shift in his art, if not its coming demise, stated:

the great object of the American orator must be to *become an accomplished* WRITER *rather than an accomplished* SPEAKER. If he consult duty, usefulness, durable reputation, a just pride, and pure exalted enjoyment, he will cultivate the art of composition, with unwearyd assiduity and zeal. It cannot be denied that the great majority of cultivated minds in our country, and the number must be continually increasing, are constantly addressing the public thro' the press; and that the few comparatively, who speak in our various assemblys, produce little or no effect on the people at large, unless their speeches are read in pamphlets or newspapers" (italics in the original; Grimke 1834:31).

The medium of verbal performance had shifted for American orators (Bauman 1977; Baskerville 1968).

Of the three types of writing which existed during the colonial and early national periods for communication across all classes, only letters seemed to remain unchanged in purpose and form by the end of the nineteenth century. Reminding students that letters were intended to take the place of conversation, one text noted: "letters constitute the principal part of written composition. They are written on every conceivable topic, in almost every temper of mind, by and to every class of persons" (Hill 1884:170-71). Even with this seeming freedom, however, late nineteenth century composition guides warned that writers should be "rather more dignified and precise in a letter than in ordinary conversation with our friends" (Hill 1884:173).

THE DEVELOPMENT OF AMERICAN WRITING INSTRUCTION

How writing was to be taught, and specifically how letter-writing was to be learned, relate closely to the functions of writing across the eighteenth and nineteenth centuries. Because the teaching of writing in schools before the mid-nineteenth century was largely confined to copying simple exercises of phrases and sentences and reciting grammar rules, the general opinion was that practical letter-writing could not be learned in school. Instead it was learned from manuals of letter-writing, self discipline in reading, practicing writing, and corresponding with those who would criticize one's style and point out errors.

Women, in particular, because they were largely excluded from formal education before the mid-nineteenth century, had to rely in great part on their own resources in learning letter-writing. Seemingly self-conscious and highly motivated, they used their correspondence with each other for practice, instruction, and recommendations for further ways of improving the mechanics and style of their letters. Their methods and results drew praise from society; it was generally agreed that women excelled in conversation and letter-writing: "Ladies...though they have never been taught a rule of syntax, yet, by a quick facility in profiting from the best books and the best company, hardly ever violate one; and often exhibit an elegant and perspicuous arrangement of style, without having studied any of the laws of composition" (More 1813:26).

Even a critic who in 1808 begrudgingly admitted the talents of women agreed that they were superior to men in their conversational and writing abilities:

Few of them has [sic] talents enough to write; but when they do, how lively, are their pictures! How animated their descriptions! But if few women write, they all talk; and every man may judge of them in this point, from every circle he goes into. Spirit in conversation depends entirely upon fancy: and women all over the world talk better than men (Thoughts on Women 1808:153).

Half a century later, when prescriptions for writing pervaded the periodicals and guided school marms and textbooks, the assessment of women's talents for writing was similar.

The fair sex, as a class, excel the lords of creation in the art of letter-writing. Their quicker perceptions, and generally superior taste, leads them instinctively to choose the most pleasing modes of expression, and to throw into their epistles a grace and attractiveness, which few masculine writers can rival. Where a man carefully studies to preserve his dignity, or to display his knowledge of the dictionary, a woman will tell the same thing in just whatever words chance to come into her head, and the probabilities are that her letter will be the more readable of the two (Haney 1867:70-71).

Women excelled not only because of the qualities ascribed to them by critics, but because of their continual efforts to improve one another's writing. The following letter from an older to a younger sister reveals this aspect of women's assessment of the merits and norms of their letter-writing:

Your affectionate letter . . . gave me pleasure not only from the tenderness of your expressions, but from the propriety and correctness of your style. Never again make any excuses about writing nor do not allow yourself the excuse of 'want of practice,' but deprive yourself of it by writing frequently: do not confine yourself to one correspondent, but enlarge your number and be attentive to all. Their [sic] is nothing which practice improves more than letter-writing; ease is its greatest beauty and how otherwise can it be acquiring [sic].
   You will not be able to correct yourself . . . in two or three letters, for the rules of grammar are too confining a particular to be always supplied; but it is by constantly reading elegant writing; whene [sic] our ear becomes accustomed, to well constructed and well divided sentences. I always find I write much better immediately after reading works of an elegant and correct style.[8]

Another letter written two decades later from one woman to another reflects the same goal of correspondence, but places responsibility for improvement on an individual's willingness to practice:

You write with ease, and with practice are capable of becoming quite a good letter writer. On your own account as well as mine, I am very desirous of having

---

[8]Margaret Smith to Susan Smith, June 6, 1797, Margaret Baynard Smith Mss. Collection, Library of Congress.

you exert yourself often, to improve your epistolary talents. The assistance of others is less necessary in this, than in any other branch of your education, and as your improvement is in your own power, you ought to make every exertion to overcome any aversion you may have to writing.[9]

The author goes on to suggest the negative role of schools in teaching writing: "A publick school, instead of correcting bad habits and propensities, which is of infinitely greater importance to your character than the acquisition of verbs, nouns, and pronouns, is much more apt to add new ones to the original stock." The simplicity, precision, and straightforwardness prized in writing were not characteristics which would readily be learned in school for application in any writing event, least of all letters. In schools, children were "enchained either to the frivolous discourse of the unlearned or abandoned to the ills of book-taught philosophy."[10] Writing in schools was not a creative, expressive, sharing-of-ideas venture, as was writing for the public in periodical reports, instruction guides, and letters. An 1836 composition guide sharply criticized schools for their inadequate methods of attempting to teach composition as though it were something entirely apart from good conversation. The author argued that pupils should be taught to write from reality, not on "vapid subjects." "Composition is nothing more than conversation put on paper." To prove his point, the author presented his "helps to young writers" in a question and answer conversational format.[11]

By the last decades of the nineteenth century, the attitude of the public on the matter of the schools' competence to teach composition was being challenged by those who wished to prescribe norms and to recommend institutional approaches to achieving these norms. Both schools and the press stressed the notion that the thinking and writing of students could and should be improved through school instruction in composition. Moreover, the moral and cultural purposes of writing came to be more and more openly assigned to teachers of English. Writing was no longer seen as a skill used by all men to instruct and to entertain their fellows. Writing came to be critical in the cultivation of taste, the creation of a satisfactory "culture." The study of rhetoric, redefined to include composition as well as oratory, should turn students into critics. Rhetoric as a science investigated, analyzed, and defined the principles of good writing; as an art, it enabled students to apply these principles to communicate their thoughts in the best way. Studying good literature reinforced morality; good men wrote good compositions: "Let the records of the world be canvassed, and we shall find that trespasses, robberies,

---

[9]Eliza A. White to Mary Jane White, March 6, 1819, Moses White Mss. Collection, Caroliniana Library, Columbia, S.C.

[10]"On the Converse and Communication of our ideas to the World," *The Massachusetts Magazine* (June 1796), 314–15.

[11]*A Help to Young Writers* 1836:14.

and murders, are not the work of refined men (Quackenbos, 1862:167). The study of rhetoric operated as "a preventive to the more heinous offences," improved the sensibilities, and enabled writers to restrain their selfishness and even violent emotions (Quackenbos 1862:168). As students cultivated "taste" through the study of composition techniques, they insured their morality and improved their intellect. Textbooks admonished students to be ever aware of the rewards of "correctness of taste [which] implies soundness of understanding" (Quackenbos 1862:175).

Style was further characterized as having essential properties which should apply to the man as well as to his art: purity, propriety, clearness, strength, harmony, and unity. The former practical purposes of composition geared to societal needs and political evaluation in the early nation shifted to a focus on individual qualities: the development of "proportions, mental flexibility, and breadth of view" (Pearson 1898:xiii). The teaching of English and the development of standards in writing and oral language came increasingly to be associated with normative judgments about standards not intrinsic to the linguistic code, but to the individual creators of language. During the last three decades of the nineteenth century, grammar books and composition texts show increased collocations of terms such as "good," "moral," "industrious," "hard-working" with "good language" or "suitable compositions." The strong implication was that those who wrote and criticized well had more intelligence, morality, and industry than did their fellow students. A class consciousness was developing on the basis of the language used and the standards of writing perpetuated in the classroom. Methods of teaching composition during this time reflect a supreme faith placed in students' abilities to feed into their compositions material which would instruct their readership. Composition students were asked to write on topics about which they had little or no real information: aspects of morality or immorality, idleness, the talent of success, or order in school (Tyack 1966).

All citizens did not accept this assertion of composition as a necessary and acceptable substitute for former emphases on oral uses of language. In 1859, the parents of a child required to write compositions in a Vermont school protested. The child was expelled for refusing to write compositions. The court upheld the expulsion, ruling that English composition was an allowable mode of teaching and interpreting other branches of knowledge. Similar cases came to several state courts throughout the last half of the nineteenth century, as parents who had been raised with an emphasis on oral discourse and the presentation of logical thinking in immediate tests of conversation and debate protested the shift to standardized norms of thinking and writing (Fulbright and Bolmeier 1962).

Nevertheless, the majority of U.S. citizens accepted the emphasis on composition in school and extension of the use of writing skills as tests of character, intellect, morality, and good taste. The pervasiveness of this view is found in arguments proposing literacy tests as restrictions on suffrage. In

1842, the first such proposal "for the public good" was made. The author of the proposal gave careful attention to why reading and writing tests should be used to limit the electorate; he argued that a voter:

> ought to be able to read and write with facility, so that he may inform himself, by study of the structure of our government, and of the principles of our government . . . and so that he may learn from the common publications of the time, the condition and wants of the country; and so that he may write his own ballot at an election, or at least so that he may learn his whole duty, and the retributions which await the performance or non-performance of it, in the oracles of divine truth (Jones, *A Treatise on the Right of Suffrage* 1842:132–33, cited in Bromage).

The first state literacy test passed in Connecticut in 1855, but it required reading only, and was obviously designed to discriminate against Irish immigrants. In 1857, Massachusetts passed a reading and writing requirement. The history of Southern literacy tests which followed the Civil War is well-known. South Carolina, Louisiana, North Carolina, Alabama, Virginia, Georgia, and Oklahoma had writing requirements of various types; some stipulated that voters write parts of the Constitution or their application for registration.

New York State's struggle to provide a "scientific literacy test" between 1915 and 1923 provides evidence that other states at least considered, even if in the final analysis they rejected, the "logic" of requiring evidence of writing ability for voting. Opponents to a proposed bill in New York argued that if the ability to write one's name was a test of good citizenship, there were many "wayward men" who had proved their ability to write not only their own names, but the names of others as well. By 1923, the New York State Board of Regents was given the task of overcoming criticisms of the literacy test's invalidity. The Regents' test was to be administered if an applicant could not present a certificate showing completion of eighth grade in a school in which English was the language of instruction. The test provided a paragraph and asked that short answers to eight questions be written. Complete sentences, and correct grammar and spelling were not required except when necessary "to show comprehension." Many of the passages required that voters interpret patriotic motives and evidences of good character in the short passages; evidence of the ability to write *and* to provide correct answers was blatantly a test of how well a citizen had learned "his whole duty."[12]

Another illustration of the pervasiveness of the view that literacy skills co-occurred with a moral patriotic character exists in discussions surrounding

---

[12]The most comprehensive survey of the content of debates surrounding literacy tests is Bromage 1930. Leibowitz 1970 provides discussion of these tests in terms of their requirements regarding English as the language in which proof of abilities to read and write had to be exhibited.

literacy tests for immigrants. Designed to exclude illiterate immigrants from admission to the United States, the test was first proposed in 1890. During the next decade, proponents argued that illiteracy was the companion of slum populations, criminals, paupers, and juvenile delinquents: "the exclusion of immigrants unable to read or write...will operate against the most undesirable and harmful part of our present population and shut out elements which no thoughtful or patriotic man could wish to see multiplied among the people of the United States."[13] Woodrow Wilson vetoed the literacy test in 1915, not because the ability to read and write was being used as "a test of character, of quality, and of personal fitness," but because it was "a test of opportunity."[14] Wilson vetoed the bill again in 1917, but it passed over his veto. This bill, however, omitted writing as a selective criterion and excluded only "all aliens over sixteen years of age, physically capable of reading, who can not read the English language, or some other language or dialect."[15]

Interpretations of the normative nature of writing and extrapolations from evidence of this ability to conclusions regarding an individual's character, logic and morality, have, in different periods of history been institutionalized in various vays. Before 1840, conversation, argument, dialogue, and the direct confrontation of opinion had—in spite of a high literacy rate in many sections of the country—been valued over writing. Periodicals of the time provided for the continuation of many of the best features of conversation in their format and clear statements of the desire that unidentified readers and writers interact through the written word in much the same way they did in direct conversation. Following the first few decades of the nineteenth century, techniques of debate, true discourse, and conversation evolved into processes adopted by individuals proving through presentation and persuasion in writing the merits of their ideas and of themselves as upright citizens. Identification of the writers helped add authority to individual pieces of writing. Proof of a man's worth and his ability to participate in the political process was interpreted through the evidence and control of thought he presented in writing.[16] Though public use of proof of literacy as a test of character and political participation has been struck down by the courts, the question remains whether or not the attitudes which established these tests

---

[13]Extract from speech, 54th Congress, 1st session, pp. 2817-20 (March 16, 1896) in Abbott 1924, pp., 192–98.

[14]President Wilson's first veto message of 1915, U.S. 63rd Congress, 3rd session House Doc. No. 1527, pp. 3–4 in Abbott 1924, pp. 213–15.

[15]Extract from "An Act to Regulate the Immigration of Aliens to, and the reisdence of aliens in, the United States," *U.S. Statutes at Large* 874 (64th Cong. 2nd session) in Abbott 1924, pp. 215–30.

[16]Another perspective on attitudes toward language and truth and a shift in attitudes on the relation of language to values is given in Rosaldo 1974. See also Northrop 1962 on law, language and morals.

remain in other cultural spheres—specifically in English classes and in the educational system at large.

THE ROLE OF SOCIAL CONTEXT
IN LEARNING TO WRITE

History does not provide us with all we want or need to know about the functions of writing in various communities, and among individuals of diffferent ages, sex, social class, and work settings. We are, however, grateful for the multitude of bits and pieces of writing of highly varied functions and formats preserved from the colonial and early national periods. Through accidents of storage, and family residence patterns, we have not only journals, diaries, business letters, and writings of a formal nature, but also scraps of children's school compositions, random notes covering topics ranging from women's dress at parties to the talents of the local cobbler, and personal letters between parents and children and parents and teachers. From today's citizens, few of these latter types of writing will be preserved for future social historians to examine, because our sense of form and correctness (plus space shortage and geographic mobility) prevent our saving these cultural artifacts. Today, *writing* is for most communities and individuals a formal public matter; "scribbling," "jotting," "drafting," are forms of private or semi-private *non-writing*. These latter forms are of use to individuals across classes and cultures as preliminaries to final written products; however, most of these will not be preserved, since they are not considered worthwhile culturally and historically by today's society. Havelock (1976) has said that it is easier to reconstruct the history of writing than of reading; this statement may not be true for the history of processes of non-literary writing outside political, business, or institutional contexts for today's society.

Through ethnographic research we can know how writing, public and private, is used in communities across classes today: which mothers leave notes for children, write grocery lists, respond in writing to PTO memos; which fathers write plans for do-it-yourself repairs, fire escape routines, or list household goods, etc. How different is the writing of children in schools from the writing which goes on in family settings? What requirements for writing are made in certain occupational settings? How supportive of types of "non-writing" noted above is the school setting? Are there any composition techniques (as opposed to spelling and punctuation skills) which small businessmen need, since most of their ordering is done through forms or by telephone?

At the outset, we suggested that educational personnel of today argue that composition is necessary for students to secure jobs, organize ideas, and express creativity. Yet many older students with vocational and avocational goals know none of these arguments can be verified in their own communities: the jobs to which they aspire do not require compositional skills; they can organize their ideas for their own needs without putting them on paper; and their creativity is expressed in music, car decoration, clothing, and oral language. We have then, the need to alter traditional and even modified "lower-track" English classes' approaches to composition which use either a literary appreciation or a "business English" basis for instruction. In both of these, there is still much reflection of the attitude that writing skills are linked with morality, good character, and/or "success."

Knowing how writing is used in the communities and work settings of different cultures can help teachers and school administrators make writing fit the social contexts in which it will be used by those individuals who choose to live out their adult lives in their "home culture." To contextualize writing in the classroom on the basis of its uses in the home communities of "lower-track" students was the goal of several writing projects in rural sections of North and South Carolina between 1970 and 1975. As an anthropologist involved in ethnographic research in several communities in which these students lived, I chose to merge this research with a longstanding commitment to teaching composition. The immediate occasion for the merger was the complaint of junior and senior high-school teachers that there was no way they could teach these students to write. The classes were all male, both black and white, reading on a third to fifth grade level, aspiring to jobs in the local textile mills (where they knew they would start at earnings exceeding those of public school teachers in their states).[17] The challenge then was to prove to these students they needed writing for any purposes beyond signing their names and filling out applications or order forms in *Popular Mechanics*.

The first task was to learn how writing was used in the mills into which these boys planned to go for jobs. Interviews and study of personnel training practices showed that over the past decade, three successive approaches to training employees had been used. The earliest was "traditional": individuals came into the mills and worked under a master weaver, loomsman, etc., to learn how to operate the machinery. This procedure gradually became unpopular with the "old-timers," because as higher and higher hourly wages began to be tied to production quotas, they resented being taken off production to break-in new employees. The supplement to their hourly wages

---

[17]It was fortuitous for the success of the project that the classes were all male, because from an ethnographic perspective, young males in the communities of the students both had more opportunities and were more willing to assume responsibility for writing than did young females. On tests of grammar and composition skills, females from these communities scored barely high enough to keep them out of "special" writing classes; however, recent female high school graduates and dropouts in the community showed little or no maintenance of their writing skills. In their communities, situations which necessitated writing by females did not arise until they were well beyond middle age.

paid for breaking-in employees was not sufficient to cover what they would have made had they been able to run their own machines, unhampered by having to instruct others. In addition, they resisted teaching new employees strategies which might enable them to meet and break production quotas. An interim practice of having foremen instruct employees was also unsuccessful, because foremen often did not know the machinery or procedures as well as the best workers, and during various seasons, there were too many employees for foremen to train adequately.

Some mills adopted a second procedure; they hired a college student to observe the procedures of each section of the mill's operations, write instructions for procedures, and illustrate these procedures and parts of the machinery. Given manuals containing these instructions and illustrations, new employees, with minimal direct personal instruction, were expected to train themselves. This procedure lasted only a short while, since most of the individuals working in the mills came from cultures in which the source of knowledge about how to do tasks was not the written medium. The correlation between actions at the machine and the procedures described step-by-step in the manual was not evident to many of these individuals. Employees with the highest levels of academic attainment were able to secure jobs, but were not able to retain them, since they were not as successful "on the floor" as those less successful in schools but more adept at managing the machines. Book training did not teach employees to work the machines for improved production or safety records.

A third and very recent attempt by some of the textile mills is a modification of an on-the-job training emphasis, and the result of an employment situation in which there are more employees than there are jobs. Prospective employees are taken through the section of the mill in which they wish to work or are needed, and asked to watch the operations. They do not interact directly with those who operate the machines, but they observe and have opportunities to ask questions of foremen. Potential employees then return to the personnel office, where they are asked to describe how to run a particular machine and what goes on in certain parts of the mill. Employees are selected on the basis of the adequacy of their oral description of the jobs they will be doing. Once they are accepted for work, they are given a machine and receive minimal supervision from a foreman. How this procedure will work is not yet known. However, what is significant is that in all three procedures described for hiring mill employees, no writing was required except a signature on the application blank after it was completed in an interview with a personnel office worker.

It was clear we could not argue writing skills were needed to get a good job. All we could draw on for transfer to the classroom was the need to present orally an organized description of process required in the third procedure. If writing was not needed in vocational settings, could we argue it was needed in the communities from which the students came? Information about writing in these communities was needed to answer this question. Ethnographic work in the communities revealed that adults had almost no situations which called for writing; individuals from mainstream institutions assumed these adults could not write and therefore wrote for them, when the occasion called for writing. Applicants at the local employment bureau and social services offices were interviewed, and institutional personnel filled in their applications. Travelling insurance salesmen filled in applications for their clients in the communities. School notes sent home were responded to with oral messages transmitted by older brothers and sisters from upper grades, or parents were told to call the school office. Writing which did exist in the community was done by middle-aged and older women, who wrote down some family records of births and deaths, recipes to share at church functions, and favorite Bible verses, poems, or sayings for use in Sunday School classes. These writings were usually kept in the family Bible or telephone book. Instead of personal letters to relatives far away, greeting cards were used. These communities bought many greeting cards, often highly elaborate ones, and their sending and receiving were highly valued. Personal messages rarely accompanied these cards. Instead direct communication was handled by telephone or through messengers who traveled back and forth between home and new locations.

It was clear that the communities themselves did not provide encouragement or support for writing. We then turned our ethnographic research to the social network of the boys themselves. There we found that pool halls, local gathering places, etc., bore evidence of writing of various types and purposes. In ways similar to these adopted by student reformers of the late sixties, these boys used their recreational centers for posting protest messages (usually commerically produced and modified to reflect a local problem or person), praise of certain "cool" personal characteristics, advertisements for parts of cars, instruments, or lost items, and calls for participation in local sports or musical events scheduled by the boys' social networks. The classroom goal became one of expanding these messages and bringing that kind of writing into the classroom.

In addition, students were asked to talk about the writing of others which created problems for them or their parents. Immediately they pointed out that information about social services, warranties and guarantees, and regulations related to urban housing were "too tough" to read. When their parents asked agents in local institutional offices to explain these writings, they talked in the same language in which the documents were written. Students were asked to try to rewrite these sources and to interview each other on the meanings of the documents in order to pinpoint specific questioning techniques needed in these "clarification episodes." Teachers stressed that certain "legal" documents used special language for the protection of the parties involved;

other documents were not legal and could be rewritten.[18] Initially, the students rewrote documents they brought from home or local community social service offices. These efforts took the students into several useful areas of language study. They challenged the merits of readability tests and basic word lists; they examined high interest-low level readers to determine their characteristics. They tried to determine what made reading "easy"—words or length of sentences, construction of discourse units or printing format and use of illustrations.

Sentences such as, "Wood when subjected to conditions of moisture tends to deteriorate," became "When wood gets wet, it rots." The new sentences appeared in posters, were circulated in the form of mock obituary notices (Willy Wood Rat dies), and community "magazines" created by the students; all formats used were those which they identified as acceptable reading materials for adults of their communities. After this initial experiment, they prepared a videotape program on other issues for use in senior citizens centers. Teachers proposed a "television script" or a summary of the program's content to supplement the videotape. Preparing this script involved the students in further examinations of the relations between structures and functions of language. They challenged each other to find words, phases, and ways of expressing themselves which would be acceptable to the elderly. Other activities which followed took them into writing the words for local songs, writing and illustrating "ethnographic readers" for students from their communities to use in elementary classes, and providing brief spots on radio programs about their favorite recording stars, etc. Local radio stations were enlisted to accept spots written by students on reports of events and how-to accounts. Students began to produce their own street-corner productions and "how-to-do-it" manuals. For materials, they obtained from local business "scratch paper" used on one side. The printed side was left either as it was or overprinted with art designs; the blank side was used for messages written by students "turned on to writing."

In a sense, history was recapitulated in this project. Students themselves found that the functions of writing they valued were those which were reports of their opinions or events, and how-to accounts on topics ranging from hunting to shooting pool. Letters, however, remained of little interest to them; they remained unconvinced that letters could prove more efficient or effective than direct telephone contact, an order form, or a greeting card. Writing as a creative outlet had no appeal for these boys; they argued they could better tell or act out a story—they needed props, gestures, and the

---

[18]Those boys who had had "bouts with the law" or disappointing purchases of stereo cr auto equipment decided to write explanations for legal notices and guarantees for members of the community. Community resource professionals were called on to explain passages and verify interpretations.

immediate feedback of the audience. They argued that the "stuff about truth in writing" was killed by teacher critics who "don't really want me to say it my way or to even hear what I have to say." For functions they valued, they learned to write—in a range of styles and for a variety of readers. They wrote for posters, elementary readers, advertisements, videotape scripts, radio programs, etc. They wrote to be read by members young and old of their own communities—a readership which trusted these students to translate public documents into common-sense language. The approach to turning these students on to writing was based on ethnographic techniques employed by teachers and students. This approach enabled students to become writers and translators for their own communities, for an audience of readers whose abilities they knew and could identify precisely. They made functional literacy truly function in the social context of their own cultures.

SUMMARY

This paper has explored the question "Why should we teach writing in school?" First we looked at the history of the functions of writing in American society and the development of writing instruction in American schools, as evidenced by social history data. We then looked at present-day functions of writing in local communities in relation to writing instruction in schools, making use of the author's recent research efforts in rural sections of North and South Carolina.

In the colonial period and until nearly midway in the nineteenth century, the focus in American writing was on individual reports, how-to accounts, and letters, all of which were viewed as the responsibility of citizens across social classes and roles. When these appeared in broadsides and periodicals, they tended to be anonymous, and high value was attached to simple conversational style rather than a literary style of writing. Many citizens felt that school instruction did not prepare students for this practical kind of writing.

In the second half of the nineteenth century, as newspapers assumed great importance, and the publication of books became an established industry, the forms shifted, and writing came to be viewed as a specialized craft. In the schools, attention shifted to correct grammar and more elaborate styles, and the ability to write well became linked to individual identification and personal characteristics of moral and cultural value. This capsule illustration of the ethnohistory of writing in American education makes us aware of this historical context which fostered current attitudes toward the functions of writing. Since the last decades of the nineteenth century, we have come to regard writing as the school subject critical to students' intellectual and social/moral maturation. Educators seem to agree generally that the experiences of literary appreciation, outlining, determining critical terms and stylistic devices, and composing are central to providing students with what they need for "successful" lives.[19]

At the present time, in spite of heated discussions about the success of schools in teaching writing, there is almost no systematic description of the functions of writing in the society as a whole or in special groups and subcultures which differ among themselves and from school culture in their uses of writing and their attitudes toward it. Ethnographic research from communities and institutions is needed in order to provide this information and to relate instruction in writing to it. Ethnographic research on rural textile mill communities in the Southeast has been used to reorganize the teaching of writing in some classes of local schools, with dramatic results for student writing and teacher attitudes. This kind of research and local application is urgently needed for many other regional, cultural, and socioeconomic settings. In this venture, both teachers and students can help by becoming culturally aware of the functions of writing in the varying contexts of their respective cultures and that of the school.

REFERENCES

Abbot, E. *Immigration: Select documents and case records.* Chicago, 1924.

Altick, R. D. *The English common Reader: A social history of the mass reading public 1800–1900.* Chicago, 1957.

Baskerville, B. 19th century burlesque of oratory. *American Quarterly,* 1968, *20,* 726–43.

Basso, K. H. The ethnography of writing. In R. Bauman & J. Sherzer (Eds.), *Explorations in the ethnography of speaking.* New York, 1974, 425–432.

Bauman, R. Linguistics, anthropology and verbal art: Toward a unified perspective with a special discussion of children's folklore. In M. Saville-Troike (Ed.), *Georgetown University round table on languages and linguistics.* Washington, D.C., 1977, 13–36.

Bauman, R., & Sherzer J. (Eds.). *Explorations in the ethnography of speaking.* New York, 1974.

Bromage, A. W. Literacy and the electorate. *American Political Science Review* 1930, *24,* 447–60.

Fulbright, E. R., & Bolmeier, E. C. *Courts and the curriculum.* Cincinnati, 1962.

Goody, J. *Domestication of the savage mind.* Cambridge, Eng., 1977.

Goody, J. *Literacy in traditional societies.* Cambridge, Eng., 1969.

Grimke, T. S. *Oration on the comparative elements and dutys of Grecian and American eloquence.* Cincinnati, 1834.

---

[19]Mathieson 1975 provides a summary of English teaching in G. at Britain from a similar perspective. The broader question of the relation of literacy to economic changes in the society is examined for Great Britain in Sanderson 1972 and Altick 1957. No similar studies exist for the reading public in American society. Useful perspectives on the future role of reading for lower classes in the United States are provided in Jennison and Sheridan 1970. A "sociological model for the study of book reading" which could be applied to the United States is given in Mann and Burgoyne 1969.

Griswold, R. W. *The prose writers of America.* Philadelphia, 1847.

Haney's guide to authorship. New York, 1867.

Havelock, E. A. *Origins of western literacy.* Ontario, 1976.

Heath, S. B. Early American attitudes toward variation in speech: A view from social history and sociolinguistics. Forum Lecture, Linguistic Society of America, 1976.

Heath, S. B. Social history and sociolinguistics. *The American Sociologist,* 1978, *13,* 84–92.

A help to young writers. Albany, N.Y., 136.

Hill, D. J. *The elements of rhetoric and composition.* New York, 1884.

Hofstader, R. *Anti-intellectualism in American life.* New York, 1963.

Hymes, D. H. Functions of speech: An evolutionary approach. In F. C. Gruber (Ed.), *Anthropology and Education.* Philadelphia, 1961, 55–83.

Hymes, D. H. The ethnography of speaking. In T. Gladwin & W. C. Sturtevant (Eds.), *Anthropology and human behavior.* Washington, D. C., 1962, 15–53.

Hymes, D., H. Introduction: toward ethnographies of communication. *American Anthropologist,* 1964, *66*(6), 1–34.

Hymes, D. H. Models of the interaction of language and social life. *Journal of Social Issues,* 1967, *23*(2), 8–28.

Jakobson, R. Concluding statement. Linguistics and poetics. In T. A. Sebeok, (Ed.), *Style in language.* Cambridge, Mass., 1960, 350–73.

Jennison, P. S., & Sheridan, R. N. (Eds.). *The future of general adult books and reading in America.* Chicago, 1970.

Jones, S. *A treatise on the right of suffrage.* 1842.

Knapp, S. L. *Lectures on American literature.* New York, 1829.

Kochman, T. Orations and literacy as factors of 'black' and 'white' communicative behavior. *International Journal of the Sociology of Language,* 1974, *3,* 91–116.

Leibowitz, A. H. English literacy: Legal sanction for discrimination. *Revista Juridica de la Universidad de Puerto Rico,* 1970, *39*(3), 313–400.

Lockridge, K. A. *Literacy in colonial New England.* New York, 1974.

Mann, P. H., & Burgoyne. J. L. *Books and reading.* London, 1969.

Mathieson, M. *The preachers of culture: A study of English and its teachers.* Totowa, N.J., 1975.

More, H. *Strictures on the modern system of female education* Vol. I. New York, 1813.

Northrop, F. S. C. Law, language and morals. *The Yale Law Journal,* 1962, *71,* 1017–48.

On the converse and communication of our ideas to the world. *The Massachusetts Magazine,* June 1796, 314–15, 336.

Parker, R. G. *Progressive exercises in English composition.* Boston, 1838.

Pearson, H. G. *The principles of composition.* Boston, 1898.

Quackenbos, G. P. *Advanced course of composition and rhetoric.* New York, 1862.

Rosaldo, M. I have nothing to hide: The language of Ilongot oratory. *Language in Society,* 1974, *2,* 192–223.

Sanderson, M. Literacy and social mobility in the industrial revolution in England. *Past and Present* 1972, *56,* 75–103.

Stone, L. Literacy and education in England 1640–1900. *Past and Present,* 1969, *42,* 69–139.

Thoughts on Women. *Literary Mirror* (1808–09) I, 153.

Tyack, D. The tribe and the common school: The district school in Ashland, Oregon in the 1860s. *Call Number,* 1966, 13–23.

3 The Status of Writing in our Society

Edward P. J. Corbett

Will writing continue to play a significant role in the political, professional, cultural, and business affairs of our society during the last quarter of this century? That question is an especially important one for teachers of English, because the answer will determine, among other things, what they will teach in the classroom. If writing is a vanishing and dispensable art, as Marshall McLuhan and others have claimed, it would be a waste of effort for English teachers to exercise their students in an anachronistic craft. It is difficult enough to motivate students to expend the effort needed to acquire even a minimum competency in writing; it would be utterly futile to try to induce students to acquire the skill if it has no pay-off value in the real world.

At the outset, certain concessions have to be made. Whatever the fate of writing, speech will continue to be the predominant mode of communication. Most people speak more words in a single week than they will write during their entire lifetime. Secondly, writing will never be as crucial a skill for surviving or thriving in our society as reading is. Functional illiterates who cannot even write their names may suffer embarrassment because of their deficiency, but they somehow manage to subsist in our technological society. But those functional illiterates who cannot even read street signs and simple directions are so severely handicapped that it is questionable whether they can survive, much less thrive, in our society. Thirdly, only a minuscule portion of the total population will regularly have to compose important, influential documents. The majority of literate people have to do some writing occasionally—letters, notes, fill-in-the-blanks forms—but only a minority have to write regularly and seriously in connection with their jobs.

Having made those concessions, I may have given the game away. I certainly have given aid and comfort to those who maintain that writing is a dispensable skill. But despite those concessions, I am not prepared to concede the game. I see too much contrary evidence all around me to concede that writing is an obsolescent skill. Writing is proliferating rather than vanishing.

For a long time, I have made it a practice to ask business and professional people I meet how much writing they have to do in connection with their jobs. Invariably, their testimony is that the amount of writing which they and their associates have to do is steadily increasing. A good deal of the writing they have to do, usually in the form of memorandums or reports, is destined for in-house consumption only. Salesmen, policemen, nurses, supervisors, foremen commonly have to file daily reports. Frequently, the higher one goes on the executive ladder, the more writing one has to do. Despite the steady resort to the telephone for transmitting messages, an astonishing amount of paper is consumed for intramural communication. If a message has to go out to several people in a hurry, that message is more likely to be transmitted in a written memorandum than by telephone or a public-address system. Because many of these written messages tend to be one-draft prose, those who compose them must develop a facility in composing a readily intelligible message off the top of their heads. Often, of course, busy executives engage in oral composition that is recorded and transcribed by a secretary. But these oral compositions are not just random talk; they have to be structured in the same way that a message in the scribal mode is composed.

One has only to note the row upon row of filling cabinets in any office to be convinced that writing is far from being an outmoded activity. Despite the emergence of the computer, written documents are still the principal means of storing and retrieving information. It is difficult to conceive of an adequate substitute for the written word as a means of preserving records of correspondence, contracts, and reports. Even the computer must be able to produce a "print-out" in order to be a useful device for storing, retrieving, and transmitting information.

When one moves out from a consideration of the amount of paper that is enscribed daily for in-house communication to a consideration of the steady stream of printed words that inundates the extramural community, the evidence for the flourishing state of writing in our society becomes staggering. There is a vast, insatiable maw out there that must be constantly fed with written words. It is a rare day when the mail does not deliver some written or printed copy from the world of "getting and spending"—promotional letters, brochures, ads, solicitations. According to *Publishers Weekly,* American book publishers produced 39,372 new titles or new editions in 1975, and the Fifteenth Edition of *Ulrich's International Periodicals Directory* reveals that there are now over 55,000 in-print magazine titles. The number of newspapers in this country has declined significantly over the last twenty-five years, but it is a rare city with a population of 100,000 or more that does not have at least one daily newspaper that absorbs all of the copy churned out by local reporters and a good deal of the copy produced by the wire services. Judging by the number of two-page advertisements that appear regularly, the major book clubs seem to be prospering, and smaller, more specialized book clubs spring up each year. Judging by the six-figure and even seven-figure prices they have been paying for reprint rights, paperback publishers seem to be prospering too. If publishers have not been able to turn as much of a profit as they did in the 1960's, it has not been so much because of a decline in potential readers as because the spiraling costs of paper and printing have pared the profit margin. And where there are readers, there must be writers to satisfy their appetite for print. Nor is that most electronic of the media, television, independent of the written word. Except for sporting events, talk shows, and variety shows, all shows on TV rely on a script. Television commercials are largely audio-visual, but the bedrock of every commerical is a production script.

To get an idea of the kind of writing that "sells" in the contemporary world, one can consult a reference work like *Writer's Market*. The 1975 edition of this work lists 5,202 paying markets in its 957 pages. We all know about those magazines with blockbuster circulations—magazines like *TV Guide, Reader's Digest, National Geographic Magazine, Better Homes and Gardens, Playboy.* But we can gain a better idea of the range of interests and tastes of readers by noting the astonishing circulation figures for some of the more specialized magazines. Apparently, "literary" people don't much support the so-called "little magazines," which typically list circulation figures of 200, 350, 800, 1200. But people with more mundane interests and tastes generously support those magazines that deal in shoptalk: *Car Craft* (300,000), *Boating* (210,000), *Gambler's World* (300,000), *Baby Care* (575,000), *The Ohio Farmer* (107,000), *Stitch 'N Sew* (200,000), *Camping & Hiking* (90,000).

The irony of those circulation figures is that English teachers do not usually engage their students in the kind of writing that finds a market in the off-beat magazines which attract tens of thousands of readers. English teachers are inclined to have students write papers about literature. There is considerable educational value, of course, in reading and writing about literary texts, and all students can benefit from that experience. But when students are exercised solely in writing literary essays, to the exclusion of more utilitarian kinds of writing, they are being scandalously shortchanged. Not one percent of them will ever have occasion to write a literary essay after they get out of school, but if they have to do any writing at all in connection with their jobs, they will certainly have to write such things as letters, memos, reports, advertising copy, instruction manuals. Somewhere in their schooling, they should be exercised in such modes of discourse. The testimony from everywhere is that the fastest-growing courses—in fact, the only growing courses—in university English departments are courses in technical or professional writing. Apparently, students more clearly perceive what kind of writing is demanded in the real world than their teachers do.

One can acknowledge that there is a tremendous demand and market for writing in the real world and still not concede that many graduates of high schools and colleges will have to do much serious writing in connection with their jobs. Certainly there are many jobs—especially manual-labor jobs—where the worker never has to do any writing. But it can just as certainly be said that the person who has acquired some competency in writing has considerably enhanced his or her chances of advancement and that the person who lacks the competency has a diminished chance of attaining any supervisory or executive position. The choice of a niche in life should be left ultimately to the students, but they should at least be made aware that they are handicapping themselves if they don't acquire a modicum of skill in writing. It is little wonder that when General Electric conducted a survey among its 24,000 employees who were college graduates, the non-engineering graduates listed English communication as the academic course which they felt contributed most to their success in the company, and the engineering graduates rated English communication second only to mathematics (General Electric, 1957).

Even if I could not demonstrate that there is still a demand or need for writing in our electronic age, I would still insist on the value of writing for developing the person. Aside from its utilitarian value, writing is an effective way of discovering and developing the self. James Britton and his colleagues articulate this viewpoint very well in the last chapter of their study of student writing conducted at the University of London Institute of Education in 1966-1971 (Britton, 1975):

> We conclude by asking, "How important is writing, anyway?" It is often claimed that in this telecommunciations age, the importance of writing is declining rapidly; indeed, that many young people leaving school today will seldom need to use it, and then only in its simplest form (say, in our categories of report and generalized narrative and, for simple instructions, regulative). The rest, it is said, will be done by word of mouth. Even if this prophecy proved largely true, we should still want to claim a *developmental* role for writing in school—that is to say, that the talk by which children will govern their lives will require mental abilities that will best be developed by the practice of writing. (p. 201)

Society may be betraying its misplaced emphasis when it bases its estimates of the worth of a person on one's spelling, grammar, and punctuation. But society can and does make some legitimate judgments about the quality of one's mind from the condition of one's writing. To paraphrase what Dr.

Johnson once said about the prospect of being hanged, writing concentrates the mind wonderfully.

If then we can justify our continuing to teach writing in our schools, what standard can we set for our students? We can certainly set the minimum standard of clarity, coherence, and some grace. But when most people hear the word *standard* in connection with writing, they are likely to have conjured up for them the whole controversial issue of "standard English." That is an issue which has to be considered in any discussion of the status of writing in our society.

Largely because of the work of descriptive linguists in the last twenty-five years or so and because of professional pronouncements like the CCCC Background Statement on the Students' Rights to Their Own Language (*College Composition and Communication,* 1974), many teachers of English—if not the general public—are now much more enlightened about, and tolerant of, variant dialects than they once were. They now realize, for instance, that especially in regard to the spoken language, it is difficult to say which class of people or even which individuals can be designated as speaking the so-called "standard English." On phonological grounds alone, can we say with any assurance which of our recent Presidents spoke "standard English?"—Truman? Eisenhower? Kennedy? Johnson? Nixon? Ford? Carter? There were phonemic oddities in the speech of all of them. Whether we consider pronunciation or pitch or tone or lexicon or usage, it is difficult to get general agreement about what the standard dialect is in the spoken medium. Moreover, many English teachers are now ready to admit that regional and social dialects of the language serve their users well in the appropriate milieu—in fact, much better, in some circumstances, than a "broadcaster's English" might serve them.

When the discussion moves to the written language, however, there is more likely to be general agreement about what is "standard" in that medium. Standard English—or, to use some alternative terms, Edited American English or Public Prose—is that form of the language in which the newspapers, magazines, books, and public speeches of this country are written. There is something slippery even in that definition—*which* newspapers, magazines, books, and public speeches?—but any questioning of that definition is likely to concern matters of style or levels of formality rather than matters of grammar or usage. In public prose, there are determinable and specifiable conventions of grammar, punctuation, and mechanics. Inveterate readers of public prose readily recognize—and are often distracted by—departures from those conventions.

In light of our recognition, on the one hand, that there is a variety of valid and useful dialects in our language and, on the other hand, that there is a uniformity in the conventions that govern edited, published prose, what should we be teaching in our schools? Well, students should certainly be made aware of and respectful of the rich variety of dialects in our language, and if time permits, they should be informed about the main grammatical and lexical differences of those dialects. But in the writing class, students will have to be exercised primarily, if not exclusively, in Edited American English. That is the power dialect in our society. That is the dialect that provides students with an entrée into the mainstream of society. Students may not want to enter that mainstream. It should be left to them to decide whether they want to swim with the current or to breast the current or to swim in the backwaters. If they decide not to master the power dialect, they must at least be made aware that they have chosen to handicap themselves. In my experience, it is the students from minority classes who most desperately want to learn the conventions of the power dialect.

I have espoused a couple of positions about writing that are anathema to some educators. Those positions strike some people as being myopic and elitist. I regard those positions as being realistic and prudent. Endorsement of one of the opposing positions—namely, that writing is an anachronism in our electronic age—relieves English teachers of one of their traditional responsibilities: teaching composition. Do they want to be relieved of that burden? If they relinquish that responsibility, what will be left for them to teach, at a time when enrollments in literature classes are declining alarmingly? Endorsement of the other opposing position—namely, that students should be allowed to write in any register of the language they are comfortable with—reduces the English teacher to the role of a mere reader, rather than a shaper, of student prose. Will teachers be content in that passive role?

If the answers to those questions is "Yes," society is bound to step in and delegate the job of teaching composition to another class of teachers. Although society is not always prepared to put its money where its priorities are, it still pays fervent lip-service to the importance of the 3 R's. We had better pay attention to those priorities.

REFERENCES

Britton, James, and others. *The Development of Writing Abilities, 11-18* (London: Macmillan Education, 1975).

"The Students' Right to Their Own Language," *College Composition and Communication,* 25 (Fall, 1974), 1-32.

"What They Think of Their Higher Education," *Educational Relations Information Bulletin* (New York: General Electric Co., 1957).

4 The Status and Politics of Writing Instruction

Richard Hendrix
Fund for the Improvement of Postsecondary Education

The writing "crisis" perceived in the mid-1970's by now has the familiar look of an educational problem in the process of being solved. While the original concern may have been overstated, it is clear that the problem of poor writing was not (as some claimed) a hoax and the solutions are not fads. In fact, both educational practice and research have been positively influenced by identifying writing ability as a key concern. Curricular reform and pedagogy have profited from an increased emphasis on writing as an essential skill and as a mode of learning. And basic research on writing is focusing on complex issues of process, development and function, which tend to be downplayed in much educational research.

But these hopeful developments unfortunately do not tell the whole story of the present status of writing in education, and the prospects for writing improvement are ambiguous. How far the movement to improve writing will progress depends on obstacles within the educational system and unresolved differences in educational, social and personal goals.

The emphasis on writing clarifies the gap between a commitment in principle to universal opportunity and the fact of unequal opportunity. Writing ability is unevenly distributed in our society along class lines. Indeed, writing and access to writing improvement is as good an indicator of the difference between, say, white collar and blue collar career tracks as we are likely to find. Failure to recognize this structural backdrop will undermine the opportunity for widespread and democratic improvement.

In this essay I want to consider the status and politics of writing instruction by exploring a series of unanswered questions. An educational activity of such significance as writing cannot proceed in a vacuum, and I want to point

53

to some of the persistent dilemmas and contradictions which writing instruction is now bumping into. These are problems of educational policy as much as of research or pedagogy, and their solution would obviously involve broader issues.

My immediate frame of reference is improvement efforts within postsecondary education. This should be widely construed to include not only college classrooms, but activities like out-of-school workshops, company training programs, and testing. In addition, writing improvement within the high schools and the new concern for clear language in public documents must be kept in mind. Although these arenas have different dimensions to them, there can still be an integrity to the concern for writing improvement as there is in the act of writing itself.

WHOSE WRITING NEEDS IMPROVEMENT?

Writing deficiencies, like other vices, are perceived in almost everyone. Yet, at a more serious level, the shortcomings in writing ability that first attracted attention were those of poorly prepared students in their late teens. Both high school and college graduates were seen as less able to write than previously. Though the evidence for this judgment was never unequivocal, there was undoubtedly a basis for it; and the wide acceptance of the perception of student decline has become an important fact in its own right.

The general observation that students write less well obscured important differences between today's students and yesterday's. It is no accident that educators began to worry about students' basic abilities shortly after the advent of open admissions policies furthered an unprecendented democratization of higher education. And one can now hear in some teachers' complaints about the poor preparation of students a wish that these "new students" would go away.

But if writing skill became a problem just as more working class students went on to college, faulty writing was also very visible in middle class students. Some of the most vigorous attacks on poor writing have come at relatively elite high schools and colleges. And there are now basic writing projects at the graduate and professional level. In a sense, better off students are profitting from the effort to cope with a much more heterogeneous student population.

Other groups of learners (unemployed high school dropouts, adult women returning to study, full-time workers, etc.) have significant basic skills needs. But schools are unlikely to recognize their special features, or they assume that they should be met elsewhere. For instance, even the most progressive postsecondary adult re-entry programs rarely provide appropriate writing assistance, yet their procedures for assessment and credentialling require writing.

There is more workplace writing than is usually recognized, and there are a variety of training programs. In this context, the writing of professional and managerial staff has been singled out, in ways which parallel the tendency of schools. The U.S. Navy offers writing instruction to officers, and reading instruction to enlisted men. One national merchandizing firm may be typical of larger companies. It offers store level employees, mainly sales clerks and beginning managers, computer assisted lessons. These usually involve short-answer responses (up to 15-20 words) geared to activities like memo-writing, accounting, inventory, reports, letters to buyers, answers to customer complaints, etc. Eighty percent of the company are store level employees, and perhaps one-half of the sales force do not have high school degrees; so the volume of training is large, and the computer is seen as economical and able to impose standardization. These lessons are said to be of high quality. At the corporate headquarters level, there are at least four seminar series a year for professional employees (mainly college graduates), ranging from grammar review to basic technical writing to flexible rhetorical approaches for various occasions and audiences. Some classes even focus on salting a speech or memo with literary quotations. Top executives receive individual tutoring on demand.

Finally, the poor quality of writing in public documents—insurance policies, regulations, instructions, and so forth—has led to workshops and courses for businessmen and bureaucrats. The Document Design Project, funded by the National Institute of Education (NIE) and directed by the American Institutes for Research, is addressing this area. There is even the beginning of an attack on specialists' writing in medicine and law, though not yet in academic writing.

The point here is not to suggest that the need for writing improvement is so widespread as to be unmanageable (although writing is as difficult as it is important for many people.) The point is that there has not been a single, sustained focus for improvement. Initially, it was especially the more poorly prepared students who were targeted. But the call for writing improvement quickly was echoed for or by others, and the need is indeed broad. The beneficiaries of the new concern with writing now include those who already have real educational advantages; this does not mean, however, that the most basic needs will be addressed.

There often seems to be an unbridgeable gap between the skills deficiencies of first generation students and the tasks of expert writers. Yet in psychological and linguistic terms there is a continuum of development between elementary skills and full command of written language. We call writing a basic skill and educators have rightly stressed producing clear, even simple prose; e.g., avoiding errors of spelling or punctuation, forming logical sentences, organizing coherent paragraphs. None of this is easy work, particularly for those whose usual language does not conform to the rules and expectations of standard written English. Further along may be such achievements as a rich vocabulary, the ability to vary structure and presentation according to the needs of different audiences, the development of an original style. It will be a major undertaking if just the ability to produce clear English prose becomes more nearly universal. But that is no reason to treat the more sophisticated aspects of writing ability as refinements, or as beyond the capacity of most learners.

WHO IS RESPONSIBLE FOR IMPROVING WRITING?

Many groups have a role in writing instruction, but they are likely to see more differences than commonalities among themselves. Because writing instruction cuts across educational levels, and also occurs outside of school, the renewed interest (and investment of resources) in writing raises issues of turf and status. Just as one example, the National Endowment for the Humanities (NEH), which actually has supported very significant writing projects, prefers not to conceive of writing as a basic skill—since basic skills are taken as prior to or outside of the humanities.

Writing instruction was for years a stepchild of English departments, who have always dominated it. As recently as fifteen years ago many colleges dropped composition altogether--partly on the basis that the high schools were handling the job, and mainly to give still greater emphasis to literary study. That development should make us hesitate about trusting that English departments, as they are presently constituted, will solve the problem.

Now there has been a resurgence of active involvement by English faculty along with others. Writing instruction could be a boon for underemployed humanists, a large and influential group. But teachers trained in literature may not necessarily be well situated to work with beginning students, nor to prepare students for the kinds of writing tasks they will likely face after school. English professors are not even necessarily good writers themselves, and their commitment to specialization has been at least as strong as any other discipline's.

On the other hand, there are useful developments in teacher training and faculty development geared to writing instruction, which come from efforts to share the responsibility with other groups of teachers. "Writing across the curriculum" programs have caught on; this was the theme of the 1979 Conference on College Composition and Communication. In this there is a recognition that English faculty cannot do it alone. Strong projects at the University of Washington, funded by the Fund for the Improvement of Postsecondary Education (FIPSE), and at Beaver College (funded by NEH), are among numerous models.

Another FIPSE supported project at Temple University trains faculty from other departments against the backdrop of retrenchment; as elsewhere, there are still students wanting writing instruction, even though enrollments overall are declining. Surely such a situation leads faculty (both in English and in other departments) to take on writing despite their own background and perhaps despite their preferences. Such a development can be a real chance for professional development--or a shotgun wedding.

Within many colleges, of course, English faculy no longer have a monopoly on writing instruction. As the numbers of needy learners grew, the range of basic language instruction broadened. Two-year and four-year colleges serving large numbers of underprepared students developed special services and Educational Opportunities Programs. Some of these blended instruction with counseling and tutoring in promising ways. The Networks dissemination project, supported by FIPSE at Bronx Community College, is an attempt to build on some of this practice. But most such programs have tended to postpone rigorous instruction in writing, and their structural isolation from regular departments has been an obstacle.

Perhaps of greater significance is the growth of communication courses, particularly in institutions serving underprepared students. Work in reading and speech can help develop abilities which presumably are related to writing. Yet given the other demands on the curriculum, writing and language study cannot come to dominate the whole curriculum. This is also a fear raised by some of the more extensive writing throughout the curriculum programs.

College faculties are made up of departments which all have high priority work to do, and there has been little common ground. The tendency of academic disciplines to develop specialized and pre-professional concerns has worked against basic writing instruction. The stirring of interest within English for graduate study in composition could be helpful if the result is higher status for practitioners concerned with significant learning problems. Literature has dominated English, yet there is valuable research and practical training for which English faculty would be well suited. But if the result is more erudite dissertations and a narrowing of the subject, the profession will have asserted its own interests over the needs of learners.

By contrast, a strong development in postsecondary writing instruction has been the organization of comprehensive writing programs which, unlike traditional curricula, are set up horizontally rather than vertically. They draw faculty and students across disciplines, involve support services and practice labs as well as courses, and concern themselves with generic writing occasions rather than with literary study. They are usually related to an institution-wide requirement, rather than a prerequisite for the English department--even though they may be administered by English faculty. The new freshman course at the University of Southern California, supported by a small FIPSE grant for training teaching assistants, is one prominent example.

The recently formed Council of Writing Program Administrators represents this fresh approach, particularly in their emphasis on practical considerations of program management. At least implicitly they are a challenge to the usual kinds of status and influence in higher education. It may be relevant that morale is higher at Conference on College Composition and Communication meetings than at the Modern Language Association meetings, especially among younger faculty. There is a new interest in team managed programs and research, which is a departure from the deep-seated individualism of the humanities. The comprehensive program structure is also in keeping with the renewed interest in general education.

At the high school level and earlier, teacher preparation is being addressed in imaginative ways. Some approaches could be a model for postsecondary instruction, thus reversing the usual situation. Best known is the Bay Area Writing Project, now being adapted nationally with NEH support, which proceeds from the assumption that teachers' own greater ease in writing will improve instruction. This compelling hypothesis should be evaluated.

There are high school programs which have recaptured younger students' willingness to write. One is the *Foxfire* literary magazine (published by Doubleday), focusing school writing on practical and even mundane subjects of real concern to students. At Queens College, a FIPSE funded project involves teamwork with teachers in neighboring high schools that is altering both secondary and college practices, partly through a curriculum involving fables and narrative structures.

Such approaches only scratch the surface, of course. Of all the levels of education, secondary schools probably have the greatest need for new program ideas and for better teacher training. And most improvement efforts are still confined either to college bound students, or to vocational training; there is little integration. The issue of responsibility for writing instruction should come back to the high schools, but not in the form of finger pointing.

Many educators would be surprised at the range of writing improvement efforts occurring outside of formal education. No thorough surveys have been done, but numerous companies have writing courses (at least for professional employees), and some unions offer basic skills programs. Furthermore, independent workshops have sprung up to serve specific professional needs. Instructors in these programs usually are not trained in composition. They may have a background in journalism or technical writing, and they typically have first-hand experience of the language and techniques of the professions they address.

Finally, we should draw into the picture the government agencies and foundations which have seen writing improvement as a priority concern. These are mainly FIPSE, NIE and NEH at the federal level, although there is not really a coordinated program among these agencies. Programs in the Office of Education (OE), which most directly affect elementary and secondary education, have so far been less prominent, partly because their range of discretion is much more confined. So far there has not been talk of a

"Right to Write" program, although in fact "Right to Read" programs funded by OE can and sometimes do include writing skills. Foundations, particularly Exxon, Sloan, and Lilly, have had an interest in writing, but have not sustained funding programs.

So there is no shortage of actors interested in improving writing, including many besides English teachers. There is, however, uncertainty about how much and how permanently any sector will take responsibility for writing instruction. Sometimes writing has been a hot potato, tossed from department to department, from college to high school to training program. Just at the moment, given the shortage of younger students as well as new pressures to require demonstrable competence, writing improvement has become more like a bridal bouquet. It remains to be seen whether that results in a better understanding and sharing of responsibility.

WHAT DOES TESTING HAVE TO DO WITH WRITING IMPROVEMENT?

The new concen with writing instruction coincides with the "back to basics" movement and an increased reliance on testing, beginning in the early grades and extending to higher education and professional certification. The renewed stress on math and language skills, and the more general willingness to require student effort, are having valuable effects. But in school settings there is always a tendency to see drill and homework as ends in themselves, and to mistake the more obvious kinds of attainment for significant learning. Writing is one of those activities most likely to be misunderstood by the back to basics perspective, since surface errors are both glaring and correctable. Donald Graves of the University of New Hampshire finds an imbalance in basic instruction in favor of grammar, punctuation and spelling drills, rather than actually having children write (Graves, 1978).

In the new emphasis on testing, writing performance is both central and vulnerable. Legislators, parents and educators have adopted the idea of competency testing as a needed quality control. Most states are now requiring that high school students demonstrate certain knowledge and abilities before graduation. All these tests involve literacy, and sometimes this is interpreted as writing.

Even the concept of basic literacy is more of a sliding scale than a fixed standard. The most recent Ford Foundation commissioned study indicates that the standard of "functional" literacy needs to be revised upward, given the increased complexity of everyday life. There are many millions of Americans who are nowhere near competency. Such estimates reflect a trend, even if they are hard to take at face value. As society demands more, more are excluded almost by definition. This is true at various levels. For example, the movement toward compulsory continuing education for professionals will probably exclude competent individuals in the name of reform.

Teachers and administrators have the problem of setting reasonable expectations. At the college level, testing requirements usually occur at the end of the sophomore year, as a prerequisite for more advanced work. A FIPSE grant to Johnson State College in Vermont enabled the careful development and field-testing of such a measure, as well as the training of faculty from all parts of the college as scorers. The test was developed in anticipation of a statewide competency requirement, for which it now serves as the model. Such groundwork would seem minimal if writing tests are to be the basis for denying degrees. Now larger campuses and systems are involved in competency testing--for instance, the University of Massachusetts at Boston, and the City University of New York (CUNY) system.

Nothing more clearly indicates the insistence that writing is an essential college-level ability than the emergence of testing requirements. Of course, requiring tests allows students more options than the earlier practice of requiring completion of composition courses, but students are likely to experience the test as more absolute and threatening, especially against the background of the relative freedom of recent years.

The problem is not that standards are out of place in education--clearly the opposite is true--but that identifying and justifying appropriate standards for writing continues to be elusive. For example, the issue of what kind of writing should be taught is significant but usually overlooked. Faculty naturally require success in the school essay, which is clearly important for academic work, but not necessarily relevant to later needs.

When we look beyond home-grown tests to national tests, it is even clearer that the increased use of testing is ambiguous in its effects, and may inhibit efforts to improve writing for those with the greatest need. There are various tests of the features of standard written English. A problem here is that the test items often refer to experience which is less familiar to minority groups, even if the grammar, punctuation or spelling being tested can be conceived of as universal. Another problem is the tendency to teach to the test, once something can be measured; so our current capacity to test for standard written English may well overstate its importance.

It also may be possible to measure more sophisticated aspects of writing. For example, there is promising work on transitions as an indication of coherence. Establishing such standards is not easy. The extensive work on sentence structure, using techniques of sentence combining to teach students to form more complex sentences, runs into disagreement that this is an appropriate measure of better writing.

The more general problems with these more objective tests are that they focus on just an aspect of writing, and that they establish standards which good writers often violate. Furthermore, the tendency toward machine scoring (preferred by testing companies for economic reasons) seriously shortchanges the assessment of writing, by not in fact requiring written responses. Here the widespread conviction that writing ability cannot truly be demonstrated except through writing must hold sway.

Recently the College Board has restored some essay tests (as indeed instructors in content areas are doing), in response to educators' demands. The absence of such tests was felt to be a partial cause of the disregard of composition. Some experimental developments in testing, such as the American College Testing Company's College Outcomes Measuring Program for general education and tests of critical thinking and analysis devised by McBer & Company, require written responses. But they are relatively expensive to administer.

Most writing instructors find that the Educational Testing Service (ETS) method of holistic assessment is the most appropriate alternative to machine scored tests. The method depends on socialization of expert readers toward consensus about good writing, but without reference to stated norms (Hirsch, 1977). According to some who participate in the scoring, this leads judgment toward conventional preferences in content, and of course toward standard usage. Yet it is hard to see the results as generalizable when the norms remain unspecified and depend on the particular mix or timing of a small group and an influential leader.

Holistic scoring is popular with English teachers because, as the name implies, it is based on overall impressions which involve common values and norms. This makes the method consistent with academic practice, and in fact some faculties are trying out collective grading activities derived from ETS's. Probably this is a worthwhile control against the arbitrariness of individual professors. And the fact that consensus is usually achieved can be taken as a validation of typical faculty judgment, although that judgment still needs explication.

The most important effect of this kind of judgment, however, is that it establishes (and continues) the norms of one fairly homogeneous group as a standard. Of course all norms belong to individuals, though some may be more universal than others. In the case of writing assessment, the norms of standard written English are very nearly the norms of white, middle class faculty. This at least is a fair description of those who make the judgments, and when the content of an essay is part of what is judged, the experience of writer and reader are at issue.

As always, we need to understand what these norms and expectations exclude. On the one hand, the relatively direct forms of written communication required in business or civic affairs are not often part of the experience of English teachers. They are likely to downgrade writing which might be very effective in non-school contexts.

Most serious is the likelihood that the typical judgments of writing teachers will penalize working class and minority students. Almost everyone expects (though few point it out) that these students will do worse with increased testing. Cultural unfairness may arise even apart from questions of content. Marcia Farr Whiteman (this volume) shows how features of black vernacular English recur in black student writing, with its own discernible logic. Speakers of nonstandard English (blacks and others) may be on their way to developing quite effective writing abilities, even while some of the surface features of their writing (e.g., noun/verb agreement) are persistently incorrect.

Until we can be sure that teachers have real insight into language, and into the emotional difficulty of cultural assimilation, it is hard to avoid the conclusion that minority and working class students have to go an extra mile in mastering writing. That fact is likely to be continuously dramatized with renewed testing. The extra effort itself may be justifiable in practical and social terms (many black parents now insist on it), but writing teachers at least need to acknowledge this situation, and rethink the relative weight given to different aspects of writing for the developing writer. Writing is hard enough to master in its own right, without becoming the arena for unacknowledged social differences.

The testing function brings us back to the prospect that the movement to improve writing may finally (and ironically) penalize those with the greatest need. This is possible because of the social role of those most concerned with writing improvement.

Holding back on specifying the norms and expectations for writing achievement prevents their examination and justification. Even the testers point out that assessment itself does not improve writing. Educators need to avoid being driven by testing, unless they want to be in the position of confirming that education is mainly a sorting and certifying activity. Writing instruction should be an opportunity for learning, expression and empowerment. But writing will simply become an obstacle and an object of mistrust for those outside the dominant culture, if we let it.

What Kind of Writing Should be Taught?

Until recent years, most educators took for granted the textbook definitions of formal expository prose alongside related forms such as business English. These forms are now more open to question. Most important, the formal school essay, while done in great volume, is done very little outside school. Indeed, the impersonal essay full of literary allusions is now less prevalent even in school. Students still write about personal experience, texts, past or current events, laboratory work, and so forth, in a way which allows them to reflect and analyze. The audience is, on the one hand, the instructor, and on the other hand, a "general" reader. This audience has patience and sensitivity. No one questions that learning to write in this way is important for school success, a serious and appropriate concern, and for intellectual growth. Learning to reflect and analyze will never be outmoded.

But out of school writing is typically for a more limited and more immediate audience, with little time to spare. This is true of memos, reports, letters (and written responses to these forms), advertisements and applications. Business English does not get at the adaptability needed for such communication, since it is mainly training in set formats.

Technical writing is clearly more powerful in its applications, though there is a tendency to go too far in the direction of specialized jargon and unique formats. The stronger programs in technical writing, such as those at Carnegie-Mellon, Massachusetts Institute of Technology and Texas A & M, avoid this extreme, and teach broad-based approaches to industrial and scientific writing. However, such courses are not usually seen as general education as much as professional training, and the technical writing itself is frequently incomprehensible for non-specialists.

We know little about everyday occasions for writing, but the time may be ripe for agreement that writing forms are quite various, though with essential commonalities. Several contributors to this volume (Heath, Szwed, Valadez) suggest an unusually wide frame of reference for discussing writing. Writing instruction probably should not focus on creating posters or graffiti, if for no other reason than the prospect that they would lose their vitality in a school setting. But we should come to understand why many people are fluent in such ephemeral writing, even when they are stymied by school or workplace writing.

Of more practical import are new attempts to determine the nature of job related writing, including NIE supported research by Lee O'Dell of SUNY Albany and Dixie Goswami of the University of Tennessee, and a new FIPSE project with the New York City Police Foundation. A successful lab-based college course, developed with FIPSE support at York College, CUNY, is now being applied experimentally at a major hospital and for customer service representatives at the Commonwealth Edison Company.

Such applications will test the extent to which a general strengthening of the ability to generate clear prose will help with fairly specific writing tasks, usually seen as self-contained in company training programs. Most writing teachers are convinced that the generic skills of organization and communication are transferable for different writing needs. This would be a hard proposition to test completely, yet there is much circumstantial evidence.

The "plain English" movement also works toward what once would have been called a *lingua communis*--especially vocabulary and syntax which are immediately understandable by readers of modest education. Such usage is independent of any specific information or style. Perhaps this should be a widespread curricular goal, replacing the former dominance of literary models.

Linda Flower of Carnegie Mellon makes an important distinction between "writer-based" and "reader-based" prose (Flower, 1979). The latter is organized according to the understanding of the audience rather than the author. This is both consistent with traditional rhetoric, and a call for writing instruction which draws the reader in in new and more direct ways: for example, through simulations which put the student in the position of writing documents on which decisions are made (e.g., a briefing document before a vote, or instructions and directions and then playing out the results).

Such work is probably more feasible for more advanced students, yet the idea that writing assignments should involve their intended function has implications for most writing instruction. This is clearly not the same as trying to keep up with a proliferation of genres and formats.

The time is past when the formal, refelctive essay was the only worthwhile kind of writing to master; but the dimension of generic application is still a crucial aspect of writing instruction. There is now a greater incentive to learn writing as public communication, and for this we need to understand the purposes of writing.

WRITING FOR WHAT PURPOSES?

Behind the longtime dominance of the school essay, was a similar certainty about the purposes of writing. Shirley Brice Heath (this volume) examines the nineteenth century evolution of writing from largely casual and informative practices (which were widespread) to more formal expressions of much greater moral import (and therefore relatively restricted). By the end of the nineteenth century the composition course in both high schools and colleges was much more than training in basic writing; it was a crucible and test of intellect and character.

The fading of composition as required study in the 1960's involved a recognition that using writing instruction as primarily cognitive and moral education had worn thin. It is meaningful that we now prefer the term "writing" to the more ambiguous (and ambitious) term "composition." The focus on basic writing more nearly meets the needs of a wide range of learners. It also allows for demonstrable gains in a very complex skill, and so learners are empowered.

In principle, this empowerment is apart from the particualr values through which composition has served as a middle class sorting device. But in practice, the unquestioned need to master surface features predominates and this alone can make writing instruction seem like training in etiquette. This seems usually to be the case in the early grades.

By the time we are adults, there are more substantial purposes for attaining the ability to write. Good writing has been seen as an outward sign, if not a guarantee, of success. Dale Carnegie was, by extension, a writing teacher, when he taught "How to Win Friends and Influence People" by public presentation. Such success includes acceptable attitudes and manners, as can be demonstrated in writing, along with originality and industriousness.

Now there is evidently less consensus about the nature of success itself. However, composition textbooks still strongly imply deeper purposes than just developing writing skill. They are now likely to work toward goals like "finding your own voice," an appropriate kind of success for the 1970's, and hardly without side benefits.

If this kind of character building seems out of place, teaching toward work-related and pragmatic concerns is not necessarily an answer. There is the same tendency as in most career education to adopt the perspective of the employer, and to align the development of writing ability with purposes which are not primarily the student's own. The purposes of organizational writing will need to be looked at critically. For example, some writing (from internal memos to insurance policies to public regulations) is obscure by design.

The emphasis on work-related writing does entail a welcome gain in relevance over the exclusive use of the formal expository essay. Other purposes for writing also have a powerful claim, and these have not yet had as prominent a place in the movement to improve writing. The traditional claim that "writing is good for you" deserves a fresher form, in terms of purposes which are more nearly the learner's own. And the association of writing instruction and intellectual (if not moral) growth runs deep, and must be based on insight into human development.

A useful parallel can be drawn with the renewed interest in liberal education, itself intimately related to writing. The problem there is to restate traditional educational purposes, in a way that takes into account the actual needs of the very different population now demanding an education of enduring personal and social value. The interest in liberal education sometimes focuses on developing generic abilities of wide application, and in this vein writing or communication is always a keystone.

Perhaps there should be a similar link for writing instruction with such roles as citizenship. Our form of government still can be seen as built on the assumption of a literate populace, despite the negative history of literacy "tests." The individual or group who can express a need or a position in writing is better able to participate. This is masked by the skepticism associated with pleas to "write your congressman" or by the stiffness of conventional petitions and speeches. But at least at the local level the fact still remains that those who can get their ideas into writing, if not into print, have a power to define and persuade.

Moreover, just as there are more kinds of writing than are likely to be appropriate subjects for instruction, there are more purposes which cause people to write than are likely to be addressed in composition courses. Ephemeral writing may have purposes ranging from self assertion to political protest. Communication by letter usually involves fairly direct purposes, whether friendly or impersonal. An ethnographer might also consider highly practical writing purposes, like list making or filling in applications or registration materials. And this may be the place to remember that writing, besides its instrumental qualities, is sometimes one of those activities which is an end in itself. Most of this need not concern writing instruction, but it does serve as a reminder that the question of purposes is never just what purposes; it is also whose.

Perhaps there should be experimentation with instructional approaches which do not assume a linear development from simple to complex (in terms of predominant models, from word to sentence to paragraph to whole essay). One route would be through creative writing, where some of the overwhelming emotional obstacles to writing development can be lessened. Interestingly, one of the most insistently basic new programs--the COMP-LAB course at York College, which requires step by step mastery beginning with the most elementary forms--also requires continual "free writing" activity, as advocated by Peter Elbow in *Writing Without Teachers* (1973). Somehow, students need to discover purposes which are their own.

Purpose is a complex issue because it involves values and politics, and this brings us closer to the limits of the new movement to improve writing. For a long time the purpose of writing instruction was clearly developmental as well as practical; yet it served to sort and select rather than to provide opportunity. At about the time that providing opportunity became the overriding concern of educational policy, writing instruction was deemphasized; perhaps partly because of its traditional gatekeeper role. Yet within a short time the perceived decline in writing ability led educators, policy makers and parents to a revived concern for teaching writing. One of the first clear and useful responses has been to make writing instruction more relevant to workplace demands. But this response leaves out very significant personal and social purposes of writing, and it may understate their importance.

A harder way to put the question of purpose, is to interpret educational policy in general as confined within larger social intentions or meanings. In the case of writing instruction, how many really able writers does society need or want? Especially if we take writing capability as something beyond mere skill--as involving critical insight, originality, control over one's own purposes--it is not at all clear that writing ability would really be accepted as a universal goal of education.

WHAT IS GOOD WRITING?

The difficult questions of standards, responsibility and purposes have a more basic form, which has largely been avoided in recent years. The question of what is good writing probably cannot have an absolute answer; this seems clear in literature, at least. Blake's dictum, "One law for the lion and the ox is oppression," has undeniable force in an age of pluralism. But the question still needs to be asked in writing instruction, if for no other reason than to indicate those features of better writing which are nearly absolute. And we should see that quality is an essential goal of writing, even if no one definition can suffice.

Of course some norms can be stated, particularly in describing the grammar, punctuation and spelling of standard written English. For expository prose, standard usage is a minimal definition of good writing, and there is no longer much argument about whether standard English is an appropriate focus of writing instruction.

Beyond the surface features of standard written English, it is probably possible to agree about the comprehensibility of a given piece of writing (Hirsch 1977). Surely effectiveness in communication is a reasonable norm for almost all writing, and more specified than in holistic scoring. In such a judgment the intended meaning is taken as a given, and the writing is good insofar as it conveys that meaning.

Communicative effectiveness is a relatively modest, though clearly meaningful, standard of good writing. It leaves out the content of the essay (and so in traditional terms its truth or orginality) and its purposes. It would be useful to know more about the effect or function of writing in actual settings, rather than in controlled test situations. There are good (or at least better) memos, regulations, reports and the like, in terms of values like clarity and usefulness to the reader. In any case, this is probably as far as assessment should go, at least through standardized testing and home-grown tests which are used to deny admissions or credentials.

But apart from the concerns of assessment, we commonly mean more than surface correctness and comprehensibility when we speak of good writing. Consider, for example, this passage from Bill Russell's autobiography (1979) on an early reading experience:

> I was breezing along through a chapter on the American Revolution when I did a double take on one sentence. It was as if somebody had stuck a foot out there on the page and tripped my mind as it went by. I looked again, and this sentence jumped out at me: Despite the hardships they suffered most slaves enjoyed a higher standard of living and a better life in America than in their primitive African homeland.
> As far as I can remember, this was the first time I was ever enraged.

In terms of standard usage and of comprehensibility, the sentence which tripped Russell up is faultless. Yet most would agree with Russell that this is not good writing because of the meaning conveyed. And obviously the effect produced is contrary to what was intended.

An analysis of this sentence shows a coldness and distance which helps make it offensive: the condescension of "primitive African homeland," the vagueness and altered context of "higher standard of living," and (at a more subtle level) the deceptive juxtaposition of "suffered" and "enjoyed"--making the latter word seem natural, when in fact it is a perversion of the slaves' experience. Such an analysis shows how much words count, whether or not the author intends their effect. And the matter is beyond just an arrangement of words; in this case, an issue of history and of justice inevitably becoming part of the writing.

It is not realistic to expect that students can develop enough control over their own writing to avoid revealing obnoxious ideas, if indeed they have them. What may be appropriate, however, is the expectation that writing instruction should include developing a critical awareness of the meaning and implications of the ideas for which an author is responsible. And that students should learn to write in ways that more nearly serve their own purposes, without earning the rage of their audience.

A partial model for a fuller understanding of good writing is the work of Brazilian priest Paulo Freire (1972). Freire makes great progress teaching illiterate peasants to read and write through a process of political education built on the experience of inequity and social and economic contradiction which is already part of the adult's consciousness. For Freire there is not the traditional split between teacher and student, since the peasant learner is clearly more authoritative about the details and meaning of his or her own experience. Although this is a Marxist education, it is not exactly an ideological one. The purposes of communication are the peasant's own and can vary, though they are dominated by the facts of oppression.

In our country, most learners are not in a revolutionary situation. But this need not obscure the lesson that the least literate can begin to use language effectively when they begin to take control of their own ideas (and perhaps not before), that being able to write involves having something meaningful to say for one's own purposes. All English teachers know the students' complaint that they have nothing to say; and most also know that students almost always do have something to say, if there is reason to do so.

By this analysis good writing must have human validity as well as correctness and clarity. Writers need to define and justify their own purposes, and to be sensitive to their audience. A way of characterizing such writing would be as a part of a broad humanistic education--once the province of the English teacher, but now usually disregarded or defined defensively (e.g., as the contrary of career education, or as only suitable for those with a "good background.")

In fact it is remarkable that much of the best recent work in writing research and instruction has not had a humanistic flavor or bias. Rather, it has had a strong scientific tendency, even when done by English faculty, and it has involved social scientists in major ways. This is clear in the experimentation with new, "teacher proof" techniques. Sentence combining, for instance, is exercises done apart from overall considerations of meaning. The autotutorial and computer based approaches are of course impersonal, and focus on drill and those aspects of writing which can be done automatically. Practitioners are now inclined to deemphasize or exclude the learning of theory and concepts of language itself or of rhetoric.

Despite a gain in practical effectiveness, the new work still has a quality of insufficiency or incompleteness. At worst, writing becomes another technocratic activity, divorced from personal or social change. Some of the behavioral studies of writing performance describe writing as if it could be produced by a machine. Raising the question of purpose in writing, and of value, can't be posponed forever because writing itself depends on them. We know that though mechanical learning can be highly successful when it is reinforced, it does not lead to invention; yet writing requires at least an understanding of ideas and their relationship, and meaningful writing is original.

Writing instruction brings us squarely to the margin of practical and moral education. This is a classic dilemma, but it does not necessarily require a choice. The integration of the useful and the ethical, as of school, work and personal life, is an old ideal which keeps recurring. The present preference for pragmatic approaches is a major advance which nevertheless is reaching its limits.

A generation ago concern about poor writing was focused differently by George Orwell (1946). Orwell demonstrated that writing inevitably reveals its origins, and that bad writing is bad politics. In doing this he assumed a hierarchal standard of good writing (somewhat ironically, considering his socialism) involving more or less fixed usage, and plain syntax and diction. Nouns were not meant to be used as verbs, nor to be piled high with adjectives. Figures of speech had to be well understood and appropriate. Otherwise, self-deception and lies were the likely result.

In the new movement to improve writing, there has been no voice like Orwell's defining valid practice. We understand language differently now, and there is not a consensus about good writing. The organizing theme of this volume, variability, is clearly different than it would have been thirty years ago. Inasmuch as it expresses the most important fact about writing practices and educational needs, it is a better theme. But Orwell's understanding of the social and political functions of writing is not outdated, and we could still learn from it.

Close to our own concerns and a truer guide than either Orwell or Freire is the work of Mina Shaughnessy, in *Errors and Expectations* (1977) and in her teaching. Shaughnessy's work with open admission students was both humanistic and rigorous. She assumed that students described by traditional faculty as "unteachable" were not that. She saw patterns to their errors which were interesting in themselves, and revealing of systematic efforts to cope with bad schooling and to express important meanings. She understood that even the most limited writers in terms of language skills, might have a great deal to say. Toward the end of her life, she was more and more interested in the problems of teaching adults to write and training teachers of writing. There were always practical problems, but never only that. She often quoted Jacques Barzun's line, that "the person who writes stands up to be shot." This is what makes writing instruction difficult, and worth doing.

It makes sense to begin with the basics, but not to end with them. The new learners who precipitated the writing "crisis" still have the most to gain by writing improvement. The best new practice in writing instruction tends to be highly realistic about beginning where the students are and consciously seeking elementary gains. But such instruction is not conceived of as sufficient, nor as a dead end.

REFERENCES

Elbow, Peter. *Writing Without Teachers.* Oxford: Oxford University Press, 1973.

Flower, Linda. "Writer-Based Prose: A Cognitive Basis for Problems in Writing," *College English,* vol. 41 (September, 1979), pp. 19–37.

Freire, Paulo. *Pedagogy of the Oppressed,* translated by Myra Bergman Ramos. New York: Herder and Herder, 1972.

Graves, Donald. *Balance the Basics: Let them Write.* New York: Ford Foundation, 1978.

Hirsch, E.D. Jr., *The Philosophy of Composition.* Chicago: University of Chicago Press, 1977.

Orwell, George. "Politics and the English Language" (1946), in *A Collection of Essays.* New York: Doubleday, 1954.

Russell, Bill and Branch, Taylor. *Second Wind.* New York: Random House, 1979.

Shaughnessy, Mina P. *Errors and Expectations: A Guide for the Teacher of Basic Writing.* New York: Oxford University Press, 1977.

5 Unpackaging Literacy

Sylvia Scribner
Michael Cole

One of the important services anthropology has traditionally provided other social sciences is to challenge generalizations about human nature and the social order that are derived from studies of a single society. The comparative perspective is especially valuable when the topic of inquiry concerns psychological "consequences" of particular social practices, such as for example, different methods of child-rearing (permissive vs. restrictive) or schooling (formal vs. nonformal) or mass communication (oral vs. literate). It is a hazardous enterprise to attempt to establish causal relationships among selected aspects of social and individual function without taking into account the totality of social practice of which they are a part. How are we to determine whether effects on psychological functioning are attributable to the particular practices selected for study, or to other practices with which they covary, or to the unique patterning of practices in the given society? When we study seemingly "same" practices in different societal contexts, we can better tease apart the distinctive impact of such practices from other features of social life.

Here we apply one such comparative approach to questions about reading and writing practices and their intellectual impact. Our approach combines anthropological field work with experimental psychological methods in a study of "literacy without schooling" in a West African traditional society. We hope our findings will suggest a new perspective from which to examine propositions about the intellectual and social significance of literacy whose uncertain status contributes to our educational dilemmas.

These dilemmas have been repeatedly stated. They revolve around implications for educational and social policy of reports that students' writing

71

skills are deficient, and that there is a "writing crisis." Is this the case and if so, is it really a matter for national concern? Does it call for infusion of massive funds in new research studies and methods of instruction? Or is it merely a signal that we should adjust our educational goals to new "technologies of communication" which reduce the need for high levels of literacy skill? (See for example Macdonald, 1973)

These questions call for judgments on the social importance of writing and thus raise an even more fundamental issue: on what grounds are such judgments to be made? Some advocate that pragmatic considerations should prevail and that instructional programs should concentrate on teaching only those specific writing skills that are required for the civic and occupational activities student groups may be expected to pursue. Many educators respond that such a position is too narrow and that it overlooks the most important function of writing, the impetus that writing gives to intellectual development. The argument for the general intellectual importance of writing is sometimes expressed as accepted wisdom and sometimes as knowledge revealed through psychological research. At one end of the spectrum there is the simple adage that "An individual who writes clearly thinks clearly," and at the other, conclusions purporting to rest on scientific analysis, such as the recent statement that "the cognitive restructurings caused by reading and writing develop the higher reasoning processes involved in extended abstract thinking" (Farrell, 1977, p. 451).

This is essentially a psychological proposition and one which is increasingly moving to the forefront of discussion of the "writing problem." Our research speaks to several serious limitations in developing this proposition as a ground for educational and social policy decisions. One of these is the frailty of the evidence for generalizations about the dependency of certain cognitive skills on writing, and the other is the restricted model of the writing process from which hypotheses about cognitive consequences tend to be generated. Before presenting our findings on Vai literacy, we shall briefly consider each of these in turn.

SPECULATIONS ABOUT COGNITIVE
CONSEQUENCES OF LITERACY

What are the sources of support for statements about intellectual consequences of literacy? In recent decades, scholars in such disciplines as philology, comparative literature and anthropology have advanced the thesis that over the course of history, literacy has produced a "great divide" in human modes of thinking. Havelock (1963) speculated that the advent of alphabetic writing systems and the spread of literacy in post-Homeric Greece changed the basic forms of human memory. Goody & Watt (1963) maintained that these same historic events laid the basis for the development of new categories of understanding and new logical operations, and in subsequent studies Goody (1977) has concluded that potentialities for graphic representation promote unique classificatory skills.

Ong's (1958) historical analyses of prose literary genres in the fifteenth century led him to conclude that the invention of the printing press gave rise to a new form of intellectual inquiry uniquely related to the printed text.

Intriguing as these speculations are, their significance for a theory of psychological consequences for *individuals* in *our* society is problematic on two counts. These scholars derive evidence for cognitive effects of literacy from historical studies of cultural and social changes associated with the advent of widespread literacy. Inferences about cognitive changes in *individuals* are shaky if they rest only on the analysis of *cultural* phenomena. The inconclusiveness of the great debate between Levy-Bruhl and Franz Boas (see Cole & Scribner, 1974) on the "logicality of primitive thought" reminds us of the limitations of reliance on cultural data as sole testimony to psychological processes. Secondly we need to distinguish between historical and contemporaneous causation (see Lewin, 1936). The development of writing systems and the production of particular kinds of text may, indeed, have laid the basis *historically* for the emergence of new modes of intellectual operation, but these over time, may have lost their connection with the written word. There is no necessary connection between the modality in which new operations come into being and the modality in which they are perpetuated and transmitted in later historical epochs. Forms of discourse initially confined to written text may subsequently come to be transmitted orally through teacher-pupil dialogue, for example, or through particular kinds of "talk" produced on television shows. One cannot leap to the conclusion that what was necessary historically is necessary in contemporaneous society. There is no basis for assuming, without further evidence, that the individual child, born into a society in which uses of literacy have been highly elaborated, must personally engage in writing operations in order to develop "literate modes of thought." That *may* be the case, but it requires proof, not simply extrapolation from cultural-historical studies.

While most psychologists have been interested in the psycholinguistic aspects of reading, some have concerned themselves with these theoretical conjectures on the cognitive consequences of writing. Vygotsky (1962) considered that writing involved a different set of psychological functions from oral speech. Greenfield (1968) has suggested that written language in the schools is the basis for the development of "context-independent abstract thought"—the distinguishing feature of school-related intellectual skills. Scribner (1968) speculated that mastery of a written language system might underlie formal scientific operations of the type Piaget has investigated. Olson (1975) argues that experience with written text may lead to a mode of thinking which derives generalizations about reality from purely linguistic, as contrasted to, empirical operations. In his view, schooling achieves importance precisely because it is an "instrument of literacy." "There is a form of human competence," he states, "uniquely associated with development of a high degree of literacy that takes years of schooling to develop" (p. 148).

These views, too, lack clear-cut empirical tests. Greenfield was extrapolating effects of written language from comparisons of schooled and unschooled child populations, but it is clear that such populations vary in many other ways besides knowledge of a written language system. Olson, to our knowledge, has developed his case from a theoretical analysis of the kind of inferential operations that the processing of written statements "necessarily" entails. Scribner employed the same method of procedure.

These are perfectly satisfactory *starting* points for a theory of the intellectual consequences of reading and writing but they do not warrant the status of conclusions. At a minimum, we would want evidence that the consequences claimed for literacy can be found in comparisons of literate and nonliterate adults living in the same social milieu whose material and social conditions of life do not differ in any systematic way.

We not only lack evidence for theoretical speculations about the relationship between writing and thinking, but in our opinion, the model of writing which underlies most psychological theorizing is too restricted to serve as a guide for the necessary research.

SOME DOMINANT CONCEPTIONS OF WRITING

Although all disciplines connected with writing acknowledge that it has different "functions," these are often conceived as external to the writing act itself—that is the functions being served by writing are not seen as intrinsic to an analysis of component skills. In theory and in practice, writing is considered a unitary (although admittedly complex) phenomenon representing some given and fixed set of processes. These processes, it is assumed, can be ferretted out and analysed by the psychologist, linguist and educator without regard to their contexts of use. The call for the present conference suggests such a view. It urges that national attention, which for some years has been directed toward the "reading process," now be turned toward an investigation of the "writing process." Writing, together with reading, are described as "abilities" which it is the task of education to enhance.

The "writing process" is typically identified with the production of written discourse or text. Non-textual uses of writing, such as the notational systems employed in mathematics and the sciences which also require complex symbol manipulation, are excluded from the domain of writing, along with other types of graphic representation which use non-linguistic elements (diagrams, codes, maps, for example).

In practice, a prototypical form of text underlies most analyses of the writing process.[1] This is the expository text or what Britton and his colleagues (Britton et al., 1975) characterize as transactional writing. Transactional writing is described as writing in which it is taken for granted that the writer means what he says and can be challenged for its truthfulness and its logicality: "...it is the typical language of science and of intellectual inquiry... of planning, reporting, instructing, informing, advising, persuading, arguing and theorising (Martin et al, 1976, p. 24, 25)."

Models of the cognitive skills involved in writing are intimately tied up with this type of text. Thus in making the claim that certain analytic and inferential operations are only possible on the basis of written text, Olson (1975) selects the analytic essay to represent the "congealed mental labor" represented in writing. Nonliterate and literate modes of thought are basically distinguished by differential experience with the production and consumption of essayist text.

The development of writing skills is commonly pictured as a course of progression toward the production of expository text. Bereiter's (mimeo) suggested model of writing, for example, rests on the assumption that there is a lawful sequence in the growth of writing competence and that this sequence progresses toward the production of a well-crafted story or a logically coherent discussion of a proposition. At the apex of progressively more complex structures of writing skills is epistemic writing-writing that carries the function of intellectual inquiry. (Similar views are expressed by Moffett, 1968).

What is apparent from this somewhat simplified sketch, is that most of our notions of what writing is about, the skills it entails and generates, are almost wholly tied up with school-based writing. Centrality of the expository text and well-crafted story in models of the writing process accurately reflects the emphasis in most school curricula. A recently completed study of secondary schools in England (Martin et al, 1976) found that writing classed as transactional (see definition above) constituted the bulk of written school work, increasing from 54% of childrens' writing in the first year to 84% in the last. Since such writing skills are both the aim of pedagogy and the enabling tools which sustain many of the educational tasks of the school, their preeminence in current research does not seem inappropriate. But we believe that near-exclusive preoccupation with school-based writing practices has

---

[1]The narrative text is also a common prototype, but we are leaving aside for the time being approaches to creative writing which have largely been initiated and developed outside the public school system.

some unfortunate consequences. The assumption that logicality is in the text and the text is in school can lead to a serious underestimation of the cognitive skills involved in non-school, non-essay writing, and, reciprocally, to an overestimation of the intellectual skills that the essayist test "necessarily" entails. This approach binds the intellectual and social significance of writing too closely to the image of the academic and the professional member of society, writ large. It tends to promote the notion that writing outside of the school is of little importance and has no significant consequences for the individual. The writing crisis presents itself as purely a pedagogical problem—a problem located in the schools to be solved in the schools through the application of research and instructional techniques. What is missing in this picture is any detailed knowledge of the role and functions of writing outside of school, the aspirations and values which sustain it, and the intellectual skills it demands and fosters. As our study of literacy among the Vai indicates, these facts are central to an evaluation of the intellectual and social significance of writing.

THREE LITERACIES AMONG THE VAI

The Vai, a Mande-speaking people of northwestern Liberia, like their neighbors, practice slash-and-burn rice farming using simple iron tools, but they have attained a special place in world history as one of the few cultures to have independently invented a phonetic writing system (Dalby, 1967; Gelb, 1952; Koelle, 1854). Remarkably, this script, a syllabary of 200 characters with a common core of 20-40, has remained in active use for a century and a half within the context of traditional rural life and in coexistence with two universalistic and institutionally powerful scripts—the Arabic and Roman alphabets. Widely available to all members of the society (though in practice confined to men), Vai script is transmitted outside of any institutional setting and without the formation of a professional teacher group.

The fact that literacy is acquired in this society without formal schooling and that literates and nonliterates share common material and social conditions allows for a more direct test of the relationship between literacy and thinking than is possible in our own society. Among the Vai we could make direct comparisons of the performance on cognitive tasks of reasonably well-matched groups of literate and nonliterate adults. To do so, however, required us from the outset to engage in an ethnographic enterprise not often undertaken with respect to literacy—the study of literacy as acquired and practiced in the society at large. Our effort to specify exactly what it is about reading and writing that might have intellectual consequences and to characterize these consequences in observable and measurable ways forced us away from reliance on vague generalizations. We found ourselves seeking more detailed and more concrete answers to questions about *how* Vai people acquire literacy skills, *what* these skills are, and *what* they do with them. Increasingly we found ourselves turning to the information we had obtained about actual literacy practices to generate hypotheses about cognitive consequences.

From this work has emerged a complex picture of the wide range of activities glossed by the term "writing," the varieties of skills these activities entail and the specificity of their cognitive consequences.

What Writing "Is" Among The Vai

Our information about Vai literacy practices comes from a number of sources: interviews with some 700 adult men and women, in which anyone literate in one of the scripts was questioned extensively on how he had learned the script and what uses he made of it; ethnographic studies of literacy in two rural towns[2]; observations and records of Vai script teaching sessions and Qur'anic schools; analyses of Vai script and Arabic documents as they relate to Vai social institutions (see Goody, Cole & Scribner, 1977).

We estimate that 28% of the adult male population is literate in one of the three scripts, the majority of these in the indigenous Vai script, the next largest group in Arabic and the smallest in English. There is a substantial number of literate men who read and write both Vai and Arabic and a small number of triliterates. Since each script involves a different orthography, completion of a different course of instruction and, in the cases of Arabic and English, use of a foreign language, multiliteracy is a significant accomplishment.[3]

As in other multiliterate societies, functions of literacy tend to be distributed in regularly patterned ways across the scripts, bringing more clearly into prominence their distinctive forms of social organization, and transmission and function. In a gross way, we can characterize the major divisions among the scripts in Vai life as follows: English is the official script of political and economic institutions operating on a national scale; Arabic is the script of religious practice and learning; Vai script serves the bulk of

---

[2]These were carried out by Michael R. Smith, an anthropologist from Cambridge University.

[3]Because this phenomenon is rarely encountered in our own culture, we tend to peg our "basic skills models" of writing very closely to the particular characteristics and structure of a single orthographic system and assumptions of pre-writing fluency in the language represented. As Fishman (1975) suggests was the case with bilingualism, studies of multiscript-using communities might well enlarge the framework in which basic research on literacy is conducted. For accounts of other nonindustrialized societies with a number of simultaneously active scripts, see Gough, 1968; Tambiah, 1968; Wilder, 1972. Schofield, 1968 reminds us that between the 16th and 19th centuries in England, early instruction in reading and writing was conducted with texts in English while higher education was conducted in classical Latin.)

personal and public needs in the villages for information preservation and communication between individuals living in different locales.

In daily practice these distinctions are often blurred, raising a host of interesting questions about the personal and situational factors which may influence the allocation of literacy work to one or another script.

English script has least visibility and least impact in the countryside. It is learned exclusively in Western-type government and mission schools, located for the most part outside of Vai country. Students leave home to pursue their education and to win their place in the modern sector. Little is seen of English texts in the villages, but paramount chiefs and some clan chiefs retain clerks to record court matters in English, and to maintain official correspondence with administrative and political functionaries.

Arabic writing, on the other hand, is an organic part of village life. Almost every town of any size has a Qur'anic school conducted by a learned Muslim (often the chief or other leading citizen). These are usually "schools without walls"—groups of boys ranging in age from approximately 4 years to 24, who meet around the fire twice a day for several hours of recitation and memorization of Qur'anic verses which are written on boards that each child holds. (Qur'anic teaching in West Africa is described in Wilks, 1968). In Islamic tradition, committing the Qur'an to memory (internalizing it in literal form) is a holy act, and the student's progress through the text is marked at fixed intervals by religious observances and feasting. Initially, learning can only proceed by "rote memorization" since the students can neither decode the written passages nor understand the sounds they produce. But students who perservere, learn to read (that is, sing out) the text and to write out passages-still with no understanding of the language. Some few who complete the Qur'an go on to advanced study under tutorship arrangements, learning Arabic as a language and studying Islamic religious, legal and other texts. In Vai country, there are a handful of outstanding scholars with extensive Arabic libraries who teach, study and engage in textual commentary, exegesis and disputation. Thus Arabic literacy can relate individuals to text on both the "lowest" (repetition without comprehension) and "highest" (analysis of textual meaning) levels. Arabic script is used in a variety of "magico-religious" practices; its secular uses include correspondence, personal journal notes and occasionally trade records. The overwhelming majority of individuals with Qur'anic training, however, do not achieve understanding of the language and their literacy activities are restricted to reading or writing out known passages of the Qur'an or frequently used prayers, a service performed for others as well as for oneself.

Approximately 90% of Vai are Muslim and, accordingly, Qur'anic knowledge qualifies an individual for varied roles in the community. Becoming literate in the Arabic language means becoming integrated into a close-knit but territorially extended social network, which fuses religious ideals, fraternal self-help, trade and economic relationships with opportunities for continuing education (see Wilks, 1968).

Knowledge of Vai script might be characterized as "literacy without education." It is typically learned within a two week to two month period with the help of a friend, relative or citizen who agrees to act as teacher. Learning consists of committing the characters to memory and practice in reading, first lists of names, later personal letters written in the Vai script. Demonstration of the ability to write a letter without errors is a common terminating point for instruction. With rare exceptions, there are no teaching materials except such letters or other written material as the teacher may have in his personal possession. "Completion of lessons" is not the endpoint of learning: there are frequent consultations between ex-student and teacher. For practiced scribe as well as novice, literacy activities often take a cooperative form (e.g. A goes to B to ask about characters he can't make out) and sometimes a contentious one (e.g., A and B dispute whether a given character is correct or in error).

Vai script uses are overwhelmingly secular. It serves the two classical functions of writing: memory (preserving information over time) and communication (transmitting it over space) in both personal and public affairs, with a heavy emphasis on the personal.[4]

From an analytic point of view, focusing on component skills, it is useful to classify script functions according to whether or not writing involves the production of text or non-text materials. Non-textual uses range from very simple activities to complex record-keeping. Among the simple activities are the uses of individual written characters as labels or marking devices (e.g., marking chairs lent for a public meeting with the names of owners, identifying one's house, clarifying information displayed in technical plans and diagrams).[5] Record-keeping, most typically a list-making activity, fulfills both social cohesion and economic functions. Lists of dowry items and death feast contributions, family albums of births, deaths, marriages—all help to regulate the kinship system of reciprocal rights and obligations. Lists enlarge the scope and planful aspects of commercial transactions: these include records of yield and income from cash-crop farming, proceeds netted in marketing, artisan records of customer orders and payments received.

A mere "listing of lists," however, fails to convey the great variation in levels of systematicity, organization and completeness displayed in records.

---

[4]Public functions of Vai script appear to be declining as English becomes mandatory for administrative and judicial matters.

[5]Gelb (1952) presents an interesting argument that social origins of non-pictorial writing systems are to be found in the use of individualized symbols as brands of ownership.

Some are barely decipherable series of names; others orderly columns and rows of several classes of information. Some genealogies consist of single-item entries scattered throughout copy books, others of sequential statements which shade off into narrative-like texts.

The more expert Vai literates keep public records from time to time when asked to do so. These are less likely to be continuing series than single list assignments: house tax payments for the current year, work contributions to an ongoing public project such as road or bridge-building, a population headcount and the like.

Personal correspondence is the principal textual use of the script. Letter-writing is a ubiquitous activity which has evolved certain distinctive stylistic devices, such as conventional forms of salutation and signature. It is not uncommon to see letters passed from hand to hand in one small town, and many people who are not personally literate participate in this form of exchange through the services of scribes. Since Vai society like other traditional cultures developed and still maintains an effective system of oral contact and communication by message and "grapevine," reasons for the popularity of letterwriting are not self-evident, especially since all letters must be personally sent and hand-delivered. Protection of secrets and guarantee of delivery are among the advantages most frequently advanced in favor of letters rather than word-of-mouth communication.

For all its popularity, letter-writing is circumscribed in ways which simplify its cognitive demands: majority of Vai literates correspond only with persons already known to them (78% of literates interviewed in our sample study reported they had never written to nor received a letter from a stranger). Many factors undoubtedly contribute to this phenomenon, among which the non-standardized and often idiosyncratic versions of script characters must figure prominently, but it is significant for hypotheses about intellectual skills that written communication among the Vai draws heavily upon shared background information against which the news is exchanged.

What about other texts? The first thing to note is that all textual material is held in private; texts are rarely circulated to be read, though on occasion and under special circumstances they might be made available for copying. Thus the relationship of Vai script literates to text is primarily as producer or writer, seldom as reader of another's work. This social arrangement has several important consequences. One is that reading is not an activity involving assimilation of novel knowledge or material; another is that existing texts reflect what people choose to write about, depending on their own interests and concepts of what writing is "for." Many texts are of a cumulative nature-that is, they are not set pieces, but rather comprise "journals" or "notebooks." Each such "book" might contain a variety of entries, some autobiographic (personal events, dreams), others impersonal and factual (facts of town history, for example). While not read as continuous texts, such materials are often used as important source books or data records and depending on their scope and age, may serve as archives.[6] Some texts fit recognizable (in terms of Western literacy) genres. There are histories, for example, fables, books of maxims, parables, and advice. In at least one instance, we have been able to obtain a set of documents of a Muslim self-help organization which included a Vai-script written constitution and bylaws (see Goody, Cole & Scribner, 1977). As in the case of lists, the range of skills reflected in texts is broad. "Histories" may be a collection of what were originally notes on scattered sheets of paper, assembled under one cover with no apparent chronological or other ordering; at the other extreme they might be well-organized and fluent narrations of a clan history or ambitious accounts of the origin and migration of the Vai people as a whole. While we do not know the relationship between written and oral history and narrative, and thus cannot determine whether written works are continuous or discontinuous with respect to the oral tradition, there clearly are individual texts which bear the stamp of creative literary and intellectual work. But it must be added that texts of this nature are the exception; most histories are brief, often fragmentary and written stories rare discoveries.

There are two types of text rarely found thus far, Britton's (1975) two polar types—the poetic, concerned with exploring personal experiences and feelings, and the transactional or expository, basically concerned with examining ideas or presenting a persuasive argument.

Vai script literates are known in the community and admired for their knowledge of books. Motivations sustaining the script are not restricted to pragmatic ones; individuals will cite its utilitarian value for correspondence, records and "secrets" but will as often speak about the importance of the "book" for self-education and knowledge and for preserving the history and reputation of the Vai people. To be looked upon with respect and to be remembered in history are important incentives to many Vai journal-writers.

It is apparent from this quick review that Vai people have developed highly diversified uses for writing and that personal values, pride of culture, hopes of gain—a host of pragmatic, ideological and intellectual factors—sustain popular literacy. The level of literacy that obtains among the Vai must, however, on balance be considered severely restricted. Except for the few Arabic scholars or secondary school English students, literacy does not lead to learning of new knowledge nor involve individuals in new methods of inquiry. Traditional processes of production, trade and education are little affected by the written word.

---

[6]It is reported (Scribner, field notes) that an entire Vai community in Monrovia was able to retain its right to disputed land because an elderly kinsman had recorded in his book the names of the original deed-holders.

Effects of Literacy

Should we conclude that these restrictions disqualify indigenous Vai literacy as "real literacy?" It clearly has social consequences for its practitioners and (we hypothesized) might have identifiable cognitive consequences as well. It seemed unlikely, however, that it would have the very general intellectual consequences which are presumed to be the result of high levels of school based literacy.

Nonetheless, this possibility was explored as part of our major survey of Vai adults at the outset of the project. In fact, we found no evidence of marked differences in performance on logical and classificatory tasks between non-schooled literates and nonliterates. Consequently, we adopted a strategy of making a functional analysis of literacy. We examined activities engaged in by those knowing each of the indigenous scripts to determine some of the component skills involved. On the basis of these analyses, we designed tasks with different content but with hypothetically similar skills to determine if prior practice in learning and use of the script enhanced performance.

Communication Skills

Since letter-writing is the most common use to which Vai script is put, it is reasonable to look here for specific intellectual consequences. In the psychological literature, written communication is considered to impose cognitive demands not encountered in face-to-face oral communication. In writing, meaning is carried entirely by the text. An effective written communication requires sensitivity to the informational needs of the reader and skill in use of elaborative linguistic techniques. We believed it reasonable to suppose that Vai literates' experience in writing and receiving letters should contribute to the development of these communicational skills. To test this proposition, we adapted a communication task used in developmental research (Flavell, 1968). With little verbal explanation, subjects were taught to play a simple board game and then were asked to explain the game without the board present to someone unfamiliar with it.

We compared a full range of literate and nonliterate groups, including junior high and high school students, under several conditions of play. Results were quite orderly. On several indices of amount of information provided in an explanation, groups consistently ranked as follows: high school students, Vai literates, Arabic literates, and nonliterates. Vai literates, more often than other non-student groups, provided a general characterization of the game before launching into a detailed account of rules of play. If there is anything to the notion that what is acquired in a particular literacy is closely related to practice of *that* literacy, the differential between Vai and Arabic literates is exactly what we would expect to find: on the average, Vai literates engage in letter-writing more frequently than Arabic literates. It is interesting, too, that both Vai and Arabic letter-writing groups were superior to all nonliterate groups.

Memory

We were also able to show specific consequences of Qur'anic learning. Regardless of what level of literacy they attain, all Arabic literates begin by learning to recite passages of the Qur'an by heart, and some spend many years in the process. Learning by memorization might promote efficient techniques for learning to memorize. To test this possibility, we employed a verbal learning task (Mandler & Dean, 1969) involving processes that our observations indicated matched those in Qur'anic memorization. In this task, a single item is presented on the first trial and a new item is added on each succeeding trial for a total of 16 trials and 16 items. The subject is required to recall the words in the order presented. Our comparison groups were the same as those used in the communication experiment. English students again ranked first, but in this task, Arabic literates were superior to Vai literates as well as to nonliterates in both amount recalled and in preservation of serial order. If this superiority were simply the manifestation of "better general memory abilities" on the part of Qur'anic scholars, we would expect Arabic literates to do better in *all* memory tasks, but this was not the case. When the requirement was to remember and repeat a story, Qur'anic students did no better, and no worse, than other groups. When the requirement was to remember a list of words under free recall conditions, there were no significant performance differentials. Superiority of Arabic literates was specific to the memory paradigm which shadowed the learning requirements of Qur'anic school.

Language Analysis

In a third domain, we were again able to demonstrate the superiority of Vai literates. Vai script is written without word division, so that reading a text requires as a first step the analysis of separate characters followed by their integration into meaningful linguistic units. Our observations of Vai literates "decoding" letters suggested that this process of constructing meaning was carried out by a reiterative routine of sounding out characters until they "clicked" into meaningful units. We supposed that this experience would foster skills in auditory perception of semantically meaningful but deformed (i.e. slowed down) utterances. Materials consisted of tape recordings in which a native speaker of Vai read meaningful Vai sentences syllable by syllable at a 2-second rate. The task was to listen and to repeat the sentence as well as to answer a comprehension question about it. Vai literates were better at comprehending and repeating the sentences than Arabic literates and nonliterates; and Vai literates with advanced skills performed at higher levels than Vai literates with beginning skills. Comparisons of performance on repetition of sentences in which words, not syllables, were the units showed no differences among literate groups but a sizeable one between all literate and nonliterate populations. The comparison of the two tasks isolates skill in syllable integration as a specific Vai script related skill.

Taken as a group, these three sets of studies provide the strongest experimental evidence to date that activities involved in reading and writing may in fact promote specific language-processing and cognitive skills.

Implications

Our research among the Vai indicates that, even in a society whose primary productive and cultural activities continue to be based on oral communication, writing serves a wide variety of social functions. Some of the pragmatic functions we have described are by no means trivial, either in indigenous terms or in terms of the concerns in economically developed countries for the promotion of "functional literacy" skills. Vai literates routinely carry out a variety of tasks using their script which are carried out no better (and perhaps worse) by their English-educated peers who have completed a costly twelve year course of school study. The record keeping activities which we described briefly in earlier sections of this paper provide the communities within which the literates live with an effective means of local administration. The fact that court cases were once recorded in the script and that religious texts are often translated into Vai as a means of religious indoctrination suggest that uses of writing for institutional purposes are fully within the grasp of uneducated, but literate, Vai people.

While the bulk of activities with the Vai script may be characterized in these pragmatic terms, evidence of scholarly and literary uses, even rudimentary ones, suggest that nonschooled literates are concerned with more than the "immediate personal gain" aspects of literacy. We could not understand in such narrowly pragmatic terms the effort of some Vai literates to write clan histories and record famous tales nor the ideological motivations and values sustaining long years of Qur'anic learning.

Of course we cannot extrapolate from Vai society to our own, but it is reasonable to suppose that there is at least as wide a range of individual aspirations and social practices capable of sustaining a variety of writing activities in our own society as among the Vai. Since our social order is so organized that access to better-paying jobs and leadership positions commonly requires writing skills, there are even more powerful economic and political incentives at work to encourage interest. It seems premature to conclude that only schools and teachers are concerned with writing and that writing would perish in this era of television if not artificially kept alive in academic settings.

An alternative possibility is that institutionalized learning programs have thus far failed to tap the wide range of "indigenous" interests and practices which confer significance on writing. Ethnographic studies of writing in different communities and social contexts—in religious, political and fraternal groups—might help broaden existing perspectives.

Our research also highlights the fact that the kind of writing that goes on in school has a very special status. It generates products that meet teacher demands and academic requirements but may not fulfill any other immediate instrumental ends. Is this an unavoidable feature of writing instruction?

When we look upon school-based writing within the context of popular uses of writing found among the Vai, we are also impressed by what appears to be the unique features of the expository or essay type text. In what nonschooled settings are such texts required and produced in our own society? Although developmental models of writing place such texts at the "highest stage" of writing ability, we find it difficult to order different types of texts and writing functions to stages of development. Our evidence indicates that social organization creates the conditions for a variety of literacy activities, and that different types of text reflect different social practices. With respect to *adult* literacy, a functional approach appears more appropriate than a developmental one. The loose generalization of developmental models developed for work with children to instructional programs with adolescents and adults is certainly questionable.

With respect to intellectual consequences, we have been able to demonstrate that literacy-without-schooling is associated with improved performance on certain cognitive tasks. This is certainly important evidence that literacy does "count" in intellectual terms, and it is especially important in suggesting *how* it counts. The consequences of literacy that we identified are all highly specific and closely tied to actual practices with particular scripts; learning the Qur'an improved skills on a specific type of memory task, writing Vai script letters improved skills in a particular communication task. Vai literates and Arabic literates showed different patterns of skills, and neither duplicated the performance of those who had obtained literacy through attendance at Western-type English schools.

The consequences we were able to identify are constrained by the type of practices common in Vai society. We did not find, for example, that performance on classification tasks and logic problems was affected by non-school literacy. This outcome suggests that speculations that such skills are the "inevitable outcome" of learning to use alphabetic scripts or write any kind of text are overstated. Our evidence leaves open the question of whether conceptual or logical skills are promoted by experience with expository text; in fact if our argument that specific uses promote specific skills is valid, we should expect to find certain skills related to practice in written exposition. The challenging question is how to identify these without reintroducing the confounding influence of schooling.

Perhaps the most challenging question of all is how to balance appreciation for the special skills involved in writing with an appreciation of the fact that there is no evidence that writing promotes "general mental abilities." We did not find superior "memory in general" among Qur'anic students nor better language integration skills "in general" among Vai literates. Moreover, improvements in performance that appear to be associated with literacy were thus far only observed in contrived experimental settings. Their applicability to other domains is uncertain. We do not know on the basis of any controlled observation whether more effective handling of an experimental communication task, for example, signifies greater communication skills in nonexperimental situations. Are Vai literates better than Arabic literates or nonliterates at communicating anything to anybody under any circumstances? We doubt that to be the case, just as we doubt that Qur'anic learning leads to superior memory of all kinds in all kinds of situations. There is nothing in our findings that would lead us to speak of cognitive consequences of literacy with the notion in mind that such consequences affect intellectual performance in all tasks to which the human mind is put. Nothing in our data would support the statement quoted earlier that reading and writing entail fundamental "cognitive restructurings" that control intellectual performance in all domains. Quite the contrary: the very specificity of the effects suggests that they may be closely tied to performance parameters of a limited set of tasks, although as of now we have no theoretical scheme for specifying such parameters. This outcome suggests that the metaphor of a "great divide" may not be appropriate for specifying differences among literates and nonliterates under contemporary conditions.

The monolithic model of what writing is and what it leads to, described at the beginning of this paper, appears in the light of comparative data to fail to give full justice to the multiplicity of values, uses and consequences which characterize writing as social practice.

REFERENCES

Bereiter, C. Integration of skill systems in the development of textual writing competence. 1977 (mimeo).

Britton, J., Burgess, T., Martin, N., McLeod, A. & Rosen, H. *The development of writing abilities.* London: McMillan Edinburgh Ltd., 1975.

Cole, M., & Scribner, S. *Culture and thought.* New York: J. Wiley & Sons, 1974.

Dalby, D. A survey of the indigenous scripts of Liberia and Sierra Leone. *African Language Studies,* 1967, *VIII,* 1–51.

Farrell, T. J. Literacy, the basics, and all that jazz. *College English,* January 1977, 443–459.

Fishman, J. A. The description of societal bilingualism. In Fishman, J. A., Cooper, R. L., Ma, R. *Bilingualism in the Barrio*. Bloomington, Indiana: Indiana University Publications, 1975, 605-611.

Flavell, J. H., Botkin, P. J., Fry, C. L., Wright, J. W., & Jarvis, P. E. *The development of role-taking and communication skills in children*. New York: Wiley, 1968.

Gelb, I. J. *A study of writing*. Chicago: The University of Chicago Press, 1952.

Goody, J. Literacy and classification: On turning the tables. In Jain, R. K. (Ed.). *Text and context: The social anthropology of tradition*. Philadelphia: Institute for the Study of Human Issues, 1977.

Goody, J., Cole, M., & Scribner, S. Writing and formal operations: A case study among the Vai. *Africa*, 1977, *47* (no. 3).

Goody, J., & Watt, I. The consequences of literacy. *Comparative Studies in Society and History*, 1963, *5*, 304-345.

Gough, K. Implications of literacy in traditional China and India. In Goody, J. (ed.). *Literacy in traditional societies*. Cambridge: Cambridge University Press, 1968, 69-84.

Greenfield, P. Oral or written langauge: the consequences for cognitive development in Africa and the United States. Presented at Symposium on Cross-Cultural Cognitive Studies, Chicago, 1968.

Havelock, E. *Preface to Plato*. Cambridge, Mass.: Harvard University Press, 1963.

Koelle, S. W. *Outlines of a grammar of the Vei language*. London: Church Missionary House, 1854.

Lewin, K. *A dynamic theory of personality*. New York: McGraw-Hill, 1936.

Macdonald, J. B. Reading in an electronic media age. In Macdonald, J. B. (ed.). *Social perspectives on reading*. Delaware: International Reading Association, 1973, 23-29.

Mandler, G., & Dean, P. Seriation: The development of serial order in free recall. *Journal of Experimental Psychology*, 1969, *81*, 207-215.

Martin, N., D'Arcy, P., Newton, B. & Parker, R. *Writing and learning across the curriculum 11-16*. London: Ward Lock Educational, 1976.

Moffett, J. *Teaching the universe of discourse*. Boston: Houghton-Mifflin, 1968.

Olson, D. R. Review of *Toward a literate society*, John B. Carroll and Jeanne Chall (eds.). *Proceedings of the National Academy of Education*, 1975, *2*, 109-178.

Ong, W. *Ramus, method, and the decay of dialogue*. Cambridge, Mass.: Harvard University Press, 1958. Reprinted by Octagon Books, 1974.

Schofield, R. S. The measurment of literacy in pre-industrial England. In Goody, J. (ed.). *Literacy in traditional societies*. Cambridge: Cambridge University Press, 1968, 311-325.

Scribner, S. Cognitive consequences of literacy. New York: Albert Einstein College of Medicine, 1968 (mimeo).

Tambiah, S. J. Literacy in a Buddhist village in north-east Thailand. In Goody, J. (ed.). *Literacy in a traditional society*. Cambridge: Cambridge University Press, 1968, 85-131.

Vygotsky, L. S. *Thought and language*. Cambridge, Mass.: M.I.T. Press, 1962.

Wilder, B. An examination of the phenomenon of the literacy skills of unschooled males in Laos. Ph.D. Dissertation. Michigan State University, 1972.

Wilks, I. The transmission of Islamic learning in the Western Sudan. In Goody, J. *Literacy in traditional societies*. Cambridge: Cambridge Universities Press, 1968, 161-197.

6 From Oral to Written Culture: The Transition to Literacy

Jenny Cook-Gumperz
John J. Gumperz
University of California, Berkeley

As the crisis of education in culturally heterogeneous industrialized societies grows, the educational failure of the poor has in some circles come to be seen primarily as a language problem. The justification given is that children who do least well in schools are for the most part speakers of dialects or languages distinct from majority speech, be they working class dialects, ethnically specific speech varieties such as Black English, or separate languages as with bilingual immigrant groups. Although the educators' preconceptions that non standard speech is somewhat "lacking in grammar" and reflects "unsystematic thinking" have by now been disproved, many continue to assume that there is something about the phonological, syntactic or semantic characteristics of the home vernaculars that impedes the learning of writing skills and that contrastive analysis of the grammatical differences between standard varieties and those spoken by the minority group can lay the foundation for pedagogical strategies to remedy this learning problem.

Research on urban language problems during the last decades has provided a great deal of descriptive information about the nature and extent of urban linguistic diversity and about socially based patterns of language usage. Yet the effect of this research on educational achievement has been minimal. We still lack theoretical justification for the claim that language differences in themselves affect the acquisition of literacy. On the contrary, as we learn more about the facts of urban language usage, we find that there is surprisingly low correlation between the actual language distance, i.e. the difference in grammatical rules that separate minority from majority group speech, and school achievement.

For Black English for example, research by Melmed (1971), Piestrup (1972) and others has shown that children whose speech shows dialect features judged deviant by "standard" English speakers are not necessarily the worst at literacy skills. Test results moreover indicate that the gap in verbal ability between minority and majority group children in many inner city schools is relatively low at the start of primary school but increases to alarming proportion by the fifth year (Gibson 1965). In bilingual school situations such as those of New York, Miami and San Francisco certain types of Spanish speaking groups such as Cubans or recent immigrants from Mexico, do quite well in school, in spite of the fact that they have little previous exposure to English, while children from local Spanish speaking groups who already speak Street English perform relatively badly.

Clearly it is not grammar as such which impedes educational success. Studies of grammatical and phonological variability alone are not likely to yield basic insights into the problems of literacy. No simple dichotomy will provide the solution . We need a fuller explanation of the historical processes that affect cultural differences and of how these differences are reflected at the level of communicative, i.e. stylistic and rhetorical, strategies to deal with the problem of why some children learn while others don't. In this paper we would like to suggest that to understand the causes of language learning problems in modern urban schools, we must examine the more basic changes in social goals and motives which accompany the transition from oral to written culture everywhere and look into the ways in which these changes interact with ethnic distinctions and with educational environments prevailing in mass education systems.

We begin with a brief discussion of some recent comparative anthropological and psychological work on literacy in small face to face non-Western societies and then go on to discuss some of our own work on discourse and contextualization strategies in home and school. The anthropological work is cited here because of the insights it provides into what it is that writing does to our perception of cultural reality and for what it tells us about the hitherto unsuspected diversity of co-existing folk and literary traditions in our own urban societies. We are not claiming that the historical processes we discuss directly affect learning; rather, we hope that these studies can provide the background we need to understand the social context within which literacy is acquired.

ORAL AND WRITTEN CULTURES

Research on the cultural effects of literacy had its origin in folklorist and literary scholars' examination of the processes by which folk epics are transmitted (Lord, 1960, Havelock, 1963). Olson (1974) in reviewing this work argues that "the introduction of writing systems has had important consequences both for the cognitive processes of individuals and for the cultural practices of social groups." Several general principles of differences important to literacy emerge. Firstly, the introduction of the writing systems changes the basic character of the storage and transmission of knowledge. In preliterate cultures, one of the key ways that knowledge is transmitted is through such oral performances as the recitation of mythological folk narratives and oral genealogies. What is stable over time in these situations are story schemata, not details of content. The storage of specific social knowledge and its transmission to the next generation are essential cultural tasks that change with the introduction of writing systems, which make possible new, essentially more *accurate* forms of recall and transmission. Goody points out that "a central difference between oral and literate cultures lies in the modes of transmission, the first allowing a surprisingly wide degree of creativity, but of a cyclical kind, the latter demanding repetition as *a condition of* incremental change" (Goody 1977). As Goody suggests in the comment we have underlined, the change from oral to written transmission brings about a shift from a view of knowledge as a constant state which can be learned through open and varied means of creative retelling; to one of knowledge as incremental, that is, where the initial learning process is repetitious in order to teach the store of knowledge available-to-date, but to which further new knowledge can be added, since the old store is "on record."

Therefore the introduction of the linear process of writing systems means a further transformation, in that knowledge is now seen as *progressive* rather than *static* in quantity. The ways of acquiring the newly progressive knowledge must be changed from the previous cyclical, oral modes of recitation. The new forms of learning and transmission that are necessitated for a writing system result in social changes.

This leads to the second major difference between the two cultures: the process of acquiring the 'stock of knowledge to date' requires a separation between the transmission and acquisition of knowledge and the practices of daily life. Eventually even the daily life of people who can add to the essential store of knowledge may be further separated. New classes of literati arise who specialize in and earn their living through the preservation, editing and interpretation of written information. In doing so, over time, these groups develop strategies of processing information and conventions for dealing with language that are quite different from those used in everyday interaction and which, as they grow more complex, must be learned through special schooling. Again a comment from Goody's recent study: "the whole process of removing children from the family, placing them under distinct authority, can be described as one of *decontextualiztion*, formalisation, for schools inevitably place an emphasis on the 'unnatural' 'unoral' decontextualized process of repetition, copying, verbatim memory. A recognition of this tendency will help us to understand the contrast with oral society, where we get little emphasis on repetition and more on recreation." Goody is here describing the growth of schools, not in our own experience, but in ancient Sumerian society. However, the division of social space that incremental learning requires continues to change the lives of children and to introduce a discontinuity between the acquisition of language as an oral skill from infancy onwards, and the acquisition of language as a literate skill. As was suggested in a previous paper (Gumperz 1977) the two modes of transmission imply a different underlying principle of learning, and more specifically of interpretation, in the use of oral or literate skills.

Decontextualization of stored knowledge and of the process of learning from daily life leads to our third and final point. The practice of learned skills, thinking and writing as separate forms of activity can give rise to different strategies of reasoning. A.R. Luria's *Cognitive Development, Its Cultural and Social Foundation* (1976) most clearly illustrates what is involved here. The book reports on tests conducted in Soviet Central Asia in which illiterate traditional peasants were compared with more educated members of local farming collectives with respect to their ways of a) categorizing and sorting everyday objects and geometrical figures and b) giving a verbal rationale for what they had done in clinical interviews. The experiments revealed systematic differences between the two groups, the illiterates being consistently more concrete, situation bound and less ready to abstract language and generalize than the literates. It is argued that the differences in question are socio-culturally conditioned and reflect changes in activities, practices and perception brought about by the collectivization process.

Luria's data, which go back to 1931-32, have since been supplemented and his basic findings have been confirmed by comparative studies in a variety of preliterate cultures (Cole and Scribner 1974, Berry and Dasen 1973). Thus Scribner and Cole (this volume) report that preliterate people when exploring a set of problems presented as syllogisms could not separate their own specific knowledge and experience from the problem presented to them. The problem, in other words, could not be considered apart from the actual conditions of the context. Preliterates could not or would not decontextualize the problem. Scribner and Cole refer to the preliterate mode of reasoning as "empiric" and contrasts it with the "theoretic" mode of literate people.

While the existence of such separate modes of reasoning is not generally accepted, the interpretation of the findings is by no means clear. Luria's and other psychologists' experiments deal with phenomena which arise in a single originally quite homogeneous community as a result of short term socio-economic change. Whatever cognitive differences result from these changes are clearly not cross-cultural distinctions as they are usually thought of, that is, distinctions among members of geographically and historically separate groups. Nothing in Luria's or any of the other investigations suggests that differences in mental abilities are involved. All adults control the same basic cognitive functions. What differs are habitual ways of perceiving relationships and conventions governing how language is used. Scribner and Cole find that even a very few years of limited schooling change the approach of people to the syllogistically presented problems (which cannot be answered in textually separate and self sufficient terms as a common sense theoretical issue). In his introduction to the Luria volume, Cole (1976) in fact argues against using developmental theories which apply to individuals to compare whole cultures cross-culturally.

Goody, in his recent volume, aptly titled *The Domestication of the Savage Mind* (1977), takes this line of reasoning one step further when he suggests that differences between oral and literate societies which continue to be explained in terms of mentalistic dichotomies (e.g., as pre-logical vs. logical [Lévy-Bruhl 1910], primitive vs. domesticated or raw and cooked [Lévi-Strauss 1962], open and closed [Horton 1967]) even by those who reject simplistic evolutionary explanations, must initially be seen in *societal* terms. He cites detailed ethnographic evidence to show that individuals in oral societies are every bit as resourceful in using the tools at hand, and as innovative in responding to changing conditions as literates.

What literacy brings about are first of all changes in communicative technology along with increases in the availability of information and in the way it is processed. Over time this gives rise to new cognitive strategies and discourse conventions which must be learned through special schooling. Thus *societies* distribute their communicative resources differently and it is within the context of these *societal* resources that individuals develop. Both Goody and Cole point out that the argument from society to individual must not be historically and ecologically contracted or the resulting social theory will be highly misleading.

The work on literacy and social change in small scale society yields a perspective for our discussion of the distinction between home and school communicative environments in complex industrial societies. But before we can make the leap from one type of system to another, it will be necessary to touch on sociological issues which emerge from the history of literacy in our own societies. Since literacy as we know it is several thousand years old, why is it that large scale educational failure has become a problem only recently? The answer lies in the changeover from elite to mass education. Until not much more than a century ago literacy had the status of a craft skill, in that it remained confined to relatively small privileged groups and written materials were expensive and difficult to obtain. A glance at the history of linguistic diversity illustrates this point. Literary styles everywhere were both grammatically and stylistically quite separate from the spoken idiom of the home. This is true for Europe, where until the end of the middle ages most writing was done in Latin, for India, where Sanskrit and Persian prevailed until the nineteenth century, as well as for areas such as China or the Arab countries where literary Chinese and Arabic were so distinct from popular colloquial speech as to require many years of special training. It was by no means unusual to have several separate literary conventions, each with their own grammatically distinct style or language to co-exist side by side within a single region. Administrative codes were separate from commercial codes and within the religious sphere competing sects tended to follow their own literary conventions. What we are dealing with therefore is not a simple distinction between spoken and written modes, but a multiplicity of coexisting, but functionally limited literary and oral folk traditions.

The grammatical distinctness and the formulaic nature of literary styles along with the many highly artificial calligraphic conventions such as those illustrated in W.J. Ong's "Latin Language Study as a Renaissance Puberty Rite" (1959), tend to function as access barriers which kept schooling and hence command over literary skills confined to small groups where learning was more a matter of personal, tutorial type contact between students and teachers and informal socialization by small group process than of formal curriculum. For those not born as members of literate groups who succeeded in crossing these barriers, becoming literate meant loosening familial ties to taking on a new cultural identity.

It was only with industrialization, the rise of middle class dominated city societies and the spread of democracy that the sharp distinctions between everyday languages and those of literary traditions began to disappear. Starting with the protestant revolution, movements set in throughout Europe to spread education and knowledge of the scriptures. New common denominator standard languages arose, which took their grammatical base from creolized varieties of local dialects spoken in urban centers and which were heavily influenced by the discourse characteristics of vernacular Bible translations.

These languages became the symbols of the newly arising national urban based cultures and in the opinion of some the ability to speak and write them properly was a prerequisite for rational thinking. Through appearance of printed grammars, style manuals, dictionaries and encyclopedias, literary knowledge for the first time became available to all who could afford the price of a book. Self improvement societies devoted to the acquisition of learning arose in provincial centers and in working class urban suburbs. Literary historians write of the rapid growth of a mass reading public after the first decades of the nineteenth century which strenghthened the growth of journalism and of new forms of popular novel writings (Williams 1961). Robert Altick (1957) writes:

> ... under the conditions of industrial life the ability to read was acquiring an importance it had never had before. The popular cultural tradition, which had

brought amusement and emotional outlets to previous generations, had largely been erased. The long hours and the monotony of work in factory and shop, the dismal surroundings in which people were condemned to spend such leisure as they had, the regimentation of industrial society with its consequent crushing of individuality, made it imperative that the English millions should have some new way of escape and relaxation, some new and plentiful means of engaging their minds and imaginations. Books and periodicals were the obvious answer.

Note however that while reading skills became widespread both in England and as Shirley Heath points out (this volume) in the United States the main function of literature for the mass public in this early period is entertainment. Reading replaces attendance at oral performance and writing is used for list making, keeping accounts, diary entries and letters. Such literary activity can be seen as an extension of the uses of speaking. It does not yet have all the characteristics of decontextualization that we tend to associate with written communication today. The following incident will illustrate this point: this account is from the stories of James Herriot, a veterinary surgeon, about his practice in the 1930's in the Yorshiredales; while making tuberclin tests of cows, he often had great difficulty in persuading the farmers to keep herd records:

I pushed along the cow and got hold of its ear, but Walter stopped me with a gentle cough.

"Nay, Mr. Herriot, you won't have to look in the ears. I have all t'numbers wrote down."

"Oh, that's fine. It'll save us a lot of time." I had always found scratching the wax away to find ear tattoos an overrated pastime. And it was good to hear that the Hugills were attending to the clerical side; there was a section in the Ministry form which said: "Are the herd records in goods order?" I always wrote "Yes," keeping my fingers crossed as I thought of the scrawled figures on the backs of the old bills, milk recording sheets, anything.

"Aye," said Walter. "I have 'em all set down proper in a book."

"Great! Can you go and get it then?"

"No need, sorr, I have it 'ere." Walter was the boss, there was no doubt about it . . .

Then he put his hand into his waistcoat pocket.

When he took it out he was holding some object but it was difficult to identify, being almost obscured by his enormous thumb. Then I saw that it was a tiny, black-covered miniature diary about two inches square—the sort of novelty people give each other at Christmans.

"Is that the herd record?" I asked.

"Yes, this is it, it's all set down here." Walter daintily flicked over the pages with a horny forefinger and squinted through his spectacles. "Now that fust cow--she's number eighty-fower."

"Splendid!" I said, "I'll just check this one and then we can go by the book." I peered into the ear. "That's funny, I make it twenty-six."

The brothers had a look. "You're right, sorr, you're right. It IS twenty-six." Walter pursed his lips. "Why, that's Bluebell's calf isn't it?"

"Nay," said Fenwick, "she's out of awd Buttercup."

"Can't be," mumbled Thomas. "Awd Buttercup was sold to Tim Jefferson afore this 'un was born. This is Branda's calf.

William shook his head. "Ah'm sure we got her as a heifer at Bob Ashby's sale."

"All right," I said, holding up a hand. "We'll put in twenty-six." I had to cut in. It was in no way an argument, just a leisurely discussion but it looked as if it could go on for some time. I wrote the number in my notebook and injected the cow. "Now how about this next one?"

"Well ah DO know that 'un," said Walter confidently, stabbing at an entry in the diary. "Cna't make no mistake, she's number five."

I looked in the ear. "Says a hundred and thirty seven here."

It started again. "She was bought in, wasn't she?" "Nay, nay, she's out of awd Dribbler," "Don't think so--Dribbler had nowt but bulls..."

I raised my hand again. "You know, I really think it might be quicker to look in all the ears. Time's getting on."...

The problem illustrated by this incident is that the relation of the numerical ordering, the written list and the named individual cows, did not quite correspond. For the farmers, when necessary, individual cows were "placed" by recalling "oral" geneologies, rather than by a single written/numerical reference accuracy was clearly not considered essential.

Until well into the present century in fact popular education concentrated on basic skills of reading, writing and arithmetic and remained quite separate from the elite system of secondary schools and universities. For the bulk of the population literacy was not vital for economic survival.

Further developments of advanced technological societies has increased the dependence on the written word; new communicative requirements have been generated by bureaucracies, from tax forms to the wording of government regulations. These changing communicative styles are also reflected in the written instructions which in our era of technical specialization have become increasingly important both at work and at home, and have necessitated a change in the functions of literacy (Habermas 1972). As part of these changes, educational systems become both socializing agents and almost exclusive selectors for economic opportunity (Halsey, Floud, Anderson, 1969).

Our own modern societies thus have again increased the dichotomy of speaking and writing and at the same time have made the achievement of literacy essential for economic survival. We have put the school in a critical gate keeping role, giving it a function which it did not have in the nineteenth or early twentieth century, without being always explicit about the nature of the communicative skills the school is to teach.

The argument has been made over the last fifteen years that the school is an adjunct to the middle class family, while presenting the minority child with an essentially discontinuous and discrepant social experience. Such arguments still depend upon the idea that some children—and by implication perhaps not others—in their early language usage are merely mini-adults. It is assumed that the development of skills, that is the transition between speaking and writing, is monologic, distributed along a single continuum or unidimensional scale. What we want to argue now is that recent studies in child discourse show that the communicative activities of speaking and writing have differentiated qualities *for all children*. We cannot excuse our societal bureaucratic decision to place the school in a critical gate keeping role by claiming that the overwhelming failure of some children on standardized tests is mainly the fault of the communicative systems used in families and schools. It is also the product of socio-economic change, radically shifting functions of literacy, and of our reliance on tests and evaluation procedures which do not account for these factors.

THE MOVE INTO LITERACY

The belief that children's language is in its beginnings from a different source and is of a basically different order from adult language is an idea held in several cultures other than our own. And as Hymes (1974) describes, societies' ideas about children's speech may show up in the adult view of language:

> attention to the interpretation put upon infant speech may reveal much of the adult culture. Both Chinookans and Ashanti believe that infants share a first language not the adult one (on native theory, the 'native language' is always a second language). For Chinookans, the baby's talk is shared with certain spirits, and shamans having those spirits interpret it lest by 'dying' it return to the spirit world from which it came; the attempt is to incorporate the infant communicatively within the community. Ashanti traditionally exclude infants from a room in which a woman is giving birth, on the ground that an infant would talk to the baby in the womb in the special language they share, and, by warning it of the hardness of life, make it reluctant to emerge and so cause a hard delivery...
>
> Interpretations of the intent of first utterances—e.g., as an attempt to name kin (Wogeo), to ask for food (Alorese), to manipulate (Chaga)—may indeed be something of a projective test for a culture, as regards adult practices and the valuation placed on speech itself. (p. 109)

The view that children's language learning is an apprenticeship to the skills and practices of an adult language; that children have in yet undeveloped initial forms a language which is learnt, processed and used in the *identical* same way as adult language, is particular to our culture. In many ways we deemphasize the differences between adults and children in regard to language; whereas the example from Hymes shows, many other societies emphasize strongly the differences, and often provide for ritual entry from the children's to the adults' language world.

Entry into school in our society provides such a ritual entry into a formal apprenticeship towards adult communicative skills. But since we do not look upon the early years of language use as different but merely as a lesser form of what is to come, this ritual entry does not have the nature of its transitional experience truly evaluated. The *oral* language experience of children is looked upon as a preparation rather than as a separate stage of experience, and we do not always give sufficient thought, nor recognition, to the social as well as the cognitive reorganization of experience and its processing that is necessary for the child to enter into literacy. As Wayne O'Neil somewhat ironically points out in his paper "Properly Literate" (1970):

> Schools render their S's able to read—some of them—and in the process destroy their proper literacy. Before they go off to school, children have engaged in five years of bringing coherent (unspoken) explanations to the world of experiences, linguistic, social, etc. that they face. They're doing pretty well at it, too. The school tries to tell them, and generally suceeds in telling them, that common sense explanations won't do ever. It's really much simpler, the school says, experience should be understood linearly not hierarchically; it's all there on the surface, not deeply and complexly organized. (p. 262)

The argument of the present paper is that the transition from the child's culture at home (and nursery school) where the child has learnt to make sense and achieve social actions within his/her own communicative system, requires a change of communicative understanding for all children. At a very important level the difference between home and school exists for all children and is not, as has been so often argued, solely a matter of cultural difference for some children or cultural deficiencies for some. The real nature of the transition can best be understood by knowing the kinds of communicative tasks and discourse processes that children develop in the years before the special communicative apprenticeship of the school begins.

The transition from oral to literacy performance occurs at two levels of generality which must be kept separate: a) the social and cognitive level, i.e., the meta-level at which individuals make sense of what they perceive by intergrating it into previous experience and b) the purely linguistic level of discourse processing. These two levels have often been confused in the literature and it has been assumed that the mere acquisition of discourse strategies will automatically result in social changes. We would like to argue that this is not the case. By making a conceptual distinction between sociocognitive strategies and discourse strategies we hope to suggest that learning environments have a selective effect on one or the other.

Children's culture is oral in its beginnings. This is perhaps almost too obvious a point but one which has received only occasional passing attention in the study of child language (Brown, 1971). Children acquire their language ability within a totally oral culture, only hearing and speaking—responding to contextually relevant sounds of others. Children's understanding and attribution of meaning, both cognitive and social, must be mediated through the oral medium, where developmental constraints on memory processing restrict the range of any task. In this way it is likely that children must build up their own system of attributing sense to events and their own mnemonics to aid their activities. In other words, they learn to rely on oral signals for recognizing what an activity is about. However, adults approach the study and evaluation of children's performance and competence from a written literate perspective. If there is a difference in the interpretation and underlying logic between the two modes, then children and adults must often experience an essential discontinuity in their understanding of each other's communications. Developmentally the transition from speaking to writing as a medium for learning about the world of others requires a change from the interpretive strategies of the oral culture in which children grow up, to the interpretive principles of *discursive* written language. The move into literacy requires children to make some basic adjustments to the way they *socially* attribute meaning to the events and processes of the every day world in order to be able to loosen their dependence upon contextually specific information and to adopt a decontextualized perspective. Among other things they must learn to rely on incrementally acquired knowledge and rather than on what is said within any one context. In another dimension the move into literacy requires children linguistically to change their process of interpretation.

Written vs. Spoken Language

For children, the essential change between written and spoken language is the change from the multi-modality of speech to lexicalized discursive sequences of written language. Wholly new principles of monitoring meaning and of recognizing the cues for further information, that is linguistic expectations, are necessary for the two modes of discourse. The problem of learning to write lies in learning a new system of what syntactic and semantic alternatives can follow where there are no prosodic cues and in learning about a system of cuing where the distinction between new and given information must by syntactically and lexically expressed rather than through prosody. Furthermore written language requires a higher concentration of new information, that is a lesser redundancy of lexical choices. For example, we all know that a transcript of an orally delivered lecture say of twelve pages would probably reduce to three or four pages of written prose. For children to monitor and reproduce written information, they must have a high degree of tolerance for lexical and semantically carried new information.

We must now give some evidence for the points we have suggested. Children's dependence on prosody as an essential part of the signalling load of any communication differs from the adult performance criteria only in so far as in everyday talk adults usually communicate in *more than one modality*. For example, in adult communication interactants mark the ending of a brief encounter both by use of verbal formulae by kinesic postural information and by signalling prosodically through a series of falling intonation patterns; in fact absence of any one of these items may fail to make the conversational partner realize that a proper ending is in progress (Sacks and Shegloff 1974). As we have commented elsewhere, during the interaction between peers, children usually do not communicate using formulaic endings at all, and if they do one modality is usually sufficient. Children use the multi-channel quality of spoken language parsimoniously with a single channel carrying the signalling load.

In the following example (Gumperz & Herasimchuk, 1972) a second grade child (T) is tutoring a first grader (S) in reading. S has been reluctant to settle down to work and T has been urging him to read.

1. T: Page thirty three
2. S: Page thirty three
   Where's thirty three?
3. T: Thirty three (announcement style)
4. S: Thirty three (reading rhythm)
5. T: Thirty three (reading rhythm)
6. S: OK well I was over there. Cōme (reading rhythm)
7. T: Thē (reading rhythm)
8. S: bā—. The? The? Thē
9. T: mōrning (reading rhythm)

Note that almost complete lack of lexicalized performatives of the kind we would expect in adult speech. T begins by announcing that the page is thirty three. S repeats her phrase twice, first copying T's intonation and then shifting to question intonation as if to ask 'you said thirty three, where is it?' T then repeats her phrase with the identical announcement intonation of (1) as if to say: 'you know where it is.' S then *reads* 'thirty three'; T copies him by way of encouragement of confirmation, where-upon S acknowledges that he has found the place and then shifts to reading rhythm on 'come' to indicate he is now reading. But the word to be read is not 'come' but 'the'. In connecting S, T copies his reading rhythms to suggest she is helping him read. S then corrects himself and starts by reading bā. Then realizing perhaps that T had said 'the', he questions her twice using question intonation and then repeats once more in reading rhythm to indicate he is now reading. T confirms that S is on the right track by reading the next word: 'mōrning' and the reading lesson proceeds.

This is but one example of a phenomenon that we have frequently noted, children's use of intonation is an *essential*, rather than background or additional part of the information signalling load for a message, so *foregrounding* the use of prosody. In this way children rely more upon and are more aware of prosodic cues, their informational and conversational cuing depends upon this, so that in the transition to written language a new system of solely syntactic and lexicalized cue-ing must be learnt.

We want now to describe some of the ways children are initiated into the 'literate' experience and some of the out-of-school informal ways that they are helped to integrate their oral, not yet totally literate experience into that of a written language form.

The LY Phenomenon

Further evidence for the point of view that prosody carries information for children which is different from what it conveys in adult speech can be gained for a phenomenon that we have often noticed in children's books (especially books intended for reading out loud to the 4+ and silent reading for the 7+). We have called this the *LY* phenomenon. This is the very frequent use of adverbs of manner as adjuncts to the usual lexicalized framing of the dialogue. These adverbs provide useful, in fact for reading aloud, often essential, informational cues as to the necessary tone of voice, for the often fairly limited and simple dialogue. In the following two examples taken at random from one of our favorite children's books about a bear called "Paddington", intended to the 4–5+.

"'What,' said Paddington *hotly*, 'Win a jackpot! I thought it was 500 pounds.

'That's just it,' said Mrs. Bird ominously, 'it's too good to be true.'"

These examples indicate the need for the reader to add appropriate intonation to the dialogue, or if necessary to re-read longer passages if, when the adverbs are scanned, the intonation pattern used, was inappropriate for the speech act described.

That even children take the information provided by the LY phenomena into account can be shown by some incidental findings from a recent study at the Centre for Applied Linguistics on children's reading skills (P. Griffin, personal communcation 1977). In a video-taped study reading task some children were observed to re-cycle passages in which their previous reading intonation did not agree with the LY word.

This stylistic device does two things. *One,* it provides essential information about the person's state of mind, attitude and situation, succinctly without verbal elaboration of descriptive detail which would slow down the pace of the story and increase the level of difficulty for the child. That is it acts as a stylistic shortcut for descriptive detail and for additional information about the characters which keeps the prose monitoring at the level of simplicity for small children. The device almost never occurs in books for children over 11 + . Secondly, the use of adverbs of manner as adjuncts to dialogue provides a model for children of the way in which information, which is very salient for them, can be encoded in words, that is *lexicalized*. The transition from spoken to written language requires children to learn to lexicalize the relationships and understandings that could be carried through these other channels in oral language; the use of LY phenomenon may indirectly be a useful providing in as a model for this process.

The WOW Phenomenon

We have argued that when children learn to monitor and use written language thay are making a transformation of their information processing and of their social interpretative strategies. We have perhaps seemed to view writings negatively in the previous discussion as having less differentiated properties from the oral use of language. However, written language once gained and understood as a skill does add to the child's experience in several important ways.

From a wider perspective than child development Goody (1977) has suggested that "writing provides, a *spatialization* of language, giving it a temporal dimension which makes it possible to subject a speech act, a sentence or a chronological record, to a more context-free manipulation." For children the move into spatialization of written language can perhaps best be demonstrated by their manipulation of *graphic stylistics*. About the ages of seven to eight, we have observed, and informally checked our observation with several teachers, that children often make dramatic use of punctuation marks and all the stylistics of visual presentation of their written messages. For example, in a recent paper by Ervin Tripp (1977) she reproduces some pages from a note book by a seven year old girl, where part of the message, which is presented as a thesis-antithesis-resolution problem is graphic.

One excellent way of discovering the child's constructive ability is to examine inventions. The following texts have a particular interest in that they are a written image of dialogue. They tell us what a 7-year old abstracted as the core of argument structure. In some cases of inventive elaboration, the source is traditional, as in semantic transformations on nursery rhymes for humor. In some, the source is a partner's contribution, as in insult exchanges, or sound play. In this case, the core structure was the dialogue of arguments. The topic changes in the text were cued by objects seen while glancing about, and the fixed elements in the formal structure may come from the poetic tradition of repeated elements in a refrain.

These examples of invention consist of a corpus of about fifty 4-page "Books of Fun Things" written by a 7-year old:

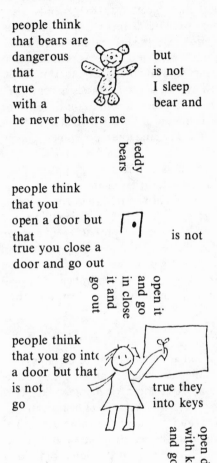

people think
that bears are
dangerous
that
true
with a
he never bothers me

but
is not
I sleep
bear and

teddy bears

people think
that you
open a door but
that
true you close a
door and go out

is not

open it
and go
in close
it and
go out

people think
that you go into
a door but that
is not
go

true they
into keys

open door
with key
and go in

people think
that dolls do not
talk but
that
true
people
don't they talk

is not
they are
so why

they're made
out of
cloth

The structure of these items was the same across dozens of exemplars. The child began with the image, drawing the object at the center of the page. The language at first was formed around the object, with long words being squashed to fit. The first and third lines were the same in form in all poems, being *people think that* and *but that is not true,* an idea that may derive from poetry with repeated lines, or song refrains. The content is a dialectic: as assertion of an opinion and its contrary and finally an explanation of the paradox or a synthesis in which both are true. The synthesis is heard as a second voice, which is visually set off at the side like another person conversing. Poets report that emblem poems are popular with children. These poems visually emulate the theme. While this child knew no emblem poems, she invented a emblem of dialogue.

Somewhat similar and perhaps less unusual are the examples of the dramatic use of punctuation oftem found in children's letters, and personal notebooks. By manipulating the surface visual form and by using graphic devices (such as exclamation marks) to carry the additional signalling load children begin to come to terms with the specific properties of written language and prepare themselves for the wider range of syntactic and semantic operations that are necessary to produce discursive written language, that is, the need to lexicalize the syntactically to embed additional information in order to achieve the linear information flow of written prose.

Lists and Other Things To Do

Having acquired the notion of language in its written form, or perhaps more accurately, in order to acquire written language, children must experience the usefulness of the written form. Not only do children keep notebooks, write notes and letters, but they realize and re-live what is perhaps historically the earliest uses of writings they make *lists,* and use these lists to organize their own lives. As Goody suggests writing skills began with the need to make lists—to record and account for object, land successions and other relationships of people to people.

For many children the move between writing and speaking has initially retained some of its older functions of record-keeping. So much are these list-making functions a part of children's lives and our adult understanding of a natural (with in our culture) usefulness of writing that lists often appear in children's books. Children's books encapsulate the knowledge that we work most to encourage within the child's language socialization. Many of the classic story books looked at as primers of competent communication would tell us more than most academic writing about the kinds and qualities of language skills we feel children most need to acquire. Here is an example of a list from a well known children's book *House at Pooh Corner:*

"'And it's no good looking at the Six Pine Trees for Piglet,' said Pooh to himself, 'because he's been organized in a special place of his own. So I shall have to look for the Special Place first. I wonder where it is.' And he wrote it down in his head like this:

ORDER OF LOOKING FOR THINGS

1. Special Place,   (To find Piglet.)
2. Piglet   (To find who Small is.)
3. Small   (To find Small.)
4. Rabbit.   (To tell him I've found Small.)
5. Small Again.   (To tell him I've found Rabbit.)

'Which makes it look like a bothering sort of day,' thought Pooh, as he stumped along."

Although children's move into various forms of written lists clearly shows the influence of "taught" skills of literacy, they are a reflection of the personal usefulness that children can see in writing rather than an imposed form. Children can turn more easily to this form of writing because of the need to organize and record things in their own lives and its affairs. Lists of favorite toys, of collections of models etc. occur very commonly as in our example Christmas and birthday present lists. Here is a very typical list written by an 8 year old for her own use in her notebook. This Christmas list shows two of the skills that writing involves and introduces into the child's life: not only the need to record and order but also the skill of *evaluating,* as a form of ordering (a lot, sort of, quite a bit, etc.).

These kinds of lists are a form of writing that children move towards very readily, and it has recently been suggested that a better way to approach the teaching of literacy skills might be to build upon this experience of notewriting, list making as an extension of the children's communicative experience (Griffith 1974). As Goody has pointed out from a wider, historical perspective, but the observation can be repeated for children, it is not the quality of writing, nor the syntactic structures or standardized spelling, that make the importance of the breakthrough into literacy, but the *transformation* of experience into just such ordered listed forms, where words written into the lists transform experience from an immediate to the *recorded* and so on to the *evaluated* form.

The Influence of Written on Spoken Language

Shirley Brice Heath (this volume) has commented on the less rigorous distinction made in the 18th and 19th century between speaking and writing—the need for the record-keeping and communicative aspects of writing meant that ordinary people kept diaries, journals, wrote letters, made lists and accounts of families, farms and animals; there was a lesser concern with standard spelling and written forms often contained irregular grammer. The needs of the modern industrial societies for a wider level of standardized literacy and the rapidly changing technologies of communication have increasingly separated out the uses of written from spoken language to a greater degree. Forms of written language have developed (See introduction to the next section) which do not allow for impression or personal idiosyncracies of the older journal styles.

With the growth of mass communication and the increasing need for communicating with individuals who differ in culture and home background, culturally neutral styles of speaking have evolved for use in instruction giving, public lectures, broadcasting and classroom lectures and similar instrumental tasks. These oral styles have taken on may of the characteristics of the modern written descriptive prose and have thus become distinct from the home languages.

The move into in understanding of language which is tempered by the written word, has an influence on children's performance in both spoken and written spoken language situations. We have argued that children experience a new and very different need for language in school situations. Here a new kind of ambiguity of meaning exists which requires children to make explicit even that information which in an everyday context could be taken for granted. The need to specify relationships in some detail applies particularly to written language. When children begin to learn this need they are already becoming more aware of the increasing nominal detail that is required in written prose (Halliday 1974).

For children, learning to read is one the critical times when the schemata for inerpretation and production of language, which are based on spoken language experience, are most exposed to change. The argument we have been developing in this paper is that for all children the literacy experience requires essential changes in the processing of verbal information, for some children however this shift of understanding of written language is sometimes facilitated by early language exeperience; the child is able early in life to gain processing experience of the written word.

This is illustrated in a recent analysis of some free play talk by two 3-½ year old middle class girls who in the course of a pretend game—of mothers with books—did some "pretend reading" to each other. That is, they took some of their books and told a story from the pictures. The told story had the prosody and intonation of a story actually read. What is more, as the anylysis shows the girls used specific *formulas*—a group of words that have a common network of syntactic patterning (Lord 1960) into which specific word choices were fitted. The formulas acted as organizing devices for the story—which was told with "normal" page turning fluency—as if being read aloud. The skill of telling a story aloud is somewhat similar to the telling of epics that are described in oral literature, and it is particularly interesting that the two girls made use of the same organizational device—of a formula into which to slot the story variations. For such young children a fluent story-telling was unusual. An example of such formula substitution follows:

$$[\quad X \qquad was \qquad Y \quad]$$

$$The\ dog \qquad was \qquad happy$$

$$The\ park \qquad was \qquad trees$$

$$it \qquad was \qquad lovely$$

Although these "sentences" are not strictly grammatical, they provided a useful format for story continuity. The main interest of this example, is the very early interchange of influence of written to spoken words in both rhythm and syntax before children have yet grasped the "essentials" of understanding a word-symbol-sound-symbol correpondence. The interpretation of written stories is done as an oral-language skill.

To summarize, children need experiences in school that favor the learning of written culture through the *medium of the oral culture,* thus building on the interpretative skills and linguistic understandings that children bring to the school experience, as a basis for further learning. The linkage has to be formed between the child's system of iconographic speech, where much of the information is carried through prosodic and paralinguistic cues, that is where such cues receive an equal informational load, and the discursive forms of written language where information that was previously carried by prosodic/paralinguistic channels must be lexicalized; and so form a part of the linear sequence of information. In fact, children need a saturation experience of orally transformed 'written' prose in as many culturally 'neutral' ways as possible (such as through the teaching of science) in order to transform, for themselves, the *rhythms* of spoken language into the written modes.

CONCLUDING REMARKS

We have suggested that there is a critical threshold in the symbolization of experience which has to be crossed between societies that have written symbols for transmitting and ordering knowledge and information and those that don't. Therefore, if we look at the various ways in which written symbols are used and look historically at the influence of written symbolization, we see that in our own society, at whatever structural or subcultural level, all groups have passed beyond that threshold. It is only when we look at forms of official language that differences appear. But it is this official language which serves as the model of school evaluation. If we consider literacy in its more general socio-historical forms we see that all peoples have their uses of literacy in the context of their social needs. The problem of literacy and school failure arises only when we narrow the definition of literacy to the acquistion of certain standard communicative strategies, such as precision in usage, decontextualization of information and careful weighing of words.

By narrowing the definition in this way we make the literacy experience discontinuous with the practices of everyday life for most people. To understand the problems of urban schools we need further explorations of this discontinuity and of its implications for residents of ethnically mixed urban societies.

REFERENCES

Altick, R. *The English common reader: A social history of the mass reading public 1800–1900.* University of Chicago Press, 1957.

Berry, J. W. & Dassen, P. R., (Eds.) *Culture and Cognition.* London, 1973.

Bond, M. *Paddington at large.* London: William Collins Ltd, 1962.

Brown, R. *A first language.* Cambridge, Mass.: Harvard University Press, 1971.

Cole, M. & Scribner, S. *Culture and Thought.* New York, 1974.

Cook-Gumperz, J. The child as practical reasoner. In M. Sanchez & B. Blount (Eds.). *Sociocultural Dimensions of Language Use.* New York: Academic Press, 1976.

Cook-Gumperz, J. Situated instructions. In S. Ervin-Tripp & C. Mitchell-Kernan (Eds.), *Child discourse.* New York: Academic Press, 1977.

Cook-Gumperz, J. & W. Corsar. Socio-ecological constraints on children's communicative strategies. *Sociology,* 1977.

Cook-Gumperz, J. & J. Gumperz. Papers on language and context. Language behavior research laboratory working paper No. 46, University of California, Berkeley, 1976.

Ervin-Tripp, S. & Mitchell-Kernan, C. (Eds.). *Child discourse*. New York: Academic Press, 1977.

Gibson, G. Aptitude tests, *Science*, 1955.

Goody, J. *The domestication of the savage mind*. Cambridge University Press, 1977.

Goody, J. Memoire et apprentissage dans les societes avec et sans ecriture: la transmission du Bagre, *L'Homme*, 1977, *17*.

Gumperz, J. & Herasimchuk, E. The conversational analysis of social meaning: A study of classroom interaction. In Sanches, M. & Blount, B. *Sociocultural dimensions of language use*. Academic Press, 1975.

Gumperz, J. Sociocultural knowledge in conversational inferene. In M. Saville-Troike (Ed.), *28th Annual Round Table Monograph Series on Languages and Linguistics*. Washington, D.C.: Georgetown University Press, 1977.

Habermas, J. *Knowledge and human interest*. New York: Beacon Press, 1973.

Halliday, M. A. K. *Learning how to mean*. London: Edward Arnold, 1974.

Halsey, A. H., Floud, J. & Anderson, C. *Education, economy and society*. Glencoe, Illinois: The Free Press, 1966.

Havelock, E. A. *Preface to Plato*. Cambridge, Mass., 1963.

Herriot, J. *All creatures great and small*. New York: Bantam Books, 1973.

Horton, R. African traditional thought and western science. In *Africa*, 1967, *37*, 50–71, 155–187.

Hymes, D. *Foundations of sociolinguistics*. University of Pennsylvania Press, 1974.

Lévy-Bruhl, L. (1910) *Les Fonctions mentales dans les sociétés inférieures*. Paris. (English transl. by L. A. Clare, *How Natives Think*. London, 1926.

Lévi-Strauss, C. (1962) *La Pensée Sauvage*. Paris. (Engl. trans. London, 1966).

Lord, A. *A Singer of tales*. Harvard University Press, 1960.

Luria, A. R. *Cognitive development, its cultural and social foundation*. Harvard University press, 1976.

Melmed, P. *Black English phonology: The question of reading interference*. Berkeley: language-behavior research laboratory, 1970.

Milne, A. A. *The house at pooh corner*. New York: E. P. Dutton, 1950; (first published 1928).

Olson, D. R. From utterance to text: The bias of language in speech and writing (typescript), 1974.

O'Neil, W. Properly literate in *Harvard Educational Review*, 1971, 260–264.

Ong, W. J. Latin language study as a Renaissance puberty rite. In *Studies in Philology*, (LVI), April 1959, pp. 103–124.

Piestrup, A. M. *Black dialect interference and accomodation of reading instructions in first grade*. Berkeley: Language-Behavior Research Laboratory, 1973.

Sacks, H., & Schegloff, E. Opening up closings. In *Semiotica*, 1973, 289–327.

7

The Voice of Varied Linguistic and Cultural Groups in Fiction: Some Criteria for the Use of Language Varieties in Writing

Elizabeth Closs Traugott
Department of Linguistics, Department of English, Stanford University

Labov has suggested that non-standard varieties are usually represented in stereotypic ways in literature because the author wants to heighten or enrich the local flavor of speech, or because

> the author hears this "marked" behavior as invariant when in fact it is variable. The two reasons actually coincide, since it can be stated more simply that people perceive speech in categorical terms, even though they behave in accordance with variable rules, and the novelist's practice reflects his perception and his intention. On the other hand, there will be unnoticed inconsistencies where the author's own grammar appears without his realizing it. (1969:62).

On the other hand, Shuy has shown that some fiction-writers, for example D. H. Lawrence in *Lady Chatterly's Lover*, use dialect variation in subtle and not necessarily stereotypic ways (1975). Fallis has also shown this for Spanish-English code-switching in Chicano poetry (1976). In fact, any cursory review of recent fiction will show that both stereotyping and finely-graded variation occur, and that which approach is taken depends on a number of variables, including most obviously the author's knowledge and intentions with respect both to subject-matter and to audience, and also including expected audience knowledge.

Labov and Fallis have suggested that the study of dialect or bilingual code-switching in literature is a valuable (but not always reliable) source of information about the varying functions of language varieties in the communities that use them. Labov has also proposed that dialect literature can be used to test a student's ability to read materials closer to, but certainly not the same as, their vernacular (1969:62). Shuy has further suggested that one can use variation theory to evaluate a literary text: identification of the variation, and study of its function and the appropriateness of its use or non-use with respect to both authorial intention and actual speech should be a part of the critic's evaluation measure. Another way to look at literature that uses different language varieties is to consider it as a resource for identifying variables of relevance to writing, and that is the task I set myself here. There is a great deal that we can learn from recent literature about the difficulties faced by anyone trying to develop techniques for representing linguistic varieties other than Standard English in ways that can be understood by a wide spectrum of readers. Even at the level of orthography, there are few conventions, and each author tends to experiment individually. More subtle is the problem of reflecting different modes of syntactic and semantic organization, including "situated meaning"—the kind of meaning that arises in social contexts.

I have chosen to discuss fiction because it has long been a vehicle for the use of regional, social, and other varieties of language, and more has already been done on such varieties in this genre than any other, yet many of the interesting linguistic questions have not yet been raised. Fiction is also a particularly useful genre to discuss because it highlights the difference between the function of linguistic varieties in a speech community in general and the function of linguistic varieties in a particular extended utterance or "text" (cf. Halliday, McIntosh, Strevens 1964; Scotton and Ury 1975). Writing in general and fiction in particular have institutionalized norms of language and correlations can be shown to exist between these norms and the statuses established between narrator and reader, and between narrator and the characters in the text, much in the same way as Labov has shown correlations to exist between social status and style (Labov 1972a). At the same time, statuses are also dynamically established and created (Gumperz 1972). Based on the frame of reference that the potentials of the linguistic norms provide, the choice is made of following them or deviating from them, in other words, of accepting the statuses assumed or of establishing new ones. In this sense authors actually "make" readers (Booth 1961:138).

A considerable amount of work has been done trying to show that the language of literature and especially fiction is by nature different from that of other genres. The Russian formalists and many critics since then have argued that literary language is deviant, or at least foregrounded, focussed on itself (cf. Jakobson 1960; Mukařovský 1964). But recent work such as Labov's on street-culture narratives (Labov 1972b), and various attempts to apply speech act theory to literature (cf. Ohmann 1971; Searle 1975; Pratt 1977; Iser 1975) have shown that the linguistic structure itself is not necessarily different (though it may be)—it is the "pragmatics" (the uses to which language is put and the appropriateness conditions for those uses) that are different and thus determine what possible linguistic structures are selected. In other words, the intention and expectation of author and reader are the key to what differences there are between fiction and non-literary language. And even these differences are far from discrete (Ohmann 1973; Pratt 1977): whether we take *In Cold Blood* or *Roots* as fact or fiction depends on whether they are intended or understood to be descriptions of facts or imitations of those facts—different readers may arrive at different conclusions. We need to allow these works to be both (a fact recognized by the Pulitzer Prize Committee when it awarded *Roots* a special prize because it fit none of the conventional categories). For our purposes it is important to keep these distinctions in mind, and especially to remember that the language of fiction can be self-creating in ways that other language types often cannot, while at the same time recognizing that good fiction, by virtue of being imitative ("mimetic") highlights the potentials of the linguistic situation and can therefore tell us much about what is conceived as important within a group or about a group. Furthermore, fiction is a form of writing. It is always pointed out that the "colloquial" language of fiction bears little or no direct relation to what is actually said, partly because speech is for the most part unpremeditated while fiction writing is very conscious. What is often forgotten, however, is that fiction has much in common with other writing since it is constrained by the same medium—it requires deliberateness, description in some form or another of what would be carried in speech by gesture, intonation and immediate, outside context,[1] and has a far higher dependence than speech on the co-operative principles of "quality" and "quantity"—the principles "Say what you believe is true" and "Don't say more or less than you need to" (Grice 1973)—since the reader can always put the writing down, whereas the addressee in the speech situation can normally not just turn away. What is important is that the written language, whether fictional or not, is, even in its most "naturalistic" style, very different from the spoken language. Channel (or "medium") seems to have far greater repercussions on the language used than whether the speech act is mimetic or not. Other crucial factors are whether the author and/or reader is monolingual/monodialectal or bilingual/bidialectal, and whether the reader is elitist or not (Mackey 1976).

From the late nineteenth century on, writing has typically been associated with the standard. This is not the place to go into the history of attitudes to language varieties, but it is useful to remind ourselves that this association is only recent. The notion of "standard" did not really exist before the seventeenth and eighteenth centuries in the English-speaking world, and when it did come into being, attitudes were primarily descriptive—the standard was identified as the language of the upper classes, and codified for

---

[1] A notable experiment in writing fiction without *He said, She said* formulae is William Gaddis, *JR* (1975).

purposes of maintenance and separation from the rising middle classes. It was only at the end of the eighteenth century in England and in the middle of the nineteenth century in America that the standard came to be regarded strictly as a target for the middle class; hence the development of prescriptive views (Lyman 1922; Leonard 1962). Until then, there was, especially in America, active interest in fostering different speech varieties in different genres and different modes, conversational, oratorical and so forth. In the mid nineteenth century, however, the emphasis turned from speaking to writing, from heterogeneity to homogeneity (Heath 1978). Indeed, the whole notion of SE in America is associated primarily with writing, a channel far more readily controlable than speech, especially through the enforcement of spelling conventions and certain morphological and syntactic rules. In its homogeneity, in its deliberate cross-cutting of ethnic, regional and social boundaries, it mandated against ethnic, regional and social identities, excluding such identities as "substandard," incorrect," even "immoral." As such it served the particular combination of unificational, prestige and frame-of-reference functions typical of standard languages everywhere (Garvin and Mathiot 1960; Macaulay 1973).

It is only recently that serious attention has once more been paid to the possibility that linguistic varieties other than the standard can be used in a multiplicity of genres, including those in the written channel—not just the obviously mimetic ones like fiction and drama, where regional, social, sex-correlated and other varieties have been used for some time, and have indeed run counter to the homogenizing principle, but also in the less obviously mimetic ones like biography and even history. The publication of *Roots* represents a cultural landmark not only in its attention to the little-discussed question of the cultural origins of black Americans, but in its concern for linguistic details in a framework which is intended both as history and fiction.

Any language utterance can be considered appropriate only in terms of external factors such as the social and ethnic group, the geographic origin, education, sex and age of both the speaker and the addressee. These variables intersect with each other, with the situation, and with a further set of variables that can be called "register": topic (linguistics, gardening, Zen Buddhism etc.), style (formal, informal, etc., depending on the degree of attention paid to speech), genre (narrative, dialogue, etc.,), and channel (spoken, written, and so forth) (cf. Ervin-Tripp 1964; Halliday, McIntosh, Strevens 1964; Hymes 1974; and papers in this volume by Gumperz and Cook-Gumperz, and Valadez). All these factors are potentially operative in any situation, but certain ones may be more important than others in a given context. There has been a tendency in the discussion of those literary works in which social, ethnic, regional, and educational varieties are linguistically marked in some way to treat them along with "colloquial" (i.e. informal) style (cf. Krapp 1925; Bridgman 1966) or to group them all together under "dialect" (cf. Page 1973).

As the work of Labov (e.g. 1972a) and Trudgill (1974a, 1974b) has shown, however, these factors are all independent, though certainly correlatable in significant ways. The tendency to treat all non-standard varieties as "colloquial" or "dialect" can perhaps be partly explained by the fact that most researchers have been primarily literary critics rather than linguists, but it is probably also partly due to the fact that linguistics itself did not make all these distinctions so clearly until the last ten years or so. It is no doubt also due to the fact that some writers either are unaware of the differences, or do not know how to represent them[2], or find it most economical to allow one variety to represent what in an actual speech situation would be more than one. But to become aware of the possibilities available in writing, and to judge the effectiveness and appropriateness of the language being used, it is important to distinguish these variables and to be conscious of the ways in which one variety can be used to represent others.

In this paper I will be concerned specifically with social and ethnic varieties as they intersect with the written channel in fictional narrative genre. Included among "varieties" are not only what are traditionally called "dialects," e.g. varieties of Black English (BE), but also different languages, e.g. Jamaican Creole, West African English, and varieties of Spanish.[3]

In the first part of this paper I sketch some of the uses to which social, regional and ethnic language varieties have been put. I then turn to the question of how constraints on speaker (author) and addressee (reader) affect the type of linguistic structure represented, and finally to examples from a number of works involving different uses of linguistic varieties, focussing on the function of linguistic varieties with respect to narrator-reader relations and with respect to relations internal to the text.

USES OF SOCIAL, ETHNIC
AND REGIONAL VARIETIES IN FICTION

Among the uses of social, ethnic and regional varieties most common in fiction are comic effect, screening unacceptable topics, characterization of folk-ways, development of character, and polemic establishment of identity.

It has been pointed out many times that uses of varieties associated with specific groups were primarily comic up to the beginning of the nineteenth century; only secondarily did they portray character or local color (cf. Bridgman 1966). Linguistic credibility is not the main issue when the effect is comic. A few lexical or phonological markers, often of a stereotypic sort, will

---

[2]A detailed account of graphic problems is to be found in Ives (1971).

[3]Cf. Fishman (1972) for the use of "varieties" in the broad sense used here.

be sufficient in many cases. Often no distinction can be made between regional, social, or ethnic varieties.

During the nineteenth century, however, new uses of linguistic varieties arose in literature, almost in converse proportion to the increasing tendency toward standardization in non-literary genres. At a time when prescriptivism was increasing and decorum in choice of both language variety and topic was becoming a vital issue, the non-standard language became for some writers the screeen for unacceptable material under the guise of comic effect, cf. George Washington Harris' development of Sut Lovingwood's "vernacular," largely marked as "uneducated" (e.g. George: *Had he hydrophobia?*...Sut: *What du yu mean by high-dry-foby?),* which puts a comic edge on "cloacal jokes" (Bridgman 1966:27). On a different level, there developed an interest in folk-ways, sometimes sympathetic and capturing the language in intricate and variable ways (cf. Ambrose Gonzales' Gullah tales).

The key to what Bridgman considers the crucial turning-point in American writing—the point at which American style came to stand on its own—is the development of non-stylistic varieties not for local color, but for character. He sees in Mark Twain's *Huckleberry Finn* (1884) the beginning of a new idiom, for in this novel Twain broke through the leveling force of the standard written language to an individual voice by using a boy as a narrator. "In that story we hear no condescending adult voice by which Huck can be judged insufficient. His idiom is the standard" (Bridgman 1966:9)—standard in the text, but 'non-standard' within the norms of society, for all children are in some sense non-standard speakers.

A good example of the way dialect in later fiction can be used to represent character can be found in Ken Kesey's *Sometimes a Great Notion*. In this novel, the dialog and even some of the narrative is largely represented in a "colloquial" mode, deliberately mimetic of spoken language, with a touch of non-standard features, such as *ain't,* and regionalisms such as *I used to wonder me* to give the flavor, not imitate, the language of loggers. There are different degrees of non-standardness, least for Leland (Lee) who regards himself as educated and socially superior to his family, a little more for Viv, the retiring wife of Hank, considerably more for Hank, Lee's brother, and most of all for old Henry, their father. The markers of these varieties are relatively few and low-keyed, and do not get in the way of reading the book. In this passage, Henry's friend Boney is asking who Lee's mother has to talk to and to share experiences with, a woman who is herself educated and totally at odds with the world she married into:

>   ...so who does *she* have?" Boney Stokes shook his head slowly at Henry, the woes of all mankind marking his face. "I just am thinkin' of the girl, Henry; because able as you still are, you can't be the stud you once was—ain't you concerned for her, day in and day out alone over yonder?"
>   Henry leered, winked, grinned into his hand. "Why shoot, Boney. Who's to say whether I'm the stud of old or not?" Modest as a turkey gobbler. "Besides,

some men are so wonderfully blest by nature that they don't need to prove theirselfs night after night; they're so fine-lookin' and so special, they can keep a woman pantin' with the *pure mem'ry* an' the *wild hope* that what has happened once is liable to happen again!"[4]

Here as elsewhere it is what is said rather than the obviously nonstandard forms that is most significant.

Occasionally, however, the dialect forms predominate, and are used in a totally different way. For example, as Lee dozes in the Greyhound bus in which he has just started to cross America from the East to Oregon in order to take up the challenge of his brother ("You are old enough now"(to log)), and indeed to revenge himself on what he considers the crudity, oppression and arrogance of his brother and father, Lee imagines his brother as an "illiterate spook." He dreams a nightmare of how he, Lee, is bullied into a protoplasmic blob and picked up in a polyethylene bag by his brother and hauled before his father. The poisonous foment of his imagination is expressed not only by the grotesqueness of the scene he imagines, but also by the language he attributes to Hank and Henry. Lee dreams of it as an insult to them, but his fabrication makes it really an insult to himself, a manifestation of his intolerance, hostility, and sense of superiority:

"Wellsir now...aye doggies...heeheehee...lookee yonder...how's 'bout *that*. What in tarnation you youngsters found floatin' in the river *this* time? I swan, *allus* draggin' in some crap or other..."

"Didn't rightly find it, Pa; sorter *conjured* it up."

"You don't tell me!" He leans forward, displaying more interest. "Nasty-lookin' outfit...what you reckon it be? Somethin' come in on the tide?"

"I'm afeared, Pa"—Hank hangs his head and scuffs his toe at the floor, shredding white pine in all directions with his spikes—"that it be"—scratches his belly, swallows—"be yer youngest son, Leland Stanford."

"*Damnation!* I told you once I told you a friggin' *hunnert* times, I don't *never!* want the name o' that *quitter!* spoke in thisyere house again! Phoo. Cain't stand the sound of him, lit-lone the *sight!* Jesus, son, what got into you to pull such a boner?"

Hank steps closer to the throne. "Paw, I knowed how ya felt. I cain't help but feel the same way myself—worst, mebee, comes down to it; I'd as leave never heard his name again the rest o' my nachrul life—but I didn't see no way gettin' around it, considerin' the situation we is in."

"What situation!"

"The labor situation."[5]

---

[4]Ken Kesey, *Sometimes a great notion.* (1965:35), reprinted by permission of Viking Penguin, Inc.

[5]Ibid, p. 74-75, reprinted by permission of the publisher, Viking Penguin, Inc.

In this century the use of non-standard varieties by writers with Anglo backgrounds has been developed primarily as an indicator of character or as a representation of social, ethnic and cultural differences. In a paper first written in 1950 and revised in 1971, Summer Ives points out that authors like Joel Chandler Harris, Mark Twain, Mary Murphree, Marjorie Kinnan Rawlings, James Russell Lowell, and others working within a tradition of standard language "were actually aware that they were depicting something peculiar, something different from their own conception of the "standard" language. The characters who speak "dialect" are set off, either socially or geographically, from the main body of those who speak the language." (1971: 146). For the non-Anglo writer, however, the situation is very different. For one, the nature of the subject matter selected is often social and political rather than psychological, at least in the formative years of writing in the particular variety in question. The function of the literary work may often itself be political and social, raising the consciousness of both those written about and of the wider audience. For the writer working in the tradition of the standard, the question is, how much that is non-standard should be added. But for the writer attempting to break through the standard tradition and to create new value systems, the question is how much to take away from the variety to which the new status is being given, whether Black English, West African Pidgin, or the language of the Chicanos in making it publicly available through writing and through the partial use of standard English. Put another way, in some sense the diglossic relation between "high" and "low" varieties in real life (Ferguson 1959) is being minimized through writing; so for the non-Anglo writer trying to minimize the stigma attached to his or her language the problem is how to close the gap and yet exploit it.

The Anglo writer for the most part has a writing tradition developed within Anglo culture. Until recently there has been no tradition for writing in Black English, even less in languages like Jamaican Creole. In countries like Jamaica and Nigeria the former colonial powers had little or nothing to do with the native culture and did nothing to promote literature in the native languages or even in the pidgin or creole languages that developed there. In Nigeria, to address the Anglo culture it was necessary to adopt English, and to slowly modify literary traditions to create a West African literature in English. The force of the written norm is particularly clear here where the problem of change within and from the low variety (the pidgin) to another considered worthy of the written medium was initially ignored by adoption of Standard English. In some cases literary history repeated itself, despite the differences in situation. Writers like Chinua Achebe started by using West African Pidgin first of all for comic effect or to reflect low social position (*Things fall apart* 1958). But in the course of his own writing career Achebe moved on to a far more complex use of West African Pidgin as a vehicle to show the multicultural nature of West African society (*A man of the people* 1966). Similarly, in the West Indies, Jamaican Creole was used only tentatively at first. Unlike West African Pidgin, it is on its way to becoming standardized (in the form of West Indian English). Relative to West African Pidgin it has far more varieties within a small area, socially, ethnically and geographically defined. It is identified with the culture and is coming to be used more and more as a literary language (cf. Ramchand 1973 on Naipaul's hesitant use of the creole as opposed to Selvon's more integrated use of it). The struggle has been harder for West African Pidgin, Jamaican Creole and for Spanish in Chicano literature, than for Black English, partly because the languages involved are fundamentally different from English, while the tradition and also the narrative frame of reference are typically English,[6] and also partly because it is only recently that writers have developed of the stature and range of experience and knowledge of a Zora Neale Hurston. She wrote novels in the 1930's reflecting the social, cultural and linguistic traditions of black people in Florida in post-Civil War days and at her time, that compete with the very best literature in any variety of English.

AUTHOR-NARRATOR-READER RELATIONS AS CONSTRAINTS ON LANGUAGE CHOICE

Although it is possible to conceive of some writing as having no intended audience (other than the author), in general any written text involves both an addressor and an addressee. In fiction the addressor/narrator is typically not to be identified with the author. However, such separation of addressor and author is by no means restricted to fiction—spokesmen for presidents, for example, or the Western Union telephonist who reads a telegram over the phone illustrate such differences. The special case of fiction is that the narrator is usually assumed not to voice the belief of the author, while the president's spokesman is expected to voice the president's beliefs (but not necessarily his actual words). In all such situations where there are two addressors, one direct and other indirect, the difference between the narrator's relation to the audience and the narrator's relation to the text must be taken into consideration. The narrator establishes a shared world with the reader through various devices such as the use of the definite article, deictic relators like *this-that, come-go,* and so forth. Thus at the beginning of William Faulkner's *The Sound and the Fury,* the narrator demands the reader's cooperation in assuming *the fence, the curling flower spaces* and *them* are shared, yet undercuts and disorients the reader by the strange use of "deictic" *come* and *went:*

---

[6]However, some Chicano writers use Spanish, not English, as the frame of reference, for example, Miguel Mendez in *Peregrinos de Atzlan* (1974). For a detailed study of the development of Chicano literature, see Leal and Barrón (1977). Sapiens (1977) discusses the use of several different varieties of Spanish in Mendez' novel, as also of *caló* and English.

> Through the fence, between the curling flower spaces, I could see them hitting. They were coming toward where the flag was and I went along the fence.[7]

Similarly, the narrator in the opening sentence of Salinger's *The Catcher in the Rye* establishes a kind of intimacy by the use of *lousy* and *crap* and the informality of the style, and assumes prior interest on the reader's part, while at the same time casting doubt on the reader's genuineness in the assumed interest—a complex social relation indeed:

> If you really want to hear about it, the first thing you'll probably want to know is where I was born and what my lousy childhood was like, and how my parents were occupied and all before they had me and that David Copperfield kind of crap, but I don't feel like going into it, if you want to know the truth.[8]

This establishment of relations with the reader is by no means restricted to first person narrative, as is clear from the markers that effect the relationships: articles, deictics, informality, and so forth. Here in the first sentence of his short story, "The beast in the jungle," the narrator assumes, just like the narrator in *The Catcher in the Rye,* that there has been a scenario before the narrative begins, specifically that the hearer/reader has asked the question *What determined the speech that startled him?* The narrator evaluates this question negatively (it *scarcely matters*), while at the same time continuing to assume shared knowledge (*him, himself, they*).

> What determined the speech that startled him in the course of their encounter scarcely matters, being probably but some words spoken by himself quite without intention—spoken as they lingered and slowly moved together after their renewal of acquaintance.[9]

In addition to narrator-reader relations there is the narrator's relation to the text, that is, the narrator's function in the internal structure of the discourse. Sometimes there will be several narrators, as in Faulkner's *The Sound and the Fury* or Kesey's *Sometimes a Great Notion*. Each narrator presents just one narrative point of view, and this is important not only in establishing relations to the reader, but also in the development of the action itself. While the meaning of a text derives in part from the interplay between textual statuses (the role relations between characters within the text) and narrator-reader statuses (the role relations established between narrator and reader), they are clearly different.

---

[7]William Faulkner, *The sound and the fury,* New York, Vintage Books, 1954,p. 1.

[8]Jerome David Salinger, *The catcher in the rye,* Boston: Little, Brown, 1951, p. 3.

[9]Henry James, "The beast in the jungle", in *Selected tales of Henry James,* London: John Baker, 1969, p. 219.

THE USE OF LANGUAGE VARIETIES
AND NARRATOR-READER RELATIONS

The author's own limitations naturally constrain the language of the narrator and that of the characters most. But assuming some kind of knowledge of non-stylistic varieties, we can distinguish between four types of situation (they are not categorically discrete, but rather prototypical norms on a continuum):

1. The author is not particularly familiar with the varieties used in the text. We can expect the use of these varieties to be stereotypic. The quality of the stereotyping varies but is often quite thin. At the weakest end of the scale is "eye-dialect" that consists of nothing but the use of "spelling errors" that in fact reflect no phonological, lexical or syntactic structure whatsoever, e.g., *ennything, exkusable, wimmen, mebbe.* [10] This form of representation always reflects stereotyping and a superior point of view. Truer to linguistic reality, but still far removed, is the use of phonological-morphological markers like *runnin',* or of stigmatized lexical forms like *ain't* which indicate no specific linguistic variety, just "general nonstandard" or "colloquial." Within the text, such stereotypings create comic effect, or local color, but little more. As far as reader-narrator relationships are concerned, the narrator often intends the reader to share the humorous point of view or the condescension, as the case may be. Failure to use even the stereotypic features effectively has no consequences within the text, but is highly damaging to narrator-reader relations, as for example when in adopting as Irish flavor an author uses *He is after X-ing it* not in the sense of *He has just X-ed it,* but as *He is X-ing it.* Another kind of failure occurs when the author footnotes a usage with a comment of the sort "They really do say this."

2. The author is familiar with the varieties in the text. In this case the use of language varieties can have the same functions as in 1), but it is more likely to be used for extended local color, characterization, and representation of cultural modes of behavior. In the first case, we tend to find stereotyping, in the latter it is likely that the linguistic markers will be used variably. How close to actual use this variability is will depend on the author's intentions with respect to the narrative and expectations with respect to the audience. In Ives' words, "nearly all examples of literary dialect are deliberately incomplete; the author is an artist, not a linguist or sociologist, and his purpose is literary rather than scientific. In working out his compromise between art and linguistics, each author has made his own decision as to how many of the peculiarities of his character's speech he can profitably represent" (1971:147). (Note here the assumption that dialect representation is "different, peculiar".) Even if incomplete, however, the variety in question

---

[10]An excellent account of eye dialect can be found in Bowdre (1971).

will typically be represented at all levels, phonological, morphological, syntactic and also pragmatic.

One particularly interesting example is from Zora Neale Hurston's novel, *Their eyes were watching God.* Published in 1937, before a tradition of writing had been established in which the narrative voice could be non-standard, adult, and serious (as opposed to non-standard, childish, and comic), this book is an account of a black woman's odyssey to self-awareness, expressed through a Standard English speaking narrator. The dialog, however, is highly variable. Many of the features selected are similar to those currently considered quantitatively characteristic of BE in Northern ghettoes (cf. Labov 1972b, Fasold, and Wolfram 1970), although the text actually represents Southern rural BE. An example is:

> Long before the year was up, Janie noticed that her husband had stopped talking in rhymes to her. He had ceased to wonder at her long black hair and finger it. Six months back he had told her, "If Ah kin haul de wood heah and chop it fuh yuh, look lak you oughta be able tuh tote it inside. Mah fust wife never bothered me 'bout choppin' no wood nohow. She'd grab dat ax and swing chips lak uh man. You done been spoilt rotten."
>
> So Janie had told him, "Ah'm just as stiff as you is stout. If you can stand not to chop and tote wood Ah reckon you can stand not to git no dinner. 'Scuse mah freezolity, Mist' Killicks, but Ah don't mean to chop de first chip."
>
> "Aw you know Ah'm gwine to chop de wood fuh yuh. Even if you is stingy as you can be wid me. Yo' Grandma and me myself done spoilt yuh now, and Ah reckon Ah have tuh keep on wid it."
>
> One morning soon he called her out of the kitchen to the barn. He had the mule all saddled at the gate.
>
> "Looka heah, LilBit, help me out some. Cut up dese seed taters fuh me. Ah got tuh go step off a place."
>
> "Where you goin?"
>
> "Over tuh Lake City tuh see uh man about uh mule."
>
> "Whut you need two mules fuh? Lessen you aims to swap off dis one."
>
> "Naw, Ah needs two mules dis yeah. Taters is going' tuh be taters in de fall. Bringin' big prices. Ah aims tuh run two plows, and dis man Ah'm talkin' 'bout is got uh mule all gentled up so even uh woman kin handle 'im."
>
> Logan held his wad of tobacco real still in his jaw like a thermometer of his feelings while he studied Janie's face and waited for her to say something.[11]

It would be excessive to detail all the variability, but a few examples will illustrate two points. One concerns the function of variability not only to

---

[11]Zora Neale Hurston, *Their eyes were watching God,* New York: Fawcett World Library, 1969, p. 25-26.

suggest authenticity but also to establish differences in characterization. The other concerns the absence of certain features of BE.

While both speakers in this passage use language variably, there is sufficient distinction between the overall tendencies to suggest that Janie's husband is (at least in her view), the less standard of the two. Part of her talking back to him consists in her paralleling his *fust wife* with *first chip*, his *gwine* with *goin'*. Her *If you can stand not to chop wood* stands out as markedly formal after Logan's *Ah kin haul de wood heah and chop it fuh you*. What might be considered sex-correlated use of prestige forms by Janie has the function in this context of establishing status and power. Logan, in turn, uses the more standard form *can* in *Even if you is as stingy as you can be wid me* in trying to reestablish his authority over her, but otherwise his language is distinctly non-standard. The shifts in speech are therefore primarily metaphorical, that is, they are attitudinal and create statuses dynamically; they are only secondarily situational, that is, a function of the events or of the social statuses already established (for this distinction see Gumperz and Hernández-Chavez 1975; Gumperz 1976).

Among variable features of BE not selected, most noticeable, perhaps, is the absence of consonant cluster deletion and of invariant *be*. One can only speculate about the reasons for this—possibly neither feature was characteristic of BE as spoken in Florida at the time Hurston was writing. This, however, is doubtful. Instead, we should probably attribute such selection to what the author conceived as the potential "multidialectal" grammar[12] of her White readers, a grammar which she may have felt did not include certain linguistic features characteristic of BE (in the case of invariant *be*, for example it has been shown that many White speakers understand it only as a form of *will be*, not of the iterative habitual (Fasold 1972)).[13]

Typically we may expect forms potentially available in readers' passive "multidialectal" grammars to be introduced without overt mention of their meaning or origin. However, "multidialectal competence" will vary not only from culture to culture but also from subculture to subculture—what is within the passive competence of British speakers is different from what is in the passive competence of American speakers. The differences between subcultures are particularly clear in the case of bilingual Chicanos. Chicano speakers (whichever their dominant language) are said to switch languages not only frequently but also quite unconsciously when speaking to other Chicanos, but to use English when non-Chicanos are present (cf. Gumperz and Hernández-Chavez 1975; Barker 1974; Lance 1975). A Chicano writing

---

[12]Differences in multidialectal competence (otherwise known as "panlectal" competence) are discussed in some detail in Labov 1972c.

[13]For more detail, see Traugott and Pratt 1980: Chap. 8.

for Chicanos would code-switch[14] in an entirely different way from a Chicano writing with an Anglo or a Spanish audience in mind. It appears then that the constraint is that the author aims at the multidialectal system of his or her potential audience and at the same time demands the expansion of that competence among readers who do not all share the same linguistic norms.

When a structure is expected not to be within the readers' competence, either extensive talk about language ("metalanguage") is used, or a third type of situation arises.

3. The author is more or less familiar with another variety but because the audience cannot be expected to be so familiar with it, it is transposed into a better-known variety. The convention of rendering foreign languages in English is age-old. However, recently several different kinds of attempts to include languages other than English within an English context have been made (for several examples see Page 1973:74-77). Even so, the foreign language is usually represented only sporadically. It is interesting to note that although code-switching would not necessarily occur in such situations in real life, many authors use (or attempt to use) the second language only in those situations characteristic of (or thought to be characteristic of) code-switching.

One example is from Ernest Hemingway's novel *For whom the bell tolls.* The action is set in Spain and the characters in the passage in question are all speaking Spanish, but most of it is rendered in English or in a modified form of English which we can call Spanish-in-English. We meet Robert Jordan, an American, the young woman Maria, with whom he has just made love, and the irrascible, jealous old woman, Pilar:

> The woman raised her head and looked up at him.
> 'Oh,' she said. 'You have terminated already?'
> 'Art thou ill?' he asked and bent down by her.
> '*Qué va,*' she said, 'I was asleep.'...
> 'Maria,' Pilar said, and her voice was as hard as her face and there was nothing friendly in her face. 'Tell me one thing of thy own volition.'
> The girl shook her head.
> Robert Jordan was thinking, if I did not have to work with this woman and her drunken man and her chicken-cut outfit, I would slap her so hard across the face that—

---

[14]"Code-switching" has been defined in many ways in the linguistic literature. Here the term is used to refer to switches from one language to another or one distinct regional or social dialect to another. It may occur sentence-internally but is not restricted to this position. It may be situational, that is, a function of who the participants are and such factors as topic or genre (academic topics may be discussed in English, intimate ones in Spanish, for example, in the Chicano community). It may also be "metaphorical", that is, it may indicate changes in attitude toward the subject or the hearer (a switch to English in the midst of an informal conversation in Spanish may indicate a switch to formality, dislike for the topic, and so forth) cf. especially Gumperz and Hernández-Chavez 1970; Gumperz 1976).

'Go ahead and tell me,' Pilar said to the girl.

'No,' Maria said, 'No.'

'Leave her alone,' Robert Jordan said and his voice did not sound like his own voice. I'll slap her anyway and the hell with it, he thought.

Pilar did not even speak to him. It was not like a snake charming a bird, nor a cat with a bird. There was nothing predatory. Nor was there anything perverted about it. There was a spreading, though, as a cobra's hood spreads. He could feel this. He could feel the menace of the spreading. But the spreading was a domination, not of evil, but of searching. I wish I did not see this, Robert Jordan thought. But it is not a business for slapping.

'Maria,' Pilar said 'I will not touch thee. Tell me now of thy own volition.'

'De tu propia voluntad,' the words were in Spanish.

The girl shook her head.

'Maria,' Pilar said. 'Now and of thy own volition. You hear me? Anything at all.'

'No,' the girl said softly. 'No and no'.[15]

The Spanish speech is marked largely by a syntax and lexicon that suggest straight translation from Spanish, and also by some phrases in Spanish. The latter have nothing whatever to do with relations between the characters and are solely features of narrator-reader relations. In general the dialog is linguistically distinct from the narrative. However, occasionally, the narrative too takes on the characteristics of translation, cf. especially *But it is not a business for slapping*. Narrative distance is abandoned for a while and Jordan's point of view is taken. Here as elsewhere the suggestion is made that, although an American, he thinks at least part of the time in Spanish.

The most interesting aspect of the linguistic varieties used in Hemingway's novel involves not relations between the characters but between narrator and reader. As has been mentioned, the sole function of the Spanish is to remind the reader that Spanish is the medium of expression. This may be the reason why there appears to be no particular metaphorical or situational motivation for the switching. It is presumably also because the Spanish is directed at the reader, not the characters, that a stylistic disjunction is permitted to occur between Spanish and Spanish-in-English. The Spanish is informal (*Qué va, Qué tal?*) or ritualistic (*De tu propia voluntad*), while the Spanish-in-English suggests formality, as is common of the representation of languages other than English (cf. especially *thou* and Latinate lexical items like *terminate*).

A characteristic of the "code-switches" in the novel is that most of the Spanish words and phrases are translated, at least the first few times they are used. *Qué va,¿Qué tal?* and similar expressions of frequent occurrence sometimes stand alone, but longer sentences are regularly translated, usually

---

[15]Ernest Hemingway, *For whom the bell tolls,* Harmondsworth, Mssex.: Penguin, 1966, pp. 168-9.

with the English second. The triad *Tell me one thing of thy own volition, De tu propia voluntad, Now and of thy own volition* are not exceptions, for the Spanish is not translated repetitiously; it is a more emphatic second attempt on Pilar's part to get an answer from Maria. Here and elsewhere in the novel where the same comment is made, we may question the function of *the words were in Spanish*. As readers we are obviously aware of the Spanish—the Gricean principle of quantity (Don't say more or less than is appropriate (Grice 1973)) has been violated. The sympathetic reader will seek to interpret the phrase some way, possibly seeing in it an indicator of Jordan's awareness of the cultural differences, or a demand that the reader listen carefully to how it sounds in Spanish and share Hemingway's reverence for the language. The purpose of the translation following rather than preceding the Spanish is presumably to require work of the reader and then to clear up any possible perceptual problems (other than the stylistic one of disjunction mentioned above).

When languages other than English are represented mainly in English, with sporadic shifts to the real language, little metalanguage is usually involved (one of the problems with Hemingway's use of Spanish is his overuse of metalanguage, particularly translation). However, when situations arise within the action of the story that involve language-switch, metalanguage is typical. It is obviously necessary when both languages are being represented in English. Page cites a particularly clever use of metalanguage totally incorporated in the conversation:

"She speaks French?"
"Not a word."
"She understands it?"
"No."
"One may then speak plainly in her presence?"
"Doubtless."[16]

but only after lengthy preparation through mixed use of English and "broken English" to set the linguistic frame of reference.

Where code-switching within a given linguistic context occurs, the metalanguage may be limited to mere mention of the languages involved, a simplicity of representation that assumes the reader understands the situational function of the shift, as exemplified in the following passage from Achebe's short story "The voter." Here, English establishes a stance of official agreement and bowing to the authority of others, while the use of Ibo represents establishment of close community ties. The situation is that Marcus is seeking election. Roof, his most trusted campaigner, is trying to

---

[16]Charlotte Brontë, *Villette,* cited in Page (1973:76).

persuade the village people to vote for Marcus; they promise to do this, but complain that Marcus had not really given them enough money when he distributed only two shillings to them apiece:

> 'We believe every word you say to be true,' said Ezenwa. 'We shall, every one of us, drop his paper for Marcus. Who would leave an ozo feast and go to a poor ritual meal? Tell Marcus he has our papers, and our wives' papers too. But what we do say is that two shillings is shameful.' He brought the lamp close and tilted it at the money before him as if to make sure he had not mistaken its value. 'Yes, two shillings is too shameful. If Marcus were a poor man—which our ancestors forbid—I should be the first to give him my paper free, as I did before. But today Marcus is a great man and does his things like a great man. We did not ask him for money yesterday; we shall not ask him tomorrow. But today is our day; we have climbed the iroko tree today and would be foolish not to take down all the firewood we need.'
>
> Roof had to agree. He had lately been taking down a lot of firewood himself. Only yesterday he had asked Marcus for one of his many rich robes—and had got it. . . .
>
> 'All right,' he said in English and then reverted to Ibo. 'Let us not quarrel about small things.' He stood up, adjusted his robes and plunged his hand once more into the bag. Then he bent down like a priest distributing the host and gave one shilling more to every man.[17]

Less work on the part of the reader, therefore less knowledge of the significance of code-switching, is required in the kind of representation in which the situational reasons for the switch are given, whether directly by the narrator or embedded within the dialog or a speech. Consider, for example, this passage, from Arturo Islas' *Dia de los muertos,* which illustrates a very different use of Spanish from Hemingway's, this time the Spanish of Mexicans and Chicanos, not of Spaniards.

> "Joo are yust alike." Angie told him. "stahborn like mulas and too proud for joor own good." She spoke English with a thick Mexican accent. She used it when she wanted to make important statements and did not realize that the way she spoke it had the opposite effect. After JoEl's first year in school, he learned to be ashamed of the way his mother abused the language. The others, including Felix, loved to tease and imitate her. Their English was perfect and their Spanish surfaced only when they addressed their older relatives or were in the company of their Mexican school friends at social events.
>
> "Come on, Mother, say it again," Magdalena pleaded.
>
> *"Me la vas a pagar, malcriada,"* Angie replied, waving a menacing hand close to her daughter's cheek.

---

[17]Chinua Achebe, "The voter," *Girls at war,* London: Heinemann, 1972, pp. 14-15.

"No, Ma, not in Spanish. Say it in English." Lena and her summer boyfriend were on the front porch, swinging back and forth, seated side by side, hardly touching. Every night at exactly nine-thirty, Angie went to the screen door behind them and said, "Magdaleen, kahm een." Lena shrieked with delight. The sad boyfriend smiled apprehensively.

"Oh, Mama, just a few more minutes." She said "mama" in the Spanish way.

"No, senorita. Joo as kahm een este meenewtoe." More howls, as the sad boyfriend said an embarrassed goodnight and slipped from the swing and the porch into the dark. Lena barely noticed, she was too taken up with her mother whom she adored.[18]

In this projected trilogy covering three generations of the "Chicano experience", the grandmother, Mama Chona, represents the immigrant generation, Mexican to the core, solely Spanish-speaking, and resentful of English. Her daughter-in-law, Angie, represents the generation who speak English at home, but recognize the necessity of speaking English, and have developed a special variety of Spanish-English. Her children identify themselves as Chicano; largely deprived of Spanish by the school-system, they are both ashamed of it and also find in it the language of affection and in some cases political identity. JoEl and Lena represent these two view-points. Language, then, has enormous social significance between generations, and the passage cited illustrates how this is worked out in the novel. Most Chicanos have two attitudes to code-switching--between generations, or between different groups, language choice signals group identification, or rejection of other groups; but between members of the same group switching from Spanish to English is largely unconscious, establishing camaraderie on some occasions, on others providing a means primarily for elaboration of narrative or personal attitude (Gumperz and Hernández-Chavez 1975, Lance 1975, Gumperz 1976). Islas explores primarily the first function of code-switching, partly because the subject-matter demands it, partly because the elaborative, emotional characteristics of the second function would probably escape an audience who was not Chicano.

In the first version of the trilogy Islas wrote the part devoted primarily to Mama Chona in Spanish, including the narrative. Consideration of the audience led to rewriting in English. In the passage cited, from the part devoted primarily to Mama Chona's son, Felix, the husband of Angie, the narrative and the dialog are mainly in English, but a conscious effort is made to incorporate Spanish into English without translation. Thus although the Spanish is limited to the same discourse types as in *For whom the bell tolls,* i.e. forms of address, expressions of affection, commands, names of cultural objects and events, the effect on the reader is entirely different. The code-

---

[18]Arturo Islas, *Dia de los muertos,* unpublished MS, Stanford University. Printed by permission of the author.

switching has an internal function in the novel, between the characters; it is not a function of narrator-reader relations. Therefore it is anchored in the context. Islas can go beyond the repetitious formulae to which Hemingway largely limits himself, elaborating a number of factors to ensure reader understanding. For one there is the metalanguage about why and how the Spanish is used. For another there is the context and often the choice of a word suggesting an English cognate, as in *Me la vas a pagar, malcriada* "You'll pay me for it, rude girl", which, if we do not understand every word, nevertheless is clearly a threat because of the menacing hand, and association with words like *malevolence, malediction,* and so forth.

Part of Islas' success in involving the reader lies in his decision to make use of the total linguistic resources of bilingualism. Thus while Hemingway limits himself to syntax and lexicon only, Islas explores ways of reflecting Spanish pronunciations of English, cf. especially lines 1 and 2. *Joo are yust alike* is not eye-dialect, but a representation of the tendency among Chicano speakers to reverse certain consonants, in this case [j] and [y]. There are some problems, however, with this experiment in representing the phonetics, since *joo* suggests a vowel different from that in *you* while *yust* suggests a vowel the same as in *just* but what is being represented is [ju] and [yUst]. No norms exist yet for representing and interpreting this particular variety of Spanish-English, and obviously much experimentation is necessary. Not only is there concern for the pronunciation. Another feature of bilingualism often noted, particularly among Chicano speakers, is the tendency to mix Spanish and English within the same sentence. This is to Islas one of the main characteristics of the language he is representing, and he includes it in most of Angie's Spanish-English, cf. *Stahborn like mulas* and *Joo mas kahm een este meenewtoe.* In the process of revealing this Spanish-English as a language interesting to listen to in its own right and of essential cultural importance, the English narrative sometimes becomes somewhat labored and formal, but even then there is little of the violation of quantity that we found in Hemingway.

The greater the number of languages being represented, the more stylized the distinctions between them are likely to become. For writers like Achebe there is the English frame in the context of which Ibo is to be represented through the medium of English, and also West African Pidgin. English is a foreign language to Achebe and to his African readers; Pidgin is too, but is widely known to them. For most English readers, however, both Ibo and the Pidgin may be equally foreign (though the latter will be somewhat more comprehensible). For both groups of readers, English and Pidgin are in the same high-low diglossic relation. While the Pidgin is represented somewhat formally in that it is standardized to some extent, (e.g., *he* is used for *i*), the Ibo is represented in *Arrow of God* and many other novels by a style that is formal in its archaism (e.g., *Was it for nothing that*...) or its use of prepositional phrases (e.g., *What would be the wisdom of deceiving the messengers of the white man? (Arrow of God* p. 190)) and other devices that parallel the structure of Ibo. While Achebe selects from styles available within English tradition, others may go so far as to invent an English close to, but not equivalent of, a literal translation. Ramchand (1973) for example, cites the following verb-final sentences in Gabriel Okara's novel, *The voice:*

> It was the day's ending and Okolo by a window stood. Okola stood looking at the sun behind the treetops falling... Okolo at the palm trees looked. [19]

and cites Okara's own words on the need to represent African ideas, philosophy and imagery to the fullest extent through translation.[20] Such deviations from the potentials of English tend to distance rather than engage the reader unless they are very carefully controlled, and therefore tend not to be very successful.

4. Finally, among situations which limit an author's choice of varieties is the situation when the language or languages being represented are of another age. As in the case of a foreign language, there may be no linguistic markers at all, but archaisms are often attempted. This issue will not concern us here.

Discussion so far has centered on the representation of speech, including not only the language of dialog and public speaking but also metalanguage about it. What about the language of the narrative frame?

Most authors have until recently selected Standard English (SE) as their frame of reference for narrative, especially where third person narrative is concerned. Varieties in first person narrative have typically been age correlated rather than socially, ethnically, or regionally correlated (cf. *The Catcher in the rye* and *Huckleberry Finn*). However, there have recently been several experiments in breaking this tradition. There seem to be a number of reasons for the selection of SE. For one, SE can distance the narrator from what is being narrated, especially from the dialog of the characters, and can be a device for establishing relative objectivity. While first and third person narratives are by no means opposites in terms of subjectivity and objectivity, involvement and non-involvement, but only tend toward these poles, they are often thought of as prime factors in the discussion of "point of view." Where literature including non-standard language is concerned, choice of language for the narrative frame can be considered another very important factor intersecting with first and third person narrative modes, but not identical with it. Use of SE tends toward greater

---

[19]Gabriel Okara, *The voice,* London: Heinemann, 1964, p. 13; cited in Ramchand (1973: 119).

[20]Gabriel Okara, "African speech... English words", *Transition*[10] (1963), cited in Ramchand (1973:118). While Ramchand discusses African "translations" into English, Ricard (1976) discusses "translations" into French.

objectivity and distance, use of other varieties to greater subjectivity and involvement.

Among recent fiction rejecting SE as the narrative frame are two novels by Al Young, *Snakes* (1970) and *Sitting Pretty* (1977). A comparison of the two works is instructive since it shows the evolution within one writer of first person narrative techniques. *Snakes* uses varieties of BE to create character within the dialog. The narrative, however, is markedly different from the dialog:

> Most of my life Ive been confused. Very little that I hear or see going on around me makes any sense. I dont always understand what people are doing. I take them on faith and play things by ear which means that Ive been let down a lot. But one of the few things that's never let me down is music–not musicians, not promoters, certainly not club owners, recording companies, critics or reviewers–Music![21]

This is actually not BE at all, but SE disguised as nonstandard English orthography, specifically by the device of omitting some apostrophes. Contractions like *I've, they've, don't, aren't* are apostrophe-less (*Ive, theyve, dont, arent*), but *it's, that's, I'd* are not, nor are the possessives. In this instance, with its function of calling attention to the conventions of SE narrative, the orthographic device is stereotypic; as in the case of most stereotyping, it is limited to a very small number of forms (those involving contraction of the negative or of the verb *have*).

Contrast with this the following opening of *Sitting Pretty*, where the same kind of orthographic device is combined with phonological-morphological features such as *-in* for *ing*, morphological markers such as absence of the third person singular *-s* (both not particularly BE features), and syntactic remarkers such as multiple negation:

> Maybe it was on accounta it was a full moon. I dont know. It's a whole lotta things I use to be dead certain about—like, day follow night and night follow day—things I wouldnt even bet on no more. It's been that way since me and Squirrel broke up and that's been yeahbout fifteen-some-odd years ago, *odd years*—July the Fourth.
> If I was to wake up tomorrow and read in the headlines where it say it aint gon be no more full moons cause the atmosphere done got too polluted or somethin like that, it wouldnt hardly faze me none.

An even greater break with tradition is represented by the third person narrative in June Jordan's *His own where:*

---

[21]Al Young, *Snakes,* New York: Holt, Rinehart and Winston, Inc., 1970, pp. 1-2.
[22]Al Young, *Sitting Pretty,* New York: Signet Books, 1977, p. 3.

First time they come, he simply say, "Come on." He tell her they are going not too far away. She go along not worrying about the heelstrap pinching at her skin; but worrying about the conversation. Long walks take some talking. Otherwise it be embarrassing just side by side embarrassing.

Buddy stay quiet, walking pretty fast, but every step right next to her. They trip together like a natural sliding down the street....

Cars make Buddy mad. Right now his father lying in the hospital from what they call A Accident. And was no accident about it, Buddy realize. The street set up that way so cars can clip the people easy kill then even. Easy.

"What you say?," she ask him.

"Damn," he answer her. "Another one. Another corner. Street-crossing-time again."

"You crazy, Buddy? What you mean?"

"I hate them. Corners. They really be a dumb way try to split the people from the cars. Don't even work. Look how a car come up and almost kill my father, minding his own business, on the corner. Corners good for nothing." Buddy frown so bad that Angela start laughing. Buddy swing around her waist.[23]

In this case the orthography is standard. No attempt is made to represent BE phonology or lexicon. The only markers of BE are the invariant forms of the verb (except for *is* which is in contrast to BE "invariant *be*", the marker of iterative habitual aspect), and occasional use of zero copula, and of multiple negation (not illustrated in the passage). Other features of the language Jordan uses in this story are not ethnic but rather features of style, of inner modes of thought. It is interesting to note that in this novel the dialog is at the beginning not markedly different from the narrative, as far as the use of BE markers is concerned. It is as though the particular markers of BE selected by Jordan are the standard for this novel, as though, in other words, the homogeneity of fiction in SE were being approached, but in another variety. However, the homogeneity is not fully realized since all the markers mentioned are used variably as the novel progresses. The language of the narrative is established in the first paragraphs as a frame of reference, with conscious intent to be different from traditional norms, and conscious attempt to focus on the ethnic identities involved, and then these markers are used more naturally, that is variably, as characterization becomes increasingly important. It is especially interesting to contrast this passage of Jordan's with Hurston's, since in some ways the language is complementary. Hurston's is highly variable, and the variability is reflected on all levels of the grammar; Jordan's is minimally variable and is reflected primarily in the syntax. Furthermore, it is precisely those syntactic structures which Hurston does not use that Jordan selects—absence of a tense marker and presence of invariant *be*. The difference results in very different types of reader

---

[23]June Jordan, *His own where,* New York: Dell Publishing Co., Inc., 1975, p. 8.

participation. Hurston develops character using the greatest possible range of forms available to the non-speaker of BE, focusing on relationships between people rather than on ethnic identity for its own sake. Jordan, however, establishes her narrative, by contrast, as ethnically identifiable first, and as character-study second.

CONCLUSION

As the differences between the writings of Achebe, Hurston, Jordan, Young, and Islas show, writing involving social and cultural linguistic varieties is still highly experimental. There are no norms for BE writing, other than reaction to the norm of writing in SE. The implications for education appear to be that as yet there is no way to appreciate BE writing, or to experiment with new modes of expression except through SE. Until writers can develop their own traditions, there seems little but misunderstanding to be gained from direct modelling in literacy programs on Black writing without reference to the SE norms it is reacting against. When a tradition for writing in BE does arise, we can expect one of its characteristics to be the highlighting of the linguistic variability that is so important in the verbal repertoire of its speakers. In other words, we can expect it to be very different indeed from much writing in SE. The same can be predicted for Chicano literature, and for the literature of other cultural groups in which strong social significance is associated with code-switching (in the broadest sense of this term, including style-shifting). Therefore, until such new traditions are developed, experience in reading and evaluation of works involving different types of variation seems essential to foster awareness of the problems involved in its use. Such reading should not be limited to the works of minorities, but should extend to the whole range of writing in English.

ACKNOWLEDGMENTS

This paper has profited much from discussions with Houston Baker, Jenny Cook Gumperz, John Gumperz, Shirley Brice Heath, Arturo Islas, Juana Mora, Mary Pratt, Alexander Sapiens, and Al Young. All errors of interpretation and of fact remain, of course, my own.

REFERENCES

Literary Texts

Achebe, C. *Things fall apart*. London: Heinemann, 1958.
Achebe, C. *Arrow of God*. London: Heinemann, 1964.

Achebe, C. *Girls at war and other stories*. London: Heinemann, 1972.

Capote, T. *In cold blood*. New York: Signet Books, 1965.

Faulkner, W. *The sound and the fury*. New York: Vintage Books, 1954. (Originally published 1929.)

Gaddis, W. *J. R.* N. Y. Knopf, 1975.

Haley, A. *Roots*. Garden City, N.Y.: Doubleday, 1976.

Harris, G. W. *Sut Lovingwood's yarns*. Ed. by M. Thomas Inge. New Haven: College and University Press, 1966.

Hemingway, E. *For whom the bell tolls*. Harmondsworth, Mssex.: Penguin. 1966.

Hurston, Z. N. *Their eyes were watching God*. New York: Fawcett World Library, 1969 (reprint of 1937 edition).

Islas, A. MS. *Dia de los meurtos*. Novel in progress.

James, H. The beast in the jungle. In *Selected tales of Henry James*. London: John Baker, 1969, 219–267.

Jordan, J. *His own where*. New York: Dell Publishing Co., Inc., 1975.

Kesey, K. *Sometimes a great notion*. New York: Bantam Books, 1965.

Mendez, M. *Peregrinos de Atzlan*. Berkeley, Ca.: Editorial Justa, 1974.

Salinger, J. D. *The Catcher in the rye*. Boston: Little, Brown, 1951.

Twain, M. *The adventures of Huckleberry Finn*. Ed. by Henry Nash Smith. Boston: Houghton, M ifflin, 1958. (Originally published 1885.)

Young, A. *Snakes*. New York: Holt, Rinehart and Winston, 1970.

Young, A. *Sitting Pretty*. New York: Signet Books, 1977.

Linguistic and Critical Works

Barker, G. C. Social functions of language in a Mexican-American community. *Acta Americana*, 1974, *5*, 185–202. (Repr. in Hernández-Chavez, Cohen and Beltramo, 1975).

Booth, W. C. *The rhetoric of fiction*. Chicago: University of Chicago Press, 1961.

Bowdre, P. H. Eye-dialect as a literary device. In J. V. Williamson & V. M. Burke (Eds.), *A various language: Perspectives on American dialects*. New York: Holt, Rinehart and Winston, 1971.

Bridgman, R. *The colloquial style in America*. New York: Oxford University Press, 1966.

Ervin-Tripp, S. An analysis of the interaction of language, logic, and listener. *American Anthropologist*, 1964, *66*(6), 86–102.

Fallis, G. V. Code-switching in bilingual Chicano poetry. *Hispania*, 1976, *59*, 877–886.

Fasold, R. W. *Tense marking in Black English*. Arlington, Va.: Center for Applied Linguistics, 1972.

Fasold, R. W., & Wolfram, W. Some linguistic features of negro dialect. In R. W. Fasold & R. W. Shuy (Eds.), *Teaching standard English in the inner city*. Washington, D.C.: Center for Applied Linguistics, 1970.

Ferguson, C. A. Diglossia. *Word*, 1959, *15*, 325–340.

Fishman, J. A. *Sociolinguistics: A brief introduction*. Rowley, Mass.: Newbury House Publishers, 1972.

Garvin, P. L., & Mathiot, M. The urbanization of the Guarani language—a problem in language and culture. In A. F. C. Wallace, (Ed.), *Men and cultures*. Philadelphia: University of Pennsylvania Press, 1960.

Grice, P. Logic and conversation. In P. Cole & J. Morgan (Eds.), *Syntax and semantics III. Speech acts*. New York: Academic Press, 1973.

Gumperz, J. Sociolinguistics and communication in small groups. In J. Pride & J. Holmes, (Eds.), *Sociolinguistics*. Harmondsworth, Mssex.: Penguin, 1972.

Gumperz, J. J. The sociolinguistic significance of conversational code-switching. Language Behavior Laboratory, University of California, Berkeley, Working Paper 46, 1976.

Gumperz, J. J. & Hernández-Chavez, E. Cognitive aspects of bilingual communication. In W. H. Whitely, (Ed.), *Language use and social change*. London: Oxford University Press, 1970. (Repr. in Hernández-Chavez, Cohen, and Beltramo, 1975.)

Halliday, M. A. K., McIntosh, A., & Strevens, P. D. The uses and users of language. Chap. IV of *The linguistic sciences and language teaching*. London: Longman, 1964.

Heath, S. B. Early American attitudes toward variation in speech: A view from social history and sociolinguistics. In C. F. Justus, (Ed.), *Language variation in America: Approaches to the study of American English*. 1978.

Hymes, D. *Foundations of sociolinguistics: An ethnographic approach*. Philadelphia: University of Pennsylvania Press, 1974.

Iser, W. The reality of fiction: A functionalist approach to literature. *New Literary History*, 1975, *7*, 7–38.

Ives, S. A theory of literary dialect. In J. V. Williamson & V. M. Burke, (Eds.), *A various language: Perspectives on American dialects*. New York: Holt, Rinehart and Winston, 1971. (Slightly revised version of an article by the same name in *Tulane Studies in English*, 1950, *2*, 137–182.)

Jakobson, R. Linguistics and poetics. In Thomas Sebeok (Ed.), *Style in language*. Cambridge, Mass.: MIT Press, 1960.

Krapp, G. P. *The English language in America*. 1925.

Labov, W. *The study of nonstandard English*. National Council of Teachers of English and Center for Applied Linguistics, 1969.

Labov, W. *Sociolinguistic patterns*. Philadelphia: University of Pennsylvania Press, 1972. (a)

Labov, W. *Language in the inner city*. Philadelphia: University of Pennsylvania Press, 1972. (b)

Labov, W. Where do grammars stop? In R. Shuy (Ed.), *Monograph series on languages and linguistics*. Washington: Georgetown University Press, 1972 (c)

Lance, D. M. Spanish-English code switching. In Hernández-Chavez, Cohen, Beltramo, 1975.

Leal, L. & Barrón P. *Chicano literature*. MS, MLS Commission on minority groups and the study of language and literature, 1977.

Leonard, S. A. *The doctrine of correctness in English usage, 1700–1800*. New York: Russell and Russell, 1962. (Reprint of 1929 edition.)

Lyman, R. V. *English grammar in American schools before 1800*. Chicago: University of Chicago Press, 1922.

Macaulay, R. Double standards. *American Anthropologist*, 1973, *75*, 1324–1337.

Mackey, F. W. Langage, dialecte et diglossie littéraire. In H. Giordan & A. Ricard (Eds.), *Diglossie et littérature*. Bordeaux-Talence: Maison des Sciences de l'homme, 1976.

Mukařovský, J. Standard language and poetic language (Paul Garvin, trans.). In Paul Garvin, (Ed.), *A Prague school reader on esthetics, literary structure and style*. Washington: Georgetown University Press, 1964.

Ohmann, R. Speech acts and the definition of literature. *Philosophy and Rhetoric*, 1971, *4*, 1–19.

Ohmann, R. Speech, literature, and the space between. *New Literary History*, 1973, *6*, 47–63.

Page, N. *Speech in the English novel*. London: Longman, 1973.

Pratt, M. *Toward a speech act theory of literary discourse*. Bloomington: Indiana University Press, 1977.

Ramchand, K. The language of the master? In R. W. Bailey and J. L. Robinson (Eds.), *Varieties of present-day English*. New York: Macmillan, 1973.

Ricard, A. Ecriture du verbal et multilinguisme. In H. Giordan and A. Ricard (Eds.), *Diglossie et littérature*. Bordeaux-Talence: Maison des sciences de l'homme.

Sapiens, A. Code-switching in Peregrinos de Aztlán. MS, Stanford University, 1977.

Scotton, C. M., & Ury, W. Bilingual strategies: The social functions of code-switching. Paper presented at the winter LSA meeting, revised version to appear in *International Journal of Sociology of Language* 1975, *12*.

Searle, J. R. The logical status of fictional discourse. *New Literary History,* 1975, *7,* 319–332.

Shuy, R. W. *Code switching in Lady Chatterly's lover.* Working papers in sociolinguistics 22. Southwest Educational Development Laboratory, Austin, Texas, 1975.

Traugott, E. C., and Pratt, M. L. *Linguistics for students of literature.* New York: Harcourt Brace Jovanovich, Inc., 1980.

Trudgill, P. *The social differentiation of English in Norwich.* London: Cambridge University Press, 1974.

Trudgill, P. *Sociolinguistics: An introduction.* Harmondsworth, Mssex.: Penguin, 1974b.

LANGUAGE DIFFERENCES AND WRITING

8

Teaching Teachers about Teaching Writing to Students from Varied Linguistic Social and Cultural Groups

Carol E. Reed
National Institute of Education

Almost all teachers of English composition know, or at least have a strong belief that they know what the major learning responsibility of the linguistically and culturally different student should be, if that student expects to succeed in the basic writing course of a college. This general conviction among college English teachers about what should be the student's responsibility for learning standard English is articulated in the heated arguments about "upholding college-level standards" for the writing of compositions—arguments especially prevalent among teachers having what I would call a more traditional or "conservative," perspective on such a student's problems with the standard written English.

Still other teachers that I would characterize as having a more liberal, or some might say "permissive," attitude toward students whose native dialect is nonstandard English project this same general conviction about what should be the student's learning responsibility. This second group of teachers will often reject their more traditionally-oriented colleagues' concern for "upholding standards" and will instead stress the need to convince such students of the absolute necessity of their adopting certain patterns of language usage as *tools* for "gaining entrance into the mainstream of society," thus enabling them to claim their ultimate rights to economic and social upward mobility.

This is the plum held out to most economically disadvantaged students, and which tends to be the guiding motivation for those bold enough to seek a college degree in the first place. And, of course, if the teachers were not already aware, they eventually become aware, when confronted with nonstandard dialect usage among students in their classrooms, that the persistent use of a nonstandard dialect at even this "high" an educational level (i.e., college) usually goes hand-in-hand with such other social correlates as race or ethnic group, as well as economic deprivation. This is perhaps the main reason that such nonstandard dialects as Black English Vernacular, Appalachian English, Puerto Rican English, West Indian Creole English (or "patois") are designated "social" dialects (as opposed to regional dialects) of English by the linguists and ethnographers who study them.

This label, "social dialect," signifies that rather than the expected regional or geographical boundaries of systematic variation within a language community (such as those we notice when we go from New England to the Mississippi delta, or from Brooklyn to Minnesota, as we listen to the speech of whites), "social" dialects reveal consistent and predictable patterns of variation irrelevant to regional boundaries. Their occurrence is more often delimited by socio-economic factors, such as cultural group, ethnic identity and social class. Thus we perceive the phenomenon that not all blacks speak Black English Vernacular. However, the masses of low-income blacks will more likely than not use the vernacular almost like a "standard," whether they live in New York or Chicago, Detroit or Los Angeles, Atlanta, Houston or Washington, D.C.

And so, as we debate the issue of the nonstandard dialect-speaking student's responsibility to learn standard English, those of us espousing the arguments for "upholding standards" tend to view that responsiblity from the perspective of how such students will "endanger" the college or university. On the other hand, those of us espousing arguments for helping students enter the mainstream of society, tend to view that responsibility from the perspective of how such students will "endanger" themselves, if they fail to heed or accept their responsibility. Of course, all of this incessant wrangling about "upholding standards" or "guaranteeing economic and social upward mobility," which goes on continuously in our respective English department meetings, centers most often around the nonstandard speaker's seemingly intractable resistance to learning how to write". . . a well-organized 500-word essay in *clear and consistent standard English* (Bruffee 1972).

The teaching of this skill, the ability to write "clear and consistent standard English" essays (putting aside for the moment the fact that we don't always agree on what constitutes clear and consistent standard English), is often perceived as the most important goal of the basic writing course within the English curriculum (whether that course is "remedial" or "credit-bearing"). As such, this most important goal becomes the *teaching* responsibility of whichever of us are "unlucky" enough or "lucky" enough (again, depending upon your point of view) to be assigned to teach that basic writing course.

Whether or not teaching the use of "clear and consistent written standard English" is, in fact, a worthy goal for a basic writing course, has been itself an issue of debate. The debate on this issue has been raging in the various journals of our profession, with notable scholars taking positions both pro and con. Perhaps the most famous argument against the teaching of standard English to nonstandard dialect speakers (and the one which has certainly spawned the most controversy) is attributable to James Sledd of the University of Texas at Austin. In an article he wrote for the N.C.T.E. *English Journal* (Sledd 1969) some years ago, he asserts his conviction that the very insistence that students who speak Vernacular Black English should learn to control the dialect of the educated elite (standard English?) represents a kind of subtle and insidious racism on the part of English teachers and the entire educational establishment.

Sledd and others of his persuasion)notably Wayne O'Neill of Harvard/M.I.T., Tom Kochman of Southern Illinois, and more recently the N.C.T.E. Conference on College Composition and Communication, which adopted a "students' right to their own language" resolution, argue that the energies of our educational system might best be spent spreading appreciation in the total society for the very real cultural pluralism and linguistic variation we live with. Such aspirations are very noble, idealistic and hard to disagree with, especially if you are Black (like myself) or otherwise victimized by discrimination according to race or ethnic group, color, sex and/or culturally-different behavior (including the wearing of "too long" hair, as well as culturally-different linguistic behavior) so often made use of in this society to obstruct or retard the development of those who can be identified as not belonging to the dominant social group.

However noble, idealistic or appealing Sledd's arguments may appear, they still do not help me answer that one nagging question I must ask myself, and which my students also ask me: "OK, we can dig where this guy Sledd is coming from, but how are we all supposed to negotiate our way through the society during the next 100 years or so it may take him and his friends to convince the American public and especially the American employer to appreciate the legitimacy of our dialect of English, and hire us, rather than discriminate against us, if we fail to demonstrate control of the standard dialect in our resumes or job applications?" To ignore these students' need for standard English, a need which they fully recognize, is to ignore the role of language as social arbiter in our society. For, if you ask students affected by this language attitude situation, which Sledd so articulately describes, you will probably find that equally uppermost in students' minds when they enroll in a college or university baccalaureate program is *not* necessarily the acquisition of a Liberal Arts education, but the acquisition of a B.A. or B.S. *diploma,* which they can then use as "legal tender" in the ever-important job market.

We've therefore come full circle and are back where we started: the *teaching* responsibility of helping students succeed with their *learning* responsibility, which is to gain reasonable control of standard written English, which can then be used as a means to a socio-economic end. If, amidst all the confusion surrounding this central issue, you are willing to accept the teaching of standard English as a necessary and viable goal for a college's basic writing course, then consider that students who use nonstandard dialects are not the only ones in the teacher-student relationship with a *learning* responsbility. If we, the teachers, are to succeed in our goal of teaching standard English to such students, I maintain that *we also* have much to learn, not only about this particularly frustrating classroom situation confronting us, but especially about the very *grammaticality* of the nonstandard dialects involved.

Contrary to any still prevalent notions among academicians and educators that nonstandard dialects are simply sloppy, slovenly or careless usage, "broken English" or "bad grammar," scholars from various academic disciplines have been studying these dialects and have revealed them to be highly systematic and socially viable, with their own perfectly valid, linguistically describable rules of phonology, morphology and syntax. Indeed, the very systematicity of such nonstandard dialects as American Black English Vernacular and its Caribbean Creole cousins suggests one reason for their persistence among the students we are confronting in our inner-city classrooms.

The research on Black English Vernacular and its varieties demand consideration from the education community in general, and from the English teacher in particular, if teachers are to be prepared to deal effectively with the educational problems of our inner-city school population. And with the advent of special admissions programs, such as the Open Admissions programs of the City University of New York and open enrollment programs at other similar institutions, learning about these problems and their linguistic and cultural implications are more and more becoming the responsibility of college English teachers.

Clearly the most significant problem facing the college English teacher today is what to do about the results of what has been a consistent failure on the part of our inner-city grade schools and secondary schools to impart standard English literacy skills to those Black students in the basic composition course whose primary mode of oral communication is Black English Vernacular. If the college English teacher is to avoid repeating the lower schools' failures, he or she cannot afford to persist in the general lack of awareness about the students' dialect, itself a full-blown, rule-governed linguistic system, which is different enough from standard English to comprise a significant interference factor blocking the students' ability to acquire standard English writing skills (i.e., the ability to approximate with reasonable consistency standard English surface features in their writing, avoiding socially stigmatized nonstandard patterns of usage such as hyper-*s* and hyper-*ed,* invariant *be* and *do* and zero copula).

Because of this interference factor, William Stewart (1964, 1967) has argued that the language learning problems of some nonstandard dialect speakers (such as speakers of Black English and Appalachian English) be dealt with as a "quasi-foreign language situation." Speakers of these dialects do not come to the classroom with the basic grammatical patterns of standard English already within their *productive* competence (as is the case for most middle socio-economic class students who use standard English as their native dialect). The nonstandard dialect speaker does, however, come to the classroom with a native speaker's knowledge of the grammatical features of his own dialect. However, if both the student and his or her teacher remain uninformed about the systematic nature of the influence these nonstandard grammatical features can exert upon the student's ability to retain the rules of standard English and produce standard English surface features consistently in writing, then the student will more likely be hindered than helped in acquiring "control" of the standard dialect, and the ability to avoid stigmatized nonstandard usage.

The dialect situation confronting the teacher of language skills is sufficiently problematic to impose upon the teacher the responsibility of becoming linguistically sophisticated enough to handle what can be called problems of "cross-dialectal interference"—those dialect-linked patterns of writing behavior we are accustomed to indiscriminately labelling "errors" or "mistakes." The perspective of English teachers has traditionally suffered from the tunnel-vision of looking at all English language phenomena evidenced in students' papers solely from the point of view of the grammar of standard English, which is linguistically just another dialect, albeit the politically prestigious one in our society. These "mistakes" or interference patterns fall somewhere in the "gray area" between nonstandard and standard dialect. Such interference patterns, which are generally manifestations of *dialect mix*, can often be seen to conform neither to the rules of the nonstandard dialect, nor to the rules of the standard grammar. Linguistic analysis of the data available from students' papers reveals these interference patterns to be somewhat systematic, since they can also be seen to occur most frequently at the points of contrast between the dialects.

College education programs attempting to prepare future teachers for the classroom must also become cognizant of the need for teachers to "... become their own ethnographers" in the classroom, as Dell Hymes so aptly suggested (Cazden, John and Hymes 1972). Such teacher-training programs must be prepared to include in their basic curricula courses which can provide the teacher (both prospective and in-service) with the kind of in-depth sociolinguistic training necessary to affect a realistic understanding of this specific language-learning problem.

What, then, is the reciprocal learning responsibility of teachers of standard English? What do they need to know about students whose native dialects are not standard English? First of all, teachers should be taking graduate school preparation, to inform themselves about the nature of language,, the processes of language change and the various sociolinguistic factors affecting the use of language which result in dialect variation.

Through such deliberate self-education, teachers would not be so vulnerable to the kinds of misconceived folk beliefs about language and the users of different language varieties which persist among educators and academicians, in spite of recent linguistic research, and which result in the scientifically tenuous assumptions underlying such labels as "non-verbal," "culturally-deprived" and "culturally-disadvantaged." These assumptions characterize the linguistically and culturally different student's seeming inability to assimilate standard English grammatical rules as evidence of a whole range of developmental deficiencies, including low intelligence, deficiency in linguistic development, or deficiency in concept-formation, and an entire spectrum of learning disabilities, including the most extreme: speech impediment or pathological speech (the "thick lips and lazy tongues" theory), brain damage and mental retardation.

College teachers especially (since their more sophisticated graduate preparation ostensibly attests to their ability to do so) should plow through the research of such scholars as Beryl Loftman Bailey, Roger D. Abrahams, Courtney Cazden, Joe L. Dillard, Ralph Fasold, Grace Holt, Benjamin Cooke, Gary Simpkins, Dell Hymes, Claudia Mitchell-Kernan, William Labov, Roger Shuy, William Stewart, Stan Legum, Walt Wolfram, and others. Publications of the results of such sociolinguistic research are now becoming available through the National Council of Teachers of English, the Center for Applied Linguistics, SWRL Educational Research and Development, the University of Pennsylvania Press, Columbia Teachers College Press, Southern Illinois University Press and other publishing concerns. We would encourage teachers to wade through and digest this research, in order to teach themselves about the rules of pronunciation, grammar and discourse of the various nonstandard dialects represented among the linguistically and culturally different students in their classrooms. Such study would demonstrate a number of important facts:

1) First, that the usage of our linguistically-different students actually does follow systematic grammatical rules which can be *learned,* and that many of the surface structure "errors" such students are making in their papers can be characterized not so much as the result of incorrectly learned standard English, but as the result of *correctly* learned nonstandard dialects.

This approach was taken with a group of grade-school teachers enrolled in an experimental course in Black English Vernacular, taught by myself and William Stewart at Columbia Teachers College during the spring of 1970 (Reed 1973). While we were working on Black English pronunciation rules in one of the language-lab drill sessions (we were using an adapted second-language teaching method), the class was quite amazed to discover that when they systematically applied the Black English rules they were learning to the pronunciation of standard English utterances, they themselves sounded very similar to the Black children they were teaching in their respective classrooms throughout New York City. Similarly, when they were engaged in doing translations from their own native standard English into equivalent Black English expressions, they quite typically made standard English-conditioned "errors" in subject-verb agreement, verb tense, and the like.

2) The second fact demonstrated by this kind of teacher-learning experience is that it is indeed possible to teach someone a second dialect, when second-language teaching methodology and attitudes are adapted to the classroom situation, without necessarily impairing or reinforcing the use of the dialect the student already knows and needs to retain for continued effective communication within his or her own speech community.

By learning about the dialect of the students he or she must teach, the English teacher also gains insight into the specific rules of that dialect which are most likely to create cross-dialectal interference problems for the students, when they attempt to approximate the standard dialect in their writing. In addition, the informed teacher will most assuredly gain a better perspective on the learning process he or she is imposing upon the students in those basic writing courses. Consequently, the teacher will be more sensitive to the difficulties inherent in learning a second communication system, especially when that other system is superficially close to one's own system. It appears to be a much more difficult task to separate two dialects of the same language (where the systematic divergence between the two is often of a more subtle nature), than it is to separate two completely divergent languages. In other words, it is easier for the learner to distinguish between Spanish and English than between Vernacular Black English and Standard English. The distance between two completely different languages helps the learner to know when he is using which, thus facilitating his ability to switch from one to the other.

How do students feel about teachers who are well-informed enough to share insights with them about their use of nonstandard dialects and the effects such usage can have on their performance in an English course? I recently gave a talk on such issues to a freshman composition class at Brooklyn College, at the invitation of the teacher of the class. After I had left, the teacher assigned a paper in which he required his students to write about their reactions to the talk. Two excerpts from those papers follow:

Talks can be boring or interesting. There can be talks on subjects you are studying and talks on things you might get involved in. All talks have very special aims, but a talk on Black english is fascinating.

> A talk on Black english is fascinating especially when you have never known such a subject existed. The lack of knowledge about Black english effects everyone. When people do not know about something special they tend to miss out on it and Black english is special because it shows the cominations of cultures.
>
> Standard English is necessary in every English speaking society, but minority groups often develop their own dialect. This dialect has been developed mainly because of the different cultural background from which they come. The Dominant American Society with its unique "Standard English" should not try to brainwash users of dialect. Rather, they should try to understand it. Society should realize that the user of dialect can be equally comfortable using Standard English and his dialect. When a person uses his dialect he should not be made to feel inferior.

The teacher of the class reported to me that the class session in which we discussed Black English and its ramifications represented the first time in the semester he had ever had students crowding around the teacher's desk *after* the bell had rung, asking lots of questions. He said it was the most positive response he had ever received from that class, which was a remedial section of the freshman composition course.

The insights reflected in those students' responses reminded me of an almost forgotten passage from Thoreau's *Walden,* in which he captures so beautifully the ethnocentrism that English-speaking societies are so often guilty of. Leading up to this passage, Thoreau chastises mankind for not recognizing that "The universe is wider than our views of it" (Thoreau 1854). He then goes on to write:

It is a ridiculous demand which England and America make, that you shall speak so that they can understand you. Neither men nor toadstools grow so. As if that were important, and there were not enough to understand you without them. As if Nature could support but one order of understandings, could not sustain birds as well as quadrupeds, flying as well as creeping things, and *hush,* and *whoa,* which Bright can understand, were the best English.

Like Thoreau, we are living in pioneer times, at least as far as linguistic knowledge is concerned. But how "extra-vagant" of us, if we refuse to "...wander far enough beyond the narrow limits of (our) daily experience" (Thoreau 1854) and grab for the information which is finally there for the grabbing, especially in light of that information's potential effect on student-teacher relationships.

From a book by Cindy Herbert (1974) entitled, *I See a Child* comes the following gem:

The relationship that develops between the teacher and student forms a foundation for what is taught and learned in the classroom. What I see in a child will strongly affect the kind of relationship that forms. A positive relationship takes conscious work to see the other person as he truly is. At first, most of the work must come from me, the teacher.

SOME SPECIFIC INFLUENCES OF NONSTANDARD DIALECT USAGE IN STUDENTS' WRITING

There are several known, systematic ways in which the use of a nonstandard dialect can interfere with a student's competence in writing standard English. Some of these are well documented. Still others are not always recognized as dialect interference by teachers of basic writing. Dialect can intrude directly into a student's writing, in the form of vocabulary, verb forms, inflectional and syntactic patterns, and colorful idiomatic expressions which are characteristic of specific speech communities and entirely predictable by the rules of nonstandard English. Such instances of direct dialect interference are well-documented and include such much-discussed nonstandard features as zero copula and invariant *be* in American Black English Vernacular and object pronominal forms with subject function in Caribbean Creoles (Reed 1972). Some examples of these are recognizable in the following sentences taken from students' writing:

(a) Some of the most intelligent men and women in the world *be* incompetent when placed in a job they know nothing about.

(b) *Him* a come for buy fish.

Nonstandard dialect can also interfere with students' ability to monitor the "correctness" of the grammatical and mechanical surface features occurring in their writing (verb forms, inflectional endings, spelling and punctuation). Students whose familiar dialect is not standard English cannot always rely on their native language to tell them whether or not a specific utterance or pattern of usage is standard English. The resulting "linguistic insecurity" can exert direct influence on the frequency of errors occurring in their papers. Such interference is reflected in the rather characteristic and systematic tendency of Black English Vernacular speakers (as well as some white speakers of nonstandard English) to exchange plural and possessive - *s* markers, as illustrated in the following example from a student's paper:

(c) I feel that no one's life should be taken from them, and if someone can take *another's persons* life from them, they don't deserve to be in the world either.

Sometimes this insecurity about what "sounds right" can surface in an overly anxious concern for avoiding stigmatized nonstandard fearures of their dialect, as in the case of example (d):

(d) They said they were told if they didn't follow orders they would *courtmarshaled* or shot as deserters.

In a commendable attempt to avoid the highly stigmatized invariant *be* form of the copula verb in Black English, the student has introduced an error by deleting a perfectly standard use of *be*. Still more evidence of this kind of insecurity about what is or is not standard usage is clearly evident in example (e):

(e) My reason are that some people have children to soon.

In the above example, the student first writes "My reason are...," crosses out the *are* and substitutes *is,* and finally crosses out *is* and settles again for *are,* leaving the verb still in error after obviously deliberating several times.

(f) Their were It was three people in charge of me. (sic).

Example (f) reveals yet another Black English Vernacular feature about which students show much insecurity—the use of *it* as the dummy subject, where standard English would require *there* (Reed et al. 1974)

In this example, we find "Their were" crossed out and replaced by the more familiar and therefore more comfortable (for the student) *"It was* three people in charge of me."

Nonstandard dialect can influence students' writing indirectly, in the sense that the dialect-mix character of the writing of vernacular speakers who have acquired some standard English rules often contains written utterances which conform neither to the grammatical rules of the nonstandard dialect, nor to the rules of standard English. In other words, there exists a whole array of *other* features, often syntactic in nature, which are entirely systematic and characteristic *in the writing* of Black English Vernacular speakers, but which can be said to be neither basilectal forms of the oral dialect, nor forms of standard English. Instead, such features as these (which can be called "cross-dialectal interference patterns") must be placed in that gray area, somewhere along the continuum between basilect and standard. As such, the frequency of occurrence of these features seems to be somewhat idiosyncratic in the writing of any given individual and cannot be predicted with consistency. Perhaps the most striking characteristic of these interference features is that they occur almost exclusively at points of contrast between the two dialects, that is, at points where the standard and nonstandard dialects diverge.

For example, such systematic divergence from the standard dialect is indicated in the following sentences excerpted from various students' papers (Reed and Baxter 1970):

(g) Duke would always fight for *his self.*

(h) Duke was a boy who lived most of *his self* in the ghetto of Harlem.

(i) I think Duke was cool because he know how to handle *hisself* in most situations.

In considering sentences like these, there are at least two aspects of this reflexive pronoun usage to note. First of all, the reflexive pronoun is almost always split into two words (e.g., *his* and *self*). Second, the first word of the reflexive is usually in the possessive case form, where standard English requires the objective case form (e.g., *his* instead of *him*).

Perhaps there is no need to mention that, traditionally, this particular deviant form has been *assumed* by teachers to be a problem of false analogy. It would seem reasonable, from the perspective of standard English, to surmise that Black English Vernacular speakers utter and write forms like *hisself* and *theirselves* as a complement to the other reflexive pronouns having their bound pronominal morphemes in the possessive case (e.g., *myself* and *yourself*).

Although this is a plausible hypothesis, it is apprently not the case. In our investigations of the dialect, we uncover the following systematic and characteristic usage among Black English Vernacular speakers:

(j) Here she come, with *her bad self.*

(k) I'm 'on give *my tired old self* a rest.

(l) Be still with *your ugly self.*

(m) She dropped the bottle on *her stupid self.*

(n) He did that for *his own self,* not me.

Such expressions as "my own self" and "his own self" are common occurrences throughout the black speech community. A Trinidadian linguist at the University of the West Indies who investigated the English of creole speakers in Dominica and St. Lucia also reports, among other structural similarities with American Black English, the systematic occurrence of split reflexive pronoun forms with an infix adjective, yielding such expressions as "his own self" and "my own self" (Carrington 1969). Moreover, this feature tends to persist in the active speech repertoire of even those Blacks who have successfully assimilated to standard English usage.

It therefore becomes increasingly clearer that in Black English Vernacular, the standard English bound morpheme *self* is considered a free morpheme that is not only modified by such personal pronouns as *his* and *their,* but also by other adjectives, especially *own.* Consequently, the fact that the reflexive often appears in students' writing as two words instead of one becomes explainable by the frequent appearance of adjectives between these forms in the students' familiar dialect. We are able to conclude, therefore, that it is the systematic nature of this distinctive feature in Black English that interferes with or blocks a student's ability to recognize the split reflexive as an "error" in standard English, and to "correct the error" or write the standard English equivalent with consistency.

Unless the teacher is also fully aware of these phenomena, he or she will not be as effective as he or she might in helping students understand and deal with their problems writing standard English and without the needed sophistication about such dialect influences, teachers may be more likely to induce confusion rather than understanding.

Yet another characteristic pattern of cross-dialectal interference is that which emerges when students who speak a vernacular Black English attempt to produce standard English plurals. In Black English Vernacular, the plural marker -s is often not added to a noun when it is preceded by a quantifier (i.e., *some, many, several, few,* and such adjectives as these which express a number or quantity). For example, in the expression "Lend me fifty cent," one notices that the noun *cent* has no plural -s marker. This is a common pattern of Black English Vernacular usage, and reflects the basic tendency in the dialect to avoid inflection as a carrier of grammatical information.

Consider the various instances of pluralization found in the following student paper:

> The Open Enrolment Program at Brooklyn College was only instituted to cool the hot tempers of Blacks and Puerto Ricans who started growing impatience for "An equal opportunity" The Administration became aware of this and open up an enrolment Program to keep the government off their backs.
>
> What was done by the administration after they started the program, was create tests, and *learning condition* that would inable the Black and Puerto Rican student to continue. This why the freshman Composition prove to be inadequate to the students needs
>
> *Some of the departments instructor* also are unfair to the new student at Brooklyn College as well as other major colleges that are predominately White. In the fall of 1970 "The New York Times Magazine," printed an article on the open enrolment program at *these so call "Major College."* Cornell's professor said that he will give the Blacks and Puerto Rican students "All A's & B's, just to hurry out of the school. This is the same attitude *most of our professor,* who thinks on racial bases. take toward *these student* The blame is not just on the lack of funds, it's on the lack of adequate *Instructor* & Professors.

Several quantifier-noun constructions can be found in the paper which conform *exactly* to the Black English Vernacular rule. However, in addition to these more direct intrusions of the vernacular dialect into the student's writing, there is also evidence of another plural construction, which can be called "conjoined-noun constructions" (Reed et al. 1974). These are constructions containing two or more plural nouns in series, where the -s marker is only partially utilized. Examples of these are the following:

(0) They are fighting like *cat and dogs.*

(p) ... it's the lack of adequate *instructor and professors.*

(q) The *boys and girl* are playing in the park.

It is, at this point in the discussion, perhaps not even necessary to point out the possible confluence between such structures as these and the previously discussed tendency in the vernacular dialect to require only contextual indicators of plurality. Since one element in a series being marked for plurality constitutes "context," it is not that difficult to comprehend the possible assumption on the part of the student writer that "one -s is enough." In any case, a *partial* assimilation to the standard, which would require both elements to carry the inflectional marker, is clearly evident.

The final aspect of cross-dialectal interference involving plurals that I wish to discuss concerns the tendency of nonstandard dialect speakers to hypercorrect for plural -s and to overgeneralize the application of the regular plural in standard English. In a sense, this tendency is probably the result of linguistic insecurity coupled with an intensive focus by teachers on drill and practice for achieving correctness. Whatever the underlying cause, however, the features which surface as a result can hardly be classified as anything but interference patterns resulting from dialect-mix. Such plural renderings as *oxes, womens, childrens, mices,* and *sheeps* all indicate an unconscious effort on the part of students to simplify the rather complex rules of standard English pluralization.

It should be clear that most of these problematic interference patterns, although being primarily *surface* features of the language, are nevertheless important, largely because they carry a high degree of social stigma. The persistence of such features as these in students' writing is literally determining the academic fate of those students, especially regarding performance of placement tests and writing proficiency examinations. And the students are aware of this fact. Because of their awareness, perhaps the strongest reason for teachers of English to be concerned about understanding dialect interference and learning to help students affected by it to overcome the barrier it represents, is that most of these students want desperately to be able to recognize and successfully eliminate such stigmatized patterns of usage from their writing. Because they want and need this ability, it should be our responsiblity as teachers and educators to help them develop the ability. Understanding the sociolinguistic and historical factors which give rise to dialect influences in students' writing prepares teachers to deal more effectively with such writing problems and the students who present them. It is especially helpful toward understanding the *persistence* of these language-related errors, even after repeated instruction in principles of standard English grammar. Teachers *must* become better prepared to help students overcome these resistant problems, because, in a very real sense, we are our students' last chance for literacy.

REFERENCES

Baxter, M. Educating educators about educating the oppressed. In *College English,* 1976, *37.*
Bruffee, K. (Ed.) *CADRE.* Newsletter of the Brooklyn College freshman writing program. Vol. 1, No. 1, 1972.

Carrington, L. Deviations from standard English in the speech of primary school children in St. Lucia and Dominica: A preliminary survey, part II. In *International Review of Applied Linguistics in Language Teaching,* Vol. VII, No. 4, 1969.

Cazden, C., John, V., & Hymes, D. (Eds.), *Functions of language in the classroom.* New York: Teachers College Press, 1972.

Herbert, C. *I see a child.* New York: Anchor/Doubleday, 1974.

Reed, C. E., "Adapting TSL techniques to the teaching of standard English to adult native speakers of American Black English Vernacular. In The T.E.S.O.L. Quarterly, Fall 1973.

Reed, C. E. Why Black English in the college curriculum. In *The Black Prism: Perspectives on the Black Experience,* 1972, 2.

Reed, C. E., & Baxter, M. Bidialectalism in the English classroom: A curriculum research project at Brooklyn college to develop materials for teaching standard English as a second dialect to speakers of Black English. In *A guide for teachers of college English.* New York: City University Office of Academic Development, 1970.

Reed, C. E., Baxter, M., Cohen, P. S., Moore, S. A., & Redrick, J. *Standard English composition for speakers of Black English vernaculuar.* New York: Language Curriculum Research Group, 1974.

Sledd, J. Bi-Dialectalism: The linguistics of white supremacy. *English Journal,* Vol. 58, No. 9, December 1969.

Sowell, T. New light on Black I.Q. *The New York Times,* Section VI, 1977, 56–62.

Stewart, W. A. Urban Negro speech: Sociolinguistic factors affecting English teaching. In R. W. Shuy (Ed.), *Social dialects and language learning.* Champaign-Urbana, Ill.: N.C.T.E., 1964.

Stewart, W. A. *Language and communication in southern Appalachia.* Washington, D.C.: Center for Applied Linguistics, 1967.

Thoreau, H. D. *Walden* (circa 1854). In O. Thomas (Ed.), *Walden and Civil Disobedience.* New York: W. W. Norton and Co., 1966.

9 Dialect Influence in Writing

Marcia Farr Whiteman
National Institute of Education

INTRODUCTION

Clearly there is much concern among educators, and among the public at large, over the apparent inability of many students to produce what is referred to as "acceptable written standard English." It is difficult to define just what "acceptable written standard English" is; however, we know by the use of "acceptable" and "standard" in this phrase that it must be written English which reflects current textbook conventions of capitalization, punctuation and spelling (i.e., the "mechanics" of writing), and that it must reflect standard English grammatical patterns (usually indicated in such areas as subject-verb agreement, negation, etc.). When a student produces writing which does not reflect control of mechanics and/or of standard grammar (even if in fact it does communicate its content effectively), it is not acceptable as "good writing" to most educators, nor to the general public.

I would like to focus in this paper on the second of these two aspects of "acceptable written standard English," that is, the occurrence in writing of features which seem to be traceable to nonstandard patterns in the writer's oral language.

Three such nonstandard features occur in the following sentences taken from a thirteen year old's essay about Mickey Mantle (NAEP: Report 10, 1972):

Mickey was T.V. star and everyone *love* him. Mickey *have* so many *friend* and the want to be like him.

153

The first noticeably nonstandard feature in the above is the omission of -*d* in *love* where the past tense is clearly intended. The second nonstandard feature is the use of *have* rather than *had* for third person singular present tense. The third nonstandard feature is the omission of -*s* in *friend* where the plural is clearly intended. All three of these features are characteristic of what is often called Vernacular Black English (VBE), which is the variety of English spoken primarily by working class Black Americans.

I would like to emphasize here that everyone speaks a "dialect," that is, one variety or another of the language he/she speaks. It is only when a "dialect" is different from our own that we notice it. Dialects of a language vary according to phonology (pronunciation) and grammar; there are also differences among dialects in the lexicon and in such aspects of language as semantics, pragmatics and rhetorical devices as well. Variation is abundant in every language, and dialects are only generalized groupings of such variation. Even though they are not in reality self-contained, isolated language systems, dialects are socially and regionally recognizable and thus are called standard English (SE), Vernacular Black English (VBE), Appalachian English (AE), etc. However, the number of features all the dialects of English share is undoubtedly greater than the number they do not share. This aspect of language variation is illustrated in figure 1 below, taken from Wolfram and Fasold (1974):

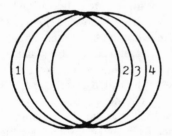

1. Standard English
2. Northern White Non-standard English
3. Southern White Non-standard English
4. Vernacular Black English

FIG. 1.   Relationship among several dialects of English.

To sum up then, every language has dialects which differ from each other at many levels of language structure, and everyone speaks one dialect or another of his/her language. These facts, however, conflict with educational goals. Standard English is called standard English precisely because it is socially and economically preeminent over other dialects of English (and not because it is inherently superior in its grammar or phonology). One educational goal of our schools, upon which most people agree, is to get students to be able to produce acceptable written standard English. If a student's natural dialect is not standard English, there will be some features of his/her oral language which are not going to be acceptable in school writing (an exception, of course, is the effective use of dialect patterns in creative writing). In this paper, I will discuss the occurrence of nonstandard features in writing and whether or not their occurrence is entirely attributable to oral language patterns of the writer.

DEFINING DIALECT INFLUENCE

It has been amply demonstrated that features which are characteristic of nonstandard dialects occur quite frequently in the expository school prose of students whose natural dialect is not standard English (Smitherman 1969, D.G. Briggs 1968, O.D. Briggs 1968, Schotta 1970, Wolfram and Whiteman 1971, and Crystal 1972). Because it has been assumed that the occurrence of these features in writing stem from the natural oral language patterns (i.e., the dialect) of the writer, this phenomenon has been called *dialect interference* (Wolfram and Whiteman 1971). This term was created by analogy with the concept of language interference, which occurs when a speaker who knows two languages uses features from one language while speaking the other language. When we are dealing with the use of features from one dialect in the attempt to produce another dialect (SE), however, we cannot assume two separate systems. Two languages may more clearly be spoken of as two separate systems, but given the evidence from linguistic variability studies (Labov 1966, Labov, et al. 1968, Wolfram 1969, 1973, Fasold 1972a, among others), it is very difficult to conceive of two dialects as distinct systems.

For this reason, it might be more appropriate to speak of *dialect influence* rather than *interference*, in order to avoid the implication that there are two separate systems interfering with each other, and to allow the recognition that the speaker of a nonstandard dialect already knows and uses many of the rules of standard English, and that there really may be only a limited number of features out of his/her total language competence which are unacceptable in written standard English. Thus *dialect influence* would refer to the use of nonstandard features in writing which are traceable to the oral language competence of the writer.

A Study of Dialect Influence

At this point, I would like to specify and characterize the major nonstandard features which occur most frequently in school writing and which seem to be traceable to dialect influence. That is, when we speak of nonstandard features in writing ("dialect influence in writing"), what specifically do we mean?

In a comprehensive investigation of dialect influence in writing (Whiteman 1976), I found that a limited number of nonstandard features occur in the writing of students who speak a nonstandard dialect of English, but that those few features occur rather frequently. Following is a list and brief description of these features:

1.   *Verbal -s absence.* The omission of the standard English *-s* suffix to indicate present tense with third person singular verbs (e.g., He *walk* to school every day) is a characteristic feature of VBE. In fact, this is a very frequently occurring feature of spoken VBE, with some speakers using it essentially categorically (i.e., at least 95% of the time). Some white nonstandard dialects use *do* and *have* (rather than *does* and *has*) as third person singular verbs, but do not generally omit the verbal *-s* suffix in this position with regular verbs like *walk, go,* etc.

2.   *Plural -s absence.* The omission of the standard English *-s* suffix to indicate plurality is also a characteristic feature of VBE; (e.g., They walk down the street with their *radio-* in their *hand-*). Most white nonstandard dialects do not omit this *-s* suffix.

3.   *Possessive -s absence.* The third *-s* suffix characteristically omitted in VBE (but not generally omitted in white nonstandard dialects) is the *-s* suffix which is used in standard English to indicate possession (e.g., Then we went over to my *girlfriend-* house).

4.   *Consonant Cluster -ed absence.* This feature (e.g., He *miss- the bus yesterday so he walk-* to school) also occurs rather frequently in the writing of nonstandard speakers, but only in certain linguistic environments. The relationship between the occurrence of this feature in writing and its occurrence in speech (it is in fact characteristic not only of VBE and white nonstandard English, but also of standard English in certain linguistic and social contexts) is somewhat complicated and will be explained in detail later in this paper. At this point it is sufficient to say that the *-ed* suffix which is used in standard English writing to indicate past tense is often absent in the writing of nonstandard speakers.

5.   *Is* and *are* absence. These two conjugated forms of the English copula (the verb *to be*) are characteristically absent in VBE (e.g., *She so calm and look so at ease* and *They tring to get away front the fire*). Copula absence is also characteristic of southern white nonstandard English in certain linguistic environments (e.g., *We gonna win this time*).

There are numerous other featuress, primarily phonological ones but also grammatical ones, which are characteristic of VBE and white nonstandard dialects of English that seem to occur rarely, if at all, in the writing of nonstandard speakers. Noticeably absent in the above list and in my (Whiteman 1976) data are most nonstandard phonological features (e.g., / f/ for /ǝ/, as in *wif* for *with*, or postvocalic *-r* absence, as in *motha'* for *mother*). The extreme rarity of phonological dialect influence in writing is shown by Table 1 below, which displays the frequencies of occurrence in writing of two typical VBE phonological features (postvocalic *–r* deletion as in *motha'* for *mother*, and monomorphemic consonant cluster simplification as in *col'* for *cold*). How this latter feature works in speech will be explained in detail later in this paper.

Also noticeably absent in my data (Whiteman 1976) are several prominent VBE grammatical features (e.g., 1) multiple negation, as in, *He can't do nothin' about it,* 2) *Ain't* or 3) iterative *be* as in, *Sometime my ears be itchin'*). The relative absence of these nonstandard features in writing, and the frequent occurrence of those discussed above, raises some interesting questions about dialect influence in writing.

First, are the occurrence of nonstandard features in writing really attributable to oral language patterns? If so, are they solely attributable, or are there other factors operating? Second, assuming that dialect influence is at least partially responsible for the occurrence of nonstandard features in writing, what kinds of features are most influential? That is, do phonological (pronunciation) features affect the spelling of words very often? Do grammatical features affect the syntax of sentences very often? If so, why do some grammatical features occur frequently whereas others occur rarely if at all?

To answer the first question, I compared nonstandard features in the speech and writing of 32 working class black and white eighth graders from southern Maryland (Whiteman 1976). The black students were speakers of VBE, and displayed the features found regularly in other studies of VBE. The white students spoke a variety of nonstandard southern white English, and regularly used features associated with that variety of English. Since the two spoken dialects, while sharing some features, were distinct in other ways (e.g., plural *-s* absence was characteristic of the speech of the blacks but not of the

TABLE 1

Frequency Rates of Postvocalic *–r* Deletion and Monomorphemic Consonant Cluster Simplification in Writing of VBE Speakers (Whiteman 1976).

	Deleted/ Simplified	*Not Deleted/ Not Simplified*	*Total*	*Percentage Deleted/Simplified*
Postvocalic *–r*	59	3292	3351	1.8
Monomorphemic Consonant Cluster	22	626	648	3.4

whites), it was possible to determine whether the occurrence in writing of some of these nonstandard features (i.e., plural -*s* absence) were traceable to dialect influence. For example, if plural -*s* absence were found in the writing of both groups of students, but only in the speech of one of the groups, then it would be apparent that dialect influence could not be solely responsible for the omission of the plural -*s* suffix in writing. If, on the other hand, plural -*s* absence occurred only in the writing of those who used it in speech, then it would be reasonable to attribute its occurrence solely to dialect influence.

The oral data were obtained in an informal interview of the type used in a number of sociolinguistic studies (Labov 1966; Shuy, Wolfram and Riley 1968; Wolfram 1969; and Fasold 1972a). Contextual factors (physical setting, peer groups, etc.) were manipulated to obtain the most natural speech possible in an interview situation. Written data were gathered from compositions written in English classrooms, with the topic controlled.

In addition to the spoken and written data from the southern Maryland students, more extensive written data were gathered from a compilation of thousands of compositions written by Americans in four age groups (9, 13, 17, 25, and over) who were additionally classified by region, sex, race, size and type of community and parental education (NAEP 1972). Racial, regional and educational classifications were used to gather two sets of compositions from the NAEP data, one written primarily by VBE speakers, and one written primarily by rural white nonstandard speakers.

An analysis of the spoken and written data from southern Maryland indicate that dialect influence apparently is responsible for some occurrences of nonstandard features in writing, but that it is not solely responsible. As can be seen in Figure 2 below, certain features occur rather frequently even when

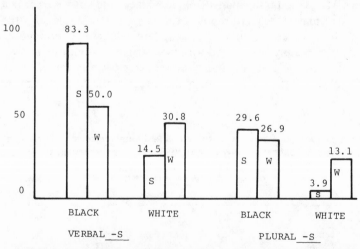

FIG. 2. Percentages of -*s* suffix absence in Speech and in writing for Southern Maryland Blacks and Whites.

they occur much less frequently in the speech of the writer. Specifically, plural -*s* was absent (e.g., They had their *radio*- in their *hand*-) 13.1% of the time in the writing of the white students, even though it was absent only 3.9% of the time in their speech. Clearly, the occurrence of this nonstandard feature in this group's writing cannot be attributed to influence from their speech patterns. Similarly, verbal -*s* was absent (e.g., He *go*- to the pool every day in the summer) 30.8% of the time in the writing the white students, but only 14.5% of the time in their speech. Again, the occurrence of this nonstandard feature in writing cannot be attributed solely to dialect influence.

In the case of verbal -*s* absence, where there is substantial occurrence of the feature in speech, some of the occurrence in writing may indeed be due to dialect influence; all of it, however, cannot be, since the percentage in writing far exceeds that found in speech. Such is not the case with plural -*s* absence; the data here give an even stronger indication that something other than dialect influence is causing occurrences of nonstandard features in writing.

I would like to explain here that the frequencies of occurrence of these two features were obtained from the two sets of data by counting actual and potential occurrences of each feature. For example, in the speech of all the white females, there were 25 occurrences of verbal -*s* absence and 60 occurrences of verbal -*s* presence. A percentage of absence is then obtained by dividing the number of absences by the total of all absences and presences. Thus, the white females did not include the verbal -*s* suffix in 25 of the 85 times that they used third singular present tense verbs, or 29.4% of the time.

These results were replicated in the analysis of more extensive written data from NAEP (1972). Both -*s* suffixes were found to be absent more frequently in the writing of whites than would be expected in their spoken dialect. Verbal -*s* absence was found 19.1% of the time and plural -*s* absence was found 11.7% of the time. Both of these frequency rates approximate those found in the writing of the southern Maryland whites (see Figure 2 above). Clearly, these results indicate a factor other than dialect influence can explain some occurrences of nonstandard forms in writing. That this factor apparently involves inflectional suffixes is shown by additional data on consonant cluster -*ed*.

Before discussing this additional data, it is necessary to explain briefly how consonant cluster simplification works in speech. In word-final position, the final member of a cluster of two consonants (e.g., ha*nd*) is often deleted. In order for this to occur, both members of the cluster must agree in voicing (i.e., both must be voiced or both must be voiceless) and the final member must be a stop (Wolfram 1969). This kind of cluster simplification occurs quite frequently in nonstandard speech, but it also occurs, less frequently, in standard varieties of English, especially if the following word begins with a consonant (e.g., *cold cuts* becomes *col' cuts* in informal standard speech). In speech, such clusters are simplified more frequently if they are *monomorphemic*, that is, if both members of the cluster belong to the same morpheme, or meaning unit. For example, the -ld cluster in cold is a monomorphemic cluster. Each consonant of a bimorphemic cluster, on the other hand, belongs to a separate morpheme (e.g., the final /st/ sounds of the word missed are a bimorphemic consonant cluster). Bimorphemic clusters, then, are represented in writing partly by the ed suffix. This is not to say that all -ed suffixes belong to bimorphemic clusters, since some of the verbs to which they are affixed do not end in consonants (e.g., played) or end in /t/ or /d/ already, requiring a pronunciation of /i-d/ (e.g., wilted or headed). It does mean, however, that there is a subset of verbs with -ed suffixes (walked, missed, jumped, etc.) which represent spoken bimorphemic consonant clusters.

This subset of verbs, in fact, occurs quite frequently in the writing of nonstandard speakers without the -ed suffix, resulting in the observation of many teachers that such students do not know the past tense. A closer look at the speech pattern of the students will reveal that it is not really a matter of not knowing the past tense, but, rather, is representative of an oral language pattern which deletes the final member of some consonant clusters.

Although such -ed absence in writing is representative of a speech pattern, the influence of speech on writing seems to end there. In speech, monomorphemic clusters (e.g., cold becoming col') are simplified more frequently than are bimorphemic clusters (e.g., missed becoming miss'). In writing, this order is reversed: bimorphemic clusters are simplified far more frequently than monomorphemic clusters. In fact, the simplification of monomorphemic clusters is so rare in writing as to be almost nonexistent; the crucial condition for simplification in writing seems to be that clusters be bimorphemic, i.e., partly represented by the inflectional suffix -ed. In the writing of the VBE speakers from the NAEP data, bimorphemic clusters were simplified 25.9% of the time; monomorphemic clusters, on the other hand, were only simplified 3.4% of the time, a striking contrast.

Discussion of Results

It seems clear from the data on verbal -s, plural -s and consonant cluster -ed that in the writing of nonstandard speakers there is a strong tendency to omit inflectional suffixes. Although these same suffixes are often omitted in nonstandard speech, it is not solely dialect influence which is responsible for their omission in writing. If it were, we would find monomorphemic clusters simplified in writing at least as often as, and perhaps more often than, bimorphemic clusters. Furthermore, we would not find -s suffixes omitted in the writing of those who rarely omit them in speech. Instead, these features (plural -s, verbal -s, and consonant -ed) seem to be omitted in writing at least partly because they are inflectional suffixes.

This conclusion is supported by a comparison of four nonstandard features (see Table 2 below) in the speech and writing of VBE speakers. In this table,

TABLE 2
Absence Rates of Four Inflectional Suffixes in Speech
(Wolfram 1969) and Writing (Whiteman 1976) of VBE
Speakers

	Speech	*Writing*
Verbal –s	up to 71.4%	37.0%
Plural –s	up to 5.8%	31.1%
Possessive –s	up to 26.8%	44.4%
Consonant Cluster –ed	up to 76.0%	25.9%

the absence rates in speech were taken from Wolfram (1969); the absence rates in writing are from the NAEP data in Whiteman (1976).

What is striking here is that, regardless of the widely varying absence rates in speech, the absence rates in writing for all four features are at the same general level. There seems to be no established relationship between the absence rates in speech and those in writing: two of the features (plural-*s* and possessive -*s*) show higher frequencies of absence in writing than in speech; the other two features (verbal -*s* and consonant cluster -*ed*) show lower frequencies in writing than in speech. The dominant pattern is that the absence levels in writing of these four inflectional suffixes cluster much more closely than their absence levels in speech, which in fact do not cluster at all. Since the primary characteristic these four features share is the fact that they are all represented in writing as inflectional suffixes, it apparently is this fact which is at least partly responsible for their frequencies of occurrence in writing.

It may be for those who are learning to write a language, as for those who are learning to speak one, inflectional suffixes are among the less crucial elements to be learned. For this reason they may be among the last elements learned; in fact they are often absent in early stages of child language (Slobin 1971) and in writing of the deaf (Charrow, this volume). Features such as these inflectional suffixes (articles and prepositions might be included also) are not only absent in the writing of relatively unskilled writers, but are also omitted by more experienced writers when they are writing quickly or under pressure. Similarly, in language contact situations which result in pidginization of one of the contact languages, such features are quickly eliminated from the language being pidginized (Fasold, 1972 b) during the learning process. Thus it would seem that, perhaps in an unconscious effort to simplify what is being learned, these features are particularly vulnerable to omission.

A pattern of age grading in the NAEP data supports this explanation. As can be seen in figures 3, 4, and 5 below, there is striking age grading in the absence rates in writing of verbal -*s*, plural -*s* and consonant cluster -*ed* for

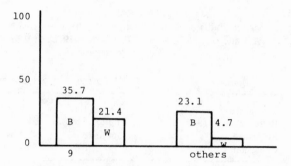

FIG. 3. Age grading for plural -s absence in writing.

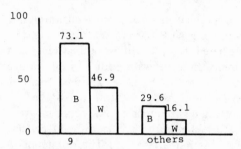

FIG. 4. Age grading for verbal -s absence in writing.

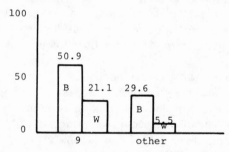

FIG. 5. Age grading for consonant cluster -ed in writing.

both blacks and whites when the nine year olds are contrasted with the older writers.

A repeated age grading pattern for all three inflectional suffixes is shown regardless of spoken dialect. Although the VBE writers can be assumed to have similar age grading in the use of these features in speech (Labov 1966, Labov, et al. 1968, Wolfram 1969, 1974 and Fasold 1972a, among others), a similar assumption would not be made for the rural white writers, since these features are not particularly characteristic of their speech. Thus the fact that the white writers show such age grading in the use of these features in their writing is strong evidence that the omission of inflectional suffixes in writing is at least partly an acquisitional phenomenon.

There is also evidence from first and second language acquisition studies (Dušková, 1969, Richards 1971, Dulay and Burt 1972, Taylor 1974, Burt and Kiparsky 1972) that supports the contention that we are dealing with an acquisitional phenomenon. Wolfram and Leap (1979), citing the above sources, suggest that there are "general acquisitional strategies" which operate in both first and second language acquisition and which often have the same effect on the language being learned (the "target" language). Thus the target language is modified by the learner during the process of acquisition in certain predictable ways. One strategy which learners apparently use to modify a target language might be referred to as redundancy reduction. Wolfram and Leap (1979) note:

> Structurally superfluous forms may be modified or eliminated as a strategy of acquisition. For example, a plural inflectional marker on a noun along with a plural quantifier in the noun phrase might be considered redundant and therefore a likely candidate for elimination.

It is quite plausible that relatively unskilled writers use a similar "redundancy reduction" strategy in their attempt to learn a new code (writing). It certainly is striking that the same inflectional suffixes are often eliminated in the learning of English as a first language, as a second language, and in the learning of written English. As was mentioned above, these suffixes are also notably absent in pidgin languages, in the sign language and writing of the deaf, in early stages of child language, and in "baby" and "foreigner" talk (Ferguson 1971). Ferguson suggests that the characteristic element in these language situations may be that of "simplicity." Perhaps the language user unconsciously attempts to simplify the code; learners might do this during the attempt to learn control of a relatively unfamiliar code. Fasold (1972b), also noting the elimination of inflectional endings in a variety of language contexts, goes on tentatively to identify the "simplification" process with the linguistic concept of marking:

> Because the "simplicity" features tend to recur in such a variety of circumstances, it is tempting to search for a universal principle to explain the phenomenon. It will not be possible to articulate such a principle too clearly, but it may well be the case that under conditions of special stress on communication situations, marked aspects tend to be lost. What are retained are the unmarked aspects which seem also to be the simplest. Under the stress of cross-language communication as in "foreigner talk" or in the formation of pidgins, or when a young child is acquiring his first language or when an adult is addressing a child in the earlier stages of acquisition, marked aspects of language tend to be dropped.

CONCLUSION

It should be clear at this point that there seems to be a general acquisitional strategy causing the omission of some inflectional suffixes in writing (as well as in a number of other communication contexts). In writing, this strategy apparently operates independently from the dialect of the writer. That is, whether or not these same inflectional suffixes are omitted in the speech of the unskilled writer, they are frequently omitted in his/her writing. We cannot, however, totally discount the role of dialect influence in writing, since there are significant differences in suffix omission in writing between dialect groups. As can be seen in Figure 6 below, frequencies of suffix absence greatly increase when that suffix absence is highly frequent in the oral dialect (in this case VBE) of the writer.

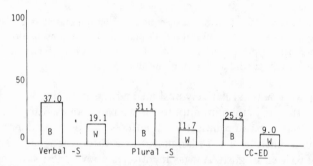

FIG. 6   Frequencies of suffix absence in writing of blacks and whites (NAEP data).

Thus we can see that dialect definitely influences writing, although it is not solely responsible for the occurrence of nonstandard features in writing. Instead, it combines with an acquisitional tendency to omit inflectional suffixes, with several results. First, nonstandard features occur more frequently in the writing of those who use them in speech. Second, some nonstandard features occur much more frequently than others. For example, nonstandard phonological features rarely occur in writing, even when these features are extremely frequent in the oral dialect of the writer. This is not surprising, in view of the fact that phonological dialect features tend to be integral parts of words (e.g., the pronunciation of such words as *mother, car* and *four* without the final, postvocalic *-r* or the pronunciation of such words as *cold, hand* and *mist* without the final consonant). As integral parts of base words, such features are apparently not so "marked" and are not so vulnerable to omission.

A third example of the combined effect of dialect influence and the acquisitional tendency to omit inflectional suffixes is the lack of occurrence in writing of nonstandard grammatical features which do not involve suffixes (e.g., *ain't*, multiple negation, iterative *be*). It could be that the acquisitional factor acts to constrain dialect influence from occurring anywhere except with suffixes. It could also be, of course, that non-suffixial dialect features are more clearly stigmatized socially and are more easily separable from standard English patterns. Thus, such features as *ain't*, multiple negation and iterative *be* might occur during the very early stages of learning to write but are rather quickly and easily spotted (by the teacher) and eliminated. To check this hypothesis, the writing of first through third graders should be looked at; unfortunately the NAEP does not provide such data, since their youngest writers are nine years old (presumably fourth graders).

Further research to extend the analysis of dialect influence in writing could focus on the writing of beginners (grades one through three). First, the writing of standard English speaking children in these early grades could be studied to see whether or not it displays the general acquisitional phenomenon of suffix omission discovered here. Also, it could be examined to determine whether or not this acquisitional phenomenon extends to such features of language as articles, prepositions, and derivative suffixes (e.g., *-ly*) as might be expected. Second, the writing of nonstandard English speaking children in these early grades could be studied to see whether or not highly stigmatized features such as *ain't* and multiple negation do occur in beginning writing but disappear by fourth grade. Finally, this early writing could be investigated for supporting or negating evidence of the age grading found here.

REFERENCES

Briggs, D. G. Deviations from standard English in papers of selected Alabama Negro high school students. Ph.D dissertation, University of Alabama, 1968.

Briggs, O. D. A study of deviations from standard English in papers of Negro freshmen at an Alabama college. Ph.D. dissertation, University of Alabama, 1968.

Burt, M. K., & Kiparsky, C. The gooficon: A repair manual for English. Rowley, Mass.: Newbury House, 1972.

Crystal, D. Dialect mixture and sorting out the concept of freshman English remediation. *The Florida FL Reporter,* Spring, Fall, 1972.

Dušková, L. On sources of errors in foreign language learning. *IRAL* 1969, *7,* 11–36.

Dulay, H., & Burt, M. K. Goofing: An indication of children's second language learning strategies. *Language Learning,* 1972, *22,* 235–252.

Fasold, R. W. Tense marking in black English: A linguistic and social analysis. Washington, D.C.: Center for Applied Linguistics, 1972a.

Fasold, R. W. Decreolization and autonomous language change. *The Florida FL Reporter,* Spring/Fall, 1972b.

Ferguson, C. A. Aspects of copula and the notion of simplicity: A study of normal speech, baby talk, and pidgins. In Dell Hymes (Ed.), *Pidginization and creolization of languages.* Cambridge: Cambridge University Press, 1971.

Labov, W. The social stratification of English in New York City. Washington, D.C.: Center for Applied Linguistics. 1966.

Labov, W., Cohen, P., Robins, C., & Lewis, J. A study of the nonstandard English of Negro and Puerto Rican speakers in New York City (Vol. I). Phonological and grammatical analysis. Final Report, U.S. Office of Education Cooperative Research Project No. 3288, 1968.

National Assessment of Educational Progress (NAEP). Report 10, Selected essays and letters. U.S. Government Printing Office, 1972.

Richards, J. C. Error analysis and second language strategies. *Language Sciences,* 1971, *17,* 12–22.

Schotta, S. G. Toward standard English through writing: An experiment in Prince Edward County, Virgina. *Tesol Quarterly,* 1970, *3,* 261–76.

Slobin, D. I. Developmental psycholinguistics. In William Orr Dingwall (Ed.), *A survey of linguistic science.* College Park, Maryland: University of Maryland, 1971.

Smitherman, G. A comparison of the oral and written styles of inner-city black students. Ph.D. dissertation, University of Michigan, 1969.

Shuy, R. W., Wolfram, W. A., & Riley, W. K. *Field techniques in an urban language study.* Washington, D.C.: Center for Applied Linguistics, 1968.

Taylor, B. P. Toward a theory of language acquisition. *Language Learning,* 1974, *24,* 23–35.

Whiteman, M. F. Dialect influence and the writing of black and white working class Americans. Ph.D. dissertation, Georgetown University, 1976.

Wolfram, W. *A sociolinguistic description of Detroit negro speech.* Washington, D.C.: Center for Applied Linguistics, 1969.

Wolfram, W., & Whiteman, M. The role of dialect interference in composition. *The Florida FL Reporter,* 1971, *9,* 34–38.

Wolfram, W. *Sociolinguistic aspects of assimilation: Puerto Rican English in New York City.* Arlington, Va.: Center for Applied Linguistics, 1973.

Wolfram, W., & Fasold, R. W. *The study of social dialects in American English.* Englewood Cliffs, N.J.: Prentice-Hall, 1974.

Wolfram, W., and Leap, W. Variability in the English of two Indian communities and its effect on reading and writing. Final report for the National Institute of Education, Grant No. NIE-G-77-0006, 1979.

10 Identity, Power and Writing Skills: The Case of The Hispanic Bilingual Student

Concepción M. Valadez
University of California, Los Angeles

INTRODUCTION

Before an effective language arts program can be planned for Hispanic bilingual students, several important characteristics of the students' language and the significance of literacy to this population should be understood. This article begins with a discussion of the term *bilingualism,* for this ambiguous word does not indicate the many levels of linguistic ability, different dialects, or speech styles, the bilingual person may be able to use. An exploration of the functions of writing for three distinct, but related groups follows, in the second part of the article, which addresses the personal needs that literacy serves barrio youth, South American peasants and Chicano college students. The final section of the article outlines concerns which language arts curriculum planners must address as they develop teaching ideas for the Spanish speaker in the classroom.

I. BILINGUALISM

The term *bilingual* is used to designate a person who speaks two languages. This definition, however, says nothing of the degree of facility with which a person uses the two languages.

There are three dimensions to this variability which merit at least some elaboration in this paper:

(a) The degree of fluency in speaking (oral production) and ability to comprehend (aural comprehension) in each language.

(b) the dialect varieties which the speaker can understand and use in each language and,

(c) the degree to which the speaker can, or will, mix the languages, or *code switch*.

Production and Comprehension

An assessment of the different dimensions of language facility among bilinguals might begin by determining the level of ability to speak each language and then relating that degree of fluency to their level of comprehension when hearing the language spoken. Language tests call these skills *oral production* and *aural comprehension*.

It is important for educators to know that many parents have elaborate conversations with their children in which the parents speak Spanish and the children speak English. There is apparent total comprehension on both sides even though the ability to produce speech in both languages is different for each speaker.

In many cases if forced, or encouraged, to speak in Spanish the child will do so, but his/her production will very likely not be fluent. There will probably be errors in phonology and syntax, and there may be hesitancy in finding the proper words. Similarly, the parent, in attempting to speak in English, may display a lack of fluency. In such cases we can say that each of the speakers is bilingual but certainly a *limited bilingual*, with a dominance in Spanish in the case of the parent and in English in the case of the child.

Limited bilingualism is frequently found among Hispanic upper elementary-age children and teenagers. It is not uncommon for children to have started school speaking only Spanish and having almost completely shifted to speaking only English by the sixth grade, yet retaining some level of comprehension in the first language.

This apparent mixed degree of facility with a language is comparable to the instances in which a person can read another language with a high degree of comprehension but cannot understand much of it in spoken form, a common former complaint directed at foreign language classes.

With respect to who is going to be called bilingual, the term is applied to the above persons and to the person who is equally fluent in both languages in both oral production and aural comprehension.

DIALECT VARIATION

Of particular importance to the teacher of Spanish–English bilinguals, as with any teacher of language arts, is the dialect variation found in a class and the relationship of the dialect of the teacher to that of the school population.

The bilingual education legislation, as well as the guidelines for developing teacher training programs, point to the need for the teacher to know standard Spanish and the local dialect of the students as well as standard English (H.E.W. 1977; State of California, Commission for Teacher Preparation, 1976). This requirement in the certification of bilingual education teachers addresses the concern of potential lack of communication that can occur if teacher and student speak different dialects. Also important is the potential harm that may occur to the children if the teacher holds negative attitudes toward the speech variety of the children or of the community being served by the bilingual program (Garcia, 1972; Shores, 1973). Without an understanding or an appreciation for the dialect of the children, bilingual teachers can unwittingly re-iterate the negative attitude monolingual English teachers have been accused of conveying—that the children's language and, by extension, the children and their home background, are not to be valued.

When speaking of dialect varieties it is necessary to distinguish between regional variations of a language, social class distinctions and informal, currently popular speech. Regional variations may include lexical distinctions as used by Mexicans or Chicanos in the Southwest and by Puerto Ricans or Cubans. An example of this might be the various words for *orange* (the fruit). In most places it is *naranja*, but in Puerto Rican Spanish it is usually *china*. The English word *kite* is *papalote* in Mexico, Texas, and California but also *huila* in Texas, *cometa* in Spain and Columbia, and *chiringa* in Puerto Rico.

Other differences may occur at the phonological level. For example, Central American Spanish velarizes final *n* sounds, with *en* becoming *eng* [eŋ]. Puerto Ricans lateralize or velarize *r* depending on its position in a word: *Ricardo* becomes *Jicaldo*.

Yet other distinctions may occur in syntactic rules, although there appears to be relatively few of these. One example from Puerto Rican Spanish involves word order and pronouns.

Puerto Rican Spanish	(1) ¿A dónde tú vas?
	(2) ¿A donde vas?
"World Standard Spanish"	(3) ¿Tú a dónde vas?
	(4) ¿A dónde vas tú?

Standard Spanish grammar rules indicate that the pronoun can be deleted since the person is included in the verb form (sentence 2 above) or it can be placed after the verb (4), and it can also be placed before the verb phrase (3). Informal usage by Puerto Ricans placing the pronoun immediately before the verb stem might appear "wrong" to speakers of other Spanish dialects, but it is in fact rule-governed behavior appropriate to the Puerto Rican dialect of Spanish.

Social class speech distinctions include the terms and morphology which can be found among Spanish speakers of low socio-economic levels throughout the Spanish speaking world.

Frequently the words in question are archaic forms, usually from 16th century Spanish,

naiden (nadie)	(nobody)
humiar (ahumar, or fumar)	(to smoke)
chupar (fumar)	(to smoke)
ansina or *asina* (asî)	(thus, as such)

common verb endings are regularizations in second person singular:

fuites (fuiste)	(you went)
comites (comiste)	(you ate)

Dialects of Spanish which these words are considered "nonstandard" in the same way in which many dialects of English are considered "nonstandard" (e.g., Vernacular Black English and Appalachian English). That is, they are characteristic of low socio-economic class speakers. Optimally, teachers should be aware of the points at which "standard" and "non standard" dialects differ and have a policy articulated on the role which "non standard" dialects are to play in their language program both in English and in Spanish. (Valadez–Love, 1973, 1976).

Attention to dialect varieties should be augmented by an explanation of another major feature of the bilingual Hispanic's speech, the ability and predilection at times, to use both languages together. *Caló*, *Spanish,* and *code switching* are terms commonly used in discussing these informal styles.

Caló ≠ Spanglish ≠ Chicano Spanish

Some teachers think that *Caló* and *Spanglish* and *Chicano Spanish* are the same thing, lumping together many very different language varieties and styles.

Caló is the label given to the speech style of a sub-culture, formerly the Pachuco, whose members feel separate from the larger Spanish speaking community. They have developed a style of communication which includes extensions or alterations of lexical terms which are also found in the larger speech community, but which are spoken in a distinct manner. Only a small segment of the Spanish-speaking population can speak or understand fluent *Caló*. Nevertheless, a limited number of phrases can be understood by many people and there is a small steady flow of this once closed code into the speech of the larger population of Spanish speakers, similar to the steady adaption into standard American English of the terms which were once strictly the domain of black musicians.

Example of Caló:

Esta noche, en mi chante, si quieres, la calmamos un escante. Mi jaina se descuenta pal cantón de su jefa, ese, y ahi pistiando te periqueo...(Tonight, at my house, let's get together for awhile. My wife will go to her mother's, and while having some drinks, I'll tell you what's happening.) (Sánchez, 1972; 48)

Spanglish is a term used loosely to mean the mixture of Spanish and English. There are several ways of addressing this mixing of languages which occurs whenever distinct linguistic systems come into contact and where there are speakers who use both languages. It should be noted that there are three clearly distinct types of mixing:

Type 1 is characterized by the extensive use of English lexical items occurring in their original form (English phonology) in otherwise Spanish utterances (Nash, 1972), e.g., *Perdi mi* LIPSTICK (I lost my lipstick); *Se necesita secretaria* PART-TIME (Needed, part-time secretary); *comprobante* TICKET *perdido* (receipt lost ticket).[1]

Type 2 is characterized by the use of English words which have become part of the Spanish language in certain regions, the sounds being totally hispanized, e.g., *asemblijol* (assembly hall); *pichel* (pitcher of beer). These words, sometimes call *loan words* or *borrowings*, are frequently used by speakers who are totally unaware of their English background.

Type 3 is characterized by a kind of alternation between languages at the phrase level.

"Me gusta mucho el arte, pos yo siempre he pintado, pero, don't ask me anthing about Michaelangelo, *de él no se nada."* Graduate Student, UCLA. October 1977.

This latter Linguistic style type 3 has been labeled *code-switching*. Probably the most widely misunderstood speech phenomenon by the general public is the effortless, moving back and forth between English and Spanish of many bilingual Chicano and Puerto Rican speakers. Research on language attitudes indicates that the shifting back and forth between languages is interpreted by many teachers as a limited ability with both. However, studies of such language behavior inicate that code switching is not necessarily due to a limited vocabulary or a lack of complex syntactic rules. Most code-

---

[1]Examples from San Juan, Puerto Rico, collected by the author in April, 1978.

switchers, in fact, can hold a sustained conversation in either language if they are speaking with a monolingual.

Gumperz and Hernández (1972) in their early work on code-switching hypothesized that sociolinguistic rules were in effect when speakers mixed their languages. The variables which appeared to most strongly influence the speakers toward this language style were the relationship between the speakers, and the topic of their conversation. That is, if the interlocutors were friends or wanted to express their camraderie they were more likely to code-switch than if there were no warmth between them. In addition, certain topics which could be considered to belong to experiences in both cultural domains would be likely to be discussed in this language mixture. Subsequent research by Gumperz and Hernández as well as by others, including Valdez-Fallis (1978), appears to support the theory that this way of speaking is used to carry specific social meaning.

In response to the notion that language mixing is done randomly, several studies have shown that there are syntactic constraints on how the languages are mixed in a phrase or sentence (Pfaff, 1976).

The role of code-switching in the development of each language is being studied also. Ana Huerta (1977) has found that acquisition of syntactic rules in each language appears to be enhanced by children who begin code-switching before they are three years old.

The above brief overview of bilingualism shows that this is a complex topic and points out the need for educators to be aware of these varying levels of complexity when planning educational programs for student populations who use two languages.

II.   THE POWER IN WRITING

Among the most common sights of the inner city is the graffiti on the walls. A drive through a Chicano barrio, be it in Union City, California or in Tucsón, Arizona, will find many store fronts, walls, and garage doors very carefully decorated with people's names, or with the name of a neighborhood gang. To many outsiders, the graffiti (called *placas* by the users of this genre) is seen as an indicator that the people who live there don't care about neatness and orderliness. Furthermore, these markings are often considered a sign of disregard for other people's property.

A close look at the graffiti shows a very carefully developed writing style. It is obvious that the graffiti authors have practiced their *placa* penmanship for long hours.

Teachers must wonder why students who can't or won't write a word at school, spend time writing *placas* all over the school and all over the neighborhood. The research of Ricardo Organista (1977) for the Los Angeles Unified School District gives some insights to the reasons barrio youth have an affinity for graffiti. Through interviews with the artists of the Estrada Court murals in East Los Angeles, Organista found the following responses from several adults who had been graffiti writers as youths as well as from contemporary graffiti writers:

> Writing my name on that wall meant I had been there. It also meant I existed, for people would see my name and say "Hey, I know him."
>   Our gang also would have our best writer put the names of all the *vatos* (guys in our gang) on a wall and then the name or initials of our gang.[1]

> Writing our names on walls meant we were claiming that area as our "turf". If someone from another neighborhood or another gang wrote over our names or crossed them out it was considered a challenge to a fight.
>   This is still pretty much the way things are now.

None of the graffiti writers considered writing on walls a destruction of property. On the contrary, they felt the graffiti a source of pride and identity. Clearly the names acted as a "coat of arms," an emblem of their power.

Paulo Freire (1970) used the empowering concept in Brazil and Chile when he was pioneering his now famous literacy techniques. The Freire method uses words which carry strong emotional loading. Words like *favela* (slum) are chosen for their linguistic properties (number of syllables, canonical form), but also for their emotional content. A discussion of the social conditions which create the slums causes the students, who are illiterate, poverty-level adults, to become personally involved with the word *favela* and what it symbolizes. Freire, then, ties social and political awareness with literacy.

Freire asked a student finishing the first level of literacy classes (at the Institute of Training and Research in Agrarian Reform) why he hadn't learned to read and write before the agrarian reform.

> "Before the agrarian reform, my friend," he said, "I didn't even think. Neither did my friends."
> "Why?" we asked.
> "Because it wasn't possible. We lived under orders. We had nothing to say," he replied emphatically.

> The simple answer of this peasant is a very clear analysis of "the culture of silence!" In "the culture of silence", to exist is only to live. The body carries out orders from above. Thinking is difficult, speaking the word, forbidden.
> "When all this land belonged to the 'latifundio'," said another man in the same

---

[1]Such as GL (Geraghty Loma), or VNE (Varrio Nuevo) or WF (White Fence).

conversation, "there was no reason to read and write. We weren't responsible for anything. The boss gave the orders and we obeyed. Why read and write? Now, it's a different story...." (Freire, 1970; 22)

In another instance, when speaking to a group of urban dwellers:

Freire: "What did you feel, my friend," when you were able to write and read your first word?"

Chilean: "I was happy because I discovered I could make words speak."

Freire, 1970; 23

A related revelation appears to have occurred to Chicanos who are writing in college literary publications (*Misquitli*, Stanford University; *Llueve Tlaloc*, Pima College, Tucson, Arizona; *Fuego de Aztlan*, University of California, Berkeley). Chicano college students are discovering that their experiences, when written on paper and shared, add a dimension of affirmation of their identity and existence in an alien environment. Frequently, these students are the first from their families to leave home for a university education. The culture they took for granted when living at home suddenly becomes an important source of strength in coping with their new surroundings.

Additionally, there are groups that meet regularly to share their writing. At these gatherings the overt objective is to critique the writing, which frequently is a newly-discovered past-time for the physics or political science student. Certainly another important function of this activity is to touch base with others from a similar cultural background now sharing an experience in an environment not always supportive or easily understood.

Themes of the writing range from the adaptive coloration expected or needed in college ("*El Camaleón*," by Francisco Santana, 1977) to male–female relationships ("Pueblo, 1950" by Bernice Zamora, 1976).

PUEBLO, 1950

I remember you, Fred Montoya.
You were the first vato to ever kiss me.
I was twelve years old.
My mother said shame on you,
my teacher said shame on you, and
I said shame on me, and nobody
said a word to you

B. Zamora, 1976

III. TEACHING WRITING IN
BILINGUAL EDUCATION PROGRAMS

With some knowledge of the linguistic variation in a particular student population and some understanding of what writing as a tool can mean to these students, the bilingual educator needs a set of operating guidelines as the instructional program is elaborated. The language arts program for bilingual children should be a personalized set of lessons based on the following information:

1. Does the student have a language preference/dominance?
   Spanish > English?
   English < Spanish?
   Spanish = English?
2. What dialects of Spanish does the student speak?
   What dialects of Spanish does the student understand?
   What dialects of English does the student speak?
   What dialects of English does the student understand?
3. Is there an E.S.L. (English as a Second Language) program the student can attend concurrently?
   Is there an S.S.L. (Spanish as a Second Language) program the student can attend concurrently?
4. Has the student received previous language arts instruction in Spanish? In English?
   How successful has any previous language instruction been?

Personalized instruction, when ideally presented in bilingual education, adds several features to traditionally defined individualized instruction. Concepts are taught in culturally meaningful context. In addition, the language used for instruction is carefully determined. Initially, the student's language arts program will be in his/her dominant language. If the dialect is not the standard one, the teaching staff must be supportive and make the student feel proud of that dialect. In addition, the teaching staff must develop a way of helping the student use that dialect to gain access to the standard variety.

One of the charges of bilingual education is to help the students learn a second language (English) well enough that instruction can be received in that language without any loss of linguistic comprehension. For the native Spanish speaker who begins school knowing no English, an E.S.L. class must be programmed into his/her school day. For the students who are dominant Spanish speaking but have some control of English, E.S.L. classes should continue and interaction with native speakers of English should be encouraged, but basic cognitive instruction should continue to be in Spanish. When the student's second language oral proficiency begins to approach some strength, that person's individual schedule should include some instruction that is given in both English and Spanish. The next level should include some units of instruction which can be all in English in a particular subject, but never should a student receive all his/her instruction in a subject totally in English unless the child is completely at ease with that language.

Because of the varied levels of training of the teaching staffs of our bilingual programs (as in all our school programs), the wide range of linguistic abilities in the student groups and the state of the art of language assessment, there are many different ways of approximating the ideal language arts program for bilingual children.

Sylvia Roberta Welner, of the Los Angeles Unified School District, has developed a handbook, *Teaching Poetry Writing to the Bilingual Child* (1976). The lessons allow for language mixing, which in turn adds to the range of feelings that can be expressed in writing:

> All poetry should be graciously accepted whether it is written in Standard Spanish, Standard English, whether it contains "pochismos," local barrio dialect, or any combination of the above. The child's language is part of his culture and is a carrier of values and interpretations of reality.

> Many bilingual children write bilingual poetry, which has also been called "bisensitive poetry." In such poetry the poet abruptly changes back and forth between languages, in order to capture images that are most authentic to the cultural context in which the event was first experienced.... Welner, 1976; iv

A second program which addresses the concerns raised above is the *Spanish Language and Concepts Program*, SWRL Educational Research and Development (1978). This program is part of a series of language arts materials being developed at SWRL for bilingual classrooms. The materials are designed using hispanic cultural content to teach reading and writing skills. Folklore as well as cultural artifacts and cultural activities found in present-day events are the context for the lessons.

It should be noted that whether a teacher can locate a ready-made language arts program for bilingual children or not, the school community, and the community at large, can be invited to assist in the bilingual classroom. Community members can be invaluable resources in many ways. English speakers, Spanish speakers and bilingual community volunteers can assist the language arts teacher by (1) sharing stories or riddles with the children, (2) listening to children compose stories or poems, (3) writing down the stories or poems as they are dictated, and (4) helping children collect oral histories.

IV. CONCLUSION

There *are* ways of getting students to write. Motivation may be fostered by providing for the students an environment in which they can feel that the language they use, be it the low-prestige local dialect, or the standard dialect, will be honored. Topics which allow the students to share moods, aspirations, and descriptions of self may be suggested. Care is advised when teachers assign sensitive topics. Students will be interested in writing on such personal topics only if they feel the instructor will not ridicule their writing, and themselves by extension.

Once the students have the motivation to write, the language arts teacher, or the literary critic, might suggest rules of rhetoric which can enhance the message the student wishes to convey. This paper is written from the speculative position that the benefits which accrue to those who discover that they can write, who feel the power that the written word gives, (as Paulo Freire teaches, and as our graffiti writers expresses), will improve academic achievement in the language arts and in other areas of the school curriculum.

At the present time, those who can write seem to hold important keys to success in school, and by extension, keys to at least a fighting chance in the outside world. Educators need to see that more of the bilingual students of our country have an opportunity to receive those keys.

REFERENCES

Burciaga, B. J. In commemoration of the American bicentennial, and Amerika Amerika. In J. A. Burciaga & B. Zamora, *Restless Serpents*. Menlo Park, Cal.: Diseñs Literarios, 1976.

California State Department of Education Commission for Teacher Preparation and Licensing. The Bilingual Education Credential. Sacramento, Cal.: 1976.

Freire, P. *Cultural Action for freedom*. Cambridge, Mass.: *Harvard Educational Review*. Monograph Series, No. 1, 1970.

García, E. Chicano Spanish dialects and education in Eduardo Hernandez-Chavez, et al. *El Lenguaje de Los Chicanos*. Arlington, Va.: Center for Applied Linguistics, 1975.

Gumperz, J., & Hernández-Chávez, E. Cognitive aspects of bilingual communication. E. Hernández-Chávez, et al., *El Lenguaje de Los Chicanos*. Arlington, Va.: Center for Applied Linguistics, 1975.

Gutiérrez, J. A. 22 Miles (1968). In C. Shular, T. Ybarra-Frausto & J. Sommers, *Literatura Chicana*. Englewood, N.J.: Prentice Hall, 1972.

Huerta, A. The acquisition of bilingualism: A code-switching approach. *Working Papers in Sociolinguistics*. Southwest Educational Development Laboratory, Austin, Tx, 1977.

Nash, R. Spanglish: Language contact in Puerto Rico. *American Speech*, 1972, *45*, 3-4.

Organista, R. R. Mexican culture and heritage unit: Contemporary California Mexican art, Los Angeles Unified School district. Contemporary Education Office, Area G, Spring, 1976.

Pfaff, C. Syntactic constraints in Spanish-English code-switching. Paper presented in Linguistic Society American conference, San Francisco, 1975.

Sánchez, R. Nuestra circunstancia linguistica. *El Grito,* 1972, *6*(1), 45–74.

Santiago, D. *The somebody in fictional autobiography.* In R. Pierce & R. K. Suid (Eds.), *Interaction: A student-centered language arts and reading program.* Houghton-Mifflin Co., 1973.

Shores, D. L. *Contemporary English, change and variation.* Lippincott, 1972.

United States Department of Health, Education and Welfare. Criteria for Governing Grants Awards. *Federal Register,* Bilingual Education Program.

Valadez-Love, C. The acquisition of Engish syntax by Spanish-English bilingual children. Doctoral Dissertation, Stanford University, 1976.

Valadez-Love, C. The role of non-standard dialects in education. Paper presented at the Northern California Conference on Bilingual Education, 1973.

Valdez-Fallis, G. Code-switching for social communication. Paper presented at the Conference of Chicano and Latino Discourse Behavior. Educational Testing Service, Princeton, N.J., 1978.

Welner, R. S. *Teaching poetry writing to the bilingual child.* Los Angeles, Cal.: Los Angeles Unified School District. Compensatory Instructional Programs Division, 1976.

Zamora, B. *Pueblo, 1950.* In B. Zamora and J. A. Burciaga, *Restless Serpents.* Menlo Park, Cal.: Diseños Literarios, 1976.

11 The Written English of Deaf Adolescents

Veda R. Charrow
American Institutes for Research

In general, reading comprehension tests have been used in assessing the English language proficiency of deaf students. In this paper, I suggest that writing samples are a far better measure of English language abilities, and as well, can serve as an excellent diagnostic tool for finding the specific problem areas of individual students. Before examining this hypothesis, I will provide a general overview of the languages taught to and employed by deaf persons, and the effect that these languages may have on their English usage.

Many persons, including many educators of the deaf, believe that the prelingually deaf person's greatest handicap is the inability to hear, and that the most important educational goal is teaching the deaf child to speak. Certainly the inability to hear is a handicap, and certainly it is useful to teach a deaf child to use his or her vocal organs to produce intelligible speech sounds. But there is a far greater handicap: illiteracy. And the most important educational task for educators of the deaf is to teach young deaf children grammatical English, whether or not the deaf child ever learns to speak intelligibly.

As things now stand, by the time deaf children have reached adolescence— a time when hearing children have mastered their societal language—the deaf children are producing written language full of errors and strange constructions. Below are two samples of deaf adolescents' writing.

Sample No. 1

Hi, I'm very happy now and also vacation. I have to swim my pool with my friends everyday.

Last week, I practice to play my golf long time. I like it very much. I played a fresbee with my friends. I dreamed about Goldfinger who throw my black hat that is as sharp as a blade. And also an ant drive in a flying saucer that called U.F.O.

Tomorrow, morning, my friend (he is deaf) will come with me at 7:30 but I will can't wake up at 7:30. Oh No! Because he will come with me and a boy and I will going to the hearing and speech school. Do you remember it was my school? We will learn English. I think I will have a lot of fun. I hope so!

Next Thursday my father and I will fly a jet and we will leaves at 4:00 p.m. We will going to Kentucky. I wish touch all in the world first times. I can free to fly because C Oil Corporation pays the bills. I promise! May be I will back home for two or three more days.

In Aug. 1, my family and I are going to Ga. That I will be very, very fun. And I will also play my golf. It will very hot.

I can make my room that is look like a space and different light. I want work my homework in my space room very easy. I throw away my old thing but my mother mad at me.

Please tell me when did I will going K school.

Your Good Friends,

Sample No. 2

The Golden Touch

King Midas who loved gold and wished to touch turn gold.

One day, Midas sat down and counted the pile of gold coins. Then he saw the strange in the room. There was the god which he asked him if he was a rich man. Midas said that may be true. He wished to touch would turn to gold.

He was very joy and ran around the castle. He touched anythings which turned to gold.

At the lunchtime he went to eat lunch and sat down with his daughter. He touched a piece of bread, milk, fish, vegetables turned to gold. He became frowned. He was hungry to eat.

His daughter saw his face was frowned and hugged him around her arms. She became gold statue. Midas became crying and said that terrible Gold touch.

Suddenly the god came. King Midas asked him that he wanted his daughter became a real child again.

The god told him to take clean water from the river. Midas throw it on the things which came real again.

He never loved the Gold Touch anymore.

Grade 8

These errors persist into adulthood, and do not appear to be eradicable even by intensive training and remedial English courses. The following sample is from a teletyped conversation of a college-educated deaf man of about 27, who furthermore, was required to use English—written, spoken and signed—extensively in the course of his work.

OK, as of now the English Department is in a bad condition now I am not supposed to say that but you may get an idea of what has happened among students here. This morning the kids had a small strike showing their complaints of what they have not learned anything from the English department ... and sure enough the English teachers are under very pressure and in this situation I know it is out of question that you have a 1 to 10 basis or a mass meeting with English teachers and then you will still find no way to convince them. Really let us wait and see what has became of them when the time comes later (after Christmas) ... I am afraid to say something but I know your visit with (high school) teachers will not be a helpful way as but with math teachers I strongly believe it will be helpful ... And second, with new revised language arts ... I will try my best to bring it up again with English teachers and hopefully they will listen me Ha ... we can discuss this in January before your coming to (city) ... I don't know any processings at (elementary) School.

I am very happy about what the kids have done but wow, it put hard on poor English teachers ... we had two hours meeting, discussing our problems about (high school) ... Really it is a big exciting among the kids and the teachers ... I know that the mess will be solved soon or later.

I don't think there will be no more strike again as long as teachers will change their ways of teaching to the kids ... really the kids have right to speak out what they are thinking of teachers ... They are only high school kids and I believe that they learned like that thing from (college) students because the (high school) is only located on the same campus of (X) college ... Anyway ... Thank you very much for chatting and hope to hear from you some day (pretty soon ha)

College Educated Deaf Adult

The writing problems of deaf children are part of a much larger problem—a problem linked to the very nature of the handicap of deafness, and the limitations it imposes upon verbal communication. It is not a problem of jargon or bad style, but a language problem per se: the impossibility for the deaf child of learning the societal language in the normal, natural manner, and the sorts of linguistic shortcircuits that occur when the language is learned in a non-normal manner, in school. The symptoms of the problem are similar to those of the foreigner who learns English after infancy from imperfect sources (Charrow and Fletcher 1974), but the problem itself is far greater than that of the foreigner and its implications more severe. The deaf adolescents' errors in written English are a direct reflection of their linguistic competence in English and their difficulties in learning the language.

It is possible that for many deaf students there is an added impediment to the learning of "correct" English, but ironically this putative impediment is also their greatest asset in communication in general: American Sign Language (ASL).

ASL is a gestural language used by most prelingually deaf persons in North America. It is the first language of about 10% of the deaf population in the country—those born to deaf parents—and of some hearing children of deaf parents as well. Children of hearing parents learn ASL from their peers, once they enter school, since it is the only language that they can learn easily in a normal way, through exposure and interaction. Although ASL employs hand shape and hand movements and facial expression, it is not to be confused with pantomime. In fact, studies by Stokoe (1971, 1972), Fisher (1973), and others have shown that ASL has the same levels of structure and the same amount of structure as spoken languages.

The structure of ASL is very different from that of English. It lacks many of the syntactic features that make English what it is: articles, plural markers, tense markers, certain prepositions, passives, heavy use of subordinate clauses, and others. Needless to say, ASL has many syntactic features that English lacks: simultaneous signs, tense and number inflections on time words, inflections for habitualness, for repetition of action, the ability to "spatialize"—to set up a scene in space—and many others. I in no way mean to disparage ASL, or to "blame" it for causing problems for deaf children. However, because its structure is so different from English (as is the struture of Yoruba, or Swahili, or any of hundreds of non-Western languages), and because it is a more normal means of communication for deaf children and adults and one which requires far less effort than spoken or even Signed English, it is quite probable that there is some interference from ASL in deaf students' English.

To further complicate matters, schools that employ "sign language" as a means of instruction, do not employ ASL. Rather, they use a brand of sign language that follows the word-order of English (Signed English) or even adds the function words and inflectional markers of English (Manual English). These are more like English in structure than like ASL, but it is unclear how well school children can understand these varieties of sign language and how much and what kind of English structure they actually learn from them.

In the past, educators and some researchers in the area of deafness tended to blame ASL for all of the errors made by deaf children in English, and forbade any use of sign in schools for the deaf. Recent studies, however, (Bonvillian, Charrow and Nelson 1973; Mindell and Vernon 1971); have indicated that children raised with ASL from infancy tend to perform better in all academic areas than those who had no sign language in their first 5 years. Schools which permitted signing, and used some form of sign language in the classroom (i.e. Signed or Manual English—ASL has never been used as a medium of instruction), produced better-educated students, who performed better in most areas (including written English) than schools which were strictly oral.

In short, it is not at all clear how and to what extent the structure of ASL affects the deaf students' English. Children of deaf and of hearing parents share the same non-standard usages, and I have been informed that deaf children with no exposure whatsoever to ASL, and hard-of-hearing children who learn English via oral methods only, still produce similar non-standard constructions (Nancy Frishberg, personal communication, 1973). It is possible, then, that many of the difficulties that the deaf child encounters in learning and using English may be due to certain redundant features of English itself—features which are not readable on the lips, and which tend to be used inconsistently in Signed English. Such grammatical features of English as determiners, tense inflections, particles, non-locative prepositions and (left-over) case markers carry a relatively low semantic load, and are most easily overlooked when raw communication is at stake.

In any event, the performance of all deaf students—even those who were raised with ASL and use Signed English in school—is far below that of hearing students of the same age, on standardized tests measuring math skills, reading, science, social science and written English (Moores 1970; Trybus and Karchmer 1977). The knowledge of ASL appears to help up to a point—in that it allows the deaf child to communicate, learn, and understand some things about language and the way it works. The deaf child without ASL essentially has no language, or only fragments of language, until he finally learns enough English to get by. By that time he is far behind the signers in language use, and in understanding the structure and functions of language in general. Thus, if the deaf child who has learned ASL from infancy is at a disadvantage in learning and using English, how much more so is the deaf child who has had no ASL and, because English is auditory/vocal, almost no English, until he is taught it, laboriously, at school. The learning of isolated English vocabulary items, which is all that can be taught in oral pre-school programs, is not the same as learning English.

In sum, I am suggesting that the deaf child makes errors in English primarily because he cannot hear English and receive a large number of correct models and patterns and immediate feedback, and therefore uses only grammatical constructions he has been explicitly taught and can remember. These are often used improperly, through improper generalization and overgeneralization of rules. If the deaf child knows ASL, he has a model for language, and can use ASL as a medium for learning English. But if differences between the two languages are not carefully pointed out to him, and if he is not made aware that ASL, Signed English and English are three different codes, he may apply some of the rules of ASL to English, and make additional errors in English.

Since ASL is not used as a medium of instruction, and since it is not even recognized as a language in many schools, its potential usefulness as a medium of instruction and as a teaching tool has been lost. Nonetheless, the value of ASL as a language for deaf persons far outweighs any of the potential problems it may cause in learning English.

My suggestion above that the deaf child's written English problems are similar to those of the foreigner who learns English as a second language is no mere metaphor. The deaf child does learn English as a second language, whether or not he has a first language, such as ASL. Like the foreign student, he learns English relatively late in childhood (he starts learning it whenever he starts school), and he does not learn it through normal exposure and interaction, but rather by means of pattern practices, vocabulary lessons, and explicit rules. In order to test whether the English that deaf college-entrance-age students had learned was similar to that of foreign college-entrants, Charrow and Fletcher (1974) administered the written part of the Test of English as a Foreign Language (TOEFL) to two groups of deaf students with some skills in English: one group consisted of children of deaf parents who had acquired American Sign Language in infancy (DP): the other consisted of deaf children of hearing parents who had learned to sign from peers and teachers after age six (HP). In general, the performance of a large comparison sample of foreign students more closely resembled the performance by deaf students with deaf parents than it did the performance of deaf students with hearing parents. (See Table 1). Charrow and Fletcher concluded that for deaf children who acquire sign language in infancy many aspects of English are learned as aspects of a second language. This study, like numerous previous studies, also demonstrated that overall English skills were higher for deaf children of deaf parents than for deaf children of hearing parents.

From these results and from writing samples of deaf high-school students, it appeared that there was a certain commonality to the errors that the deaf students were making in English. Teachers, too, often referred to certain constructions in the written and spoken English of deaf students as "deafisms". This suggested to me that perhaps the errors in the English of deaf students should not be considered errors, but rather the earmarks of a non-standard dialect, similar to vernacular Black English. This seemed all the more reasonable since many of these "errors" and "deafisms" persist even with remedial English classes at the college level; they become "frozen" and even institutionalized. I therefore suggested that there may be enough commonality among deaf adolescents' English errors to justify the existence of a "Deaf English" non-standard dialect, or of a regular deaf pidginization of

TABLE 1

Means, Standard Deviations, and *T* for TOEFL Scores of 13 HP, 13 DP and 113,975 Foreign Students (S)

	Group	Mean	S.D.	T score
	HP	28.15	3.69	
English Structure (ES)	DP	39.85	6.36	5.74*
	S[a]	49	8	
	HP	34.92	5.11	
Vocabulary (V)	DP	43.85	6.09	4.05*
	S	48	11	
	HP	34.15	2.12	
Reading Comprehension (RC)	DP	30.31	5.02	−.59
	S	48	8	
	HP	31.00	3.39	
Writing Ability (WA)	DP	38.54	6.72	3.62*
	S	48	8	
	HP	128.23	10.69	
Total Score (T)	DP	159.54	19.04	5.17*
	S[b]	—	—	

[a]Means and standard deviations for foreign students were taken from the TOEFL manual (Test of English, 1970, p. 6).

[b]Distribution of total scores for foreign students across the four subtests was not available.

*$p < .01$, $df = 24$.

English. In an experiment based on this idea (Charrow 1975), students were tested on recall of sentences in the hypothesized "Deaf English" (DE) and of corresponding standard English (SE) sentences. Hearing subjects had more difficulty in recalling "Deaf English" sentences than in recalling standard English sentences, but deaf subjects found the former as easy to recall as the latter. In addition, it appeared that the sentences were processed in different ways by the deaf and the hearing children, since they committed different kinds of errors. I proposed that whereas hearing persons rely on obligatory grammatical rules of English, the deaf have inconsistent or variable rules for certain English constructions, somewhat like the variable rules found among pidgin-users.

Some of the findings of this study are summarized in Table 2.

Some of the differences between the two groups of deaf children are interesting, such as present and past tense markers and mass nouns: The HP group made more errors, more consistently, in these items than the DP group. Perhaps the greater consistency in these errors is due to their greater reliance

TABLE 2

Means, Standard Deviations, for each Group for Percentages of Errors in 11
Parts of Speech in SE and 9 Parts of Speech in DE

Source of Variance Part of Speech	Subtest	Normals $\bar{X}$	SD	HP $\bar{X}$	SD	DP $\bar{X}$	SD
Present tense marker	SE	5	5	12	6	11	6
	DE	16	16	25	12.5	20	16
Past tense marker	SE	4	4	17	8.5	13	11
	DE	20	7	24	16	27	6
Copula	SE	1	2	15	12	16	11
	DE	19	15	23	14	23	20
Preposition	SE	4	3	17	7	16	8
	DE	32	16	21	9	23	11
Present participle	SE	3	6	21	20	35	37
	DE	6	14	12	11	11	11
Past participle	SE	3	6	21	15	29	25
	DE	42	31	10	11	6	10
Definite article	SE	5	9	34	20	31	39
	DE	7	10	8	8	12	9
Indefinite article	SE	4	4	20	8	12	6
	DE	21	14	32	11	27	14
Plural	SE	1	4	20	10	20	17
	DE	23	19	36	15	36	16
Mass	SE	0	0	25	12	14	15
Future	SE	0	0	6	12	4	9

N.B.-Underlined items are those in which the Mean is equal to approximately
2 or more times the SD—i.e., items with a reasonable amount of variability.

upon English than deaf children of deaf parents, and hence the possibility that
once they have fixed upon a form, even if it is incorrect, it will be more
resistant to interference from ASL.

An interesting general note concerning this experiment is that although
standardized tests placed the deaf junior-high-school students' reading level
as fourth grade, they made errors in written English that the control group of
hearing fourth graders never made. Thus, although they were considered as
being able to read at a fourth grade level, they were not able to write at a
fourth grade level, and therefore a writing test is probably a better measure of
proficiency in Standard English than a reading comprehension test. (It is
interesting to note, also, that a fourth -grade reading level is significantly better
than average for deaf students of this age).

In conclusion, the written English of deaf adolescents is a valuable
indicator and diagnostic tool. Speaking ability is no measure of the deaf

adolescents' proficiency in English. Reading comprehension tests are only an indirect measure. It is the writing of deaf adolescents, and of all prelingually deaf and hearing-impaired persons, that can provide the evidence for the extent of their knowledge of English, and their progress in overcoming the true handicaps of deafness. It is not the inability to hear that causes the most persistent problems of prelingually deaf persons, but the enormous constraints that that inability puts upon the learning and use of the societal language. Until better ways are found of teaching prelingually deaf children to read and write grammatical English, they will remain illiterate or semi-literate in a society that is increasingly dependent upon literacy.

REFERENCES

Bonvillian, J. D., Charrow, V. R., & Nelson, K. E. Psycholinguistic and educational implications of deafness. *Human development,* 1973, *16,* 321–345.

Charrow, V. R. A Psycholinguistic Analysis of Deaf English. *Sign Language Studies,* 1975, *7,* 139–150.

Charrow, V. R., & Fletcher, J. D. English as the second language of deaf children. *Developmental Psychology,* 1974, *10,* 463–470.

Fischer, S. Verbs in American Sign Language. Salk Institute, San Diego, 1973, unpublished.

Mindel, E. D., & Vernon, M. *They grow in silence.* National Association of the Deaf, Silver Spring, Maryland, 1971.

Moores, D. An investigation of the psycholinguistic functioning of deaf adolescents. *Exceptional Child,* 1970, *36,* 645–652.

Stokoe, W. C., Jr. *The study of sign language.* National Association of the Deaf, Silver Spring, Md., 1971.

Stokoe, W. C. Jr. *Semiotics and human sign languages.* The Hague: Mouton, 1972.

Trybus, R. J., & Karchmer, M. A. School achievement scores of hearing impaired children: National data on achievement status and growth patterns. *American Annals of the Deaf,* Directory Issue, 1977.

12 Practical Aspects of Teaching Composition to Bidialectal Students: The Nairobi Method

Shirley A. Lewis

The Nairobi Method of teaching composition was developed (See Hoover, et. al., 1974) to meet the writing needs of the predominantly working class, bidialectal, black students of East Palo Alto (Nairobi) California. It has been used quite successfully with Nairobi students in a series of alternative school settings including Nairobi Community College, Nairobi High School and a variety of tutorial centers. These students range in age from seventeen to sixty. Most have had unsuccessful past school experience, many score low both on national and locally designed achievement and diagnostic tests, and some have had litle work or social experience outside the local community. Nearly all identify self-improvement as a goal which they expect to realize by participating in yet another educational endeavor.

The Nairobi Method is built upon a set of beliefs about the students for which it was designed. One such belief is that although some people seem to learn to write regardless or even in spite of teaching methods, most Nairobi students have not. Therefore these students must be taught a well designed, clearly structured method that has consistently proved successful in the past.

Another belief concerns the students' feelings. Since the majority of Nairobi students have had unpleasant and unsuccessful experiences in previous schools, they enter Nairobi feeling sensitive and skeptical about how they wil be perceived and treated by teachers—even at Nairobi. The Nairobi Method requires teachers to be competent in their fields of study and encouraging and supportive in their instructional approach.

These two beliefs form the basis of the Nairobi Method. The goal of the Nairobi method is to generate a community oriented, culturally appropriate learning atmosphere in which students will make academic advancement. The composition method consists of a series of steps designed to facilitate the accomplishment of this goal.

Provide Motivational Models.   The first step in the Nairobi Method is a motivational one. The teacher acquaints the students with oral and written examples of the communication styles of such black writers and orators as W. E. B. DuBois, Malcolm X, Martin Luther King and Amiri Baraka. These materials are used to counteract negative stereotyping by showing that black language is logical, intellectual, rich, and capable of expressing any kind of idea. They are also used to inspire and encourage students to believe that they too can—and should—write.

Value All Styles of Language.   Classifications of speech variety usage are discussed in early meetings of the composition classes. Students are told that there is variation in all languages. Two varieties of Black English are identified as Vernacular Black English (VBE) and Standard Black English (SBE).

VBE is described as that speech variety whose grammatical, phonological and lexical features mark the speaker as black and/or Southern and which in some cases is socially stigmatized (Lewis and Hoover, 1979).

Origins of VBE are discussed, including the influences of European and African languages. For example, some scholars (Johnson, 1930; Brooks, 1971, and Traugott, 1972) contend that the primary source of VBE is early English or other British Isle speech. According to this view, black Americans learned the English of indentured servants, foremen, and other members of the white, lower working class with whom they had close and consistent contact. Some features used currently by many blacks, such as uninflected third person singular verb forms (she go), durative "be" (he be working), and done as past marker (be done gone), are attributed to early British provincial speech.

The Africanization theory holds that VBE is primarily the result of West African influences. Some scholars (Dalby, 1972; Turner, 1969) have traced many lexical items common to Black English and to other varieties of English directly to Africa. Examples such as *jazz, hippy,* and *bad mouth* are cited as examples of African lexical influence.

Structural similarities of many West African languages to equivalent features of VBE are described to the students. Such VBE characteristics as uninflected verb stems (she go, yesterday he walk home), aspective tense (she been gone), absence of copula (she a girl), occur in many West African languages (Welmers, 1973; Dalby, 1971; Turner, 1969).

Other Black English characteristics such as inversion (using words with double meanings, such as bad for good, mean for nice) (Holt, 1972) and intonational conveyance of meaning such as ow'on no (I don't know); uh-huh (yes); huh-uh (no) (Dalby, 1972; Taylor, 1974) are related to African communication styles.

Standard Black English (SBE) is defined as having grammar that fits the pattern of standardized, textbook or educated English and phonology which is less like that of VBE and other forms of vernacular English but with intonational patterns that in some way identify the speaker as black (Taylor, 1971). SBE is identified as the preferred, most appropriate speech variety form for the classroom. The point is emphasized that written Standard Black English is identical to other written standard speech varieties, while spoken SBE often identifies the speaker as black. The teachers use themselves as model SBE speakers, and students often identify other SBE speakers including television announcers, movie stars, and fellow students.

The discussion of speech variety is concluded by stressing to students that all languages and all speech varieties are systematic, logical and capable of expressing any idea or concept. In the process, students gain an appreciation for all language including their own.

Get Involved Early. The next step is to immediately involve the students in the process of writing by having them write autobiographies. Students are asked to tell what the term autobiography means, to cite some autobiographical works and to name some people about whom they are interested. The students tell what they would like to know about these figures, and the teacher lists these topics on the board. The students are then asked to write about similar subject areas in their own autobiographies including why they came to college, what they hope to gain and what they intend to do upon completing their studies.

Participate As a Group. The teacher informs the class that an essential feature in the Nairobi Writing Method is group participation. The group approach is used to select topics, research data and prepare drafts. In addition, students read drafts out loud so that fellow students and the teacher may help them make revisions. The teacher and sometimes fellow students emphasize that the value of the participational approach lies in the ability of the group as a body to give and take constructive criticism, and all members of the class are encouraged to engage actively in this process.

Stress the Importance of "Discipline". Nairobi teachers maintain a structured classroom environment and encourage students to be self-disciplined. Students are expected to do all assignments and to have them ready by the required time. Teachers stress that participation is an essential part of the group approach to learning and that students have to attend class in order to participate. Those students who may be more "advanced" in certain areas and who might therefore be tempted to go elsewhere during class time, are utilized as co-teachers or group leaders to help other students and to otherwise assist the teacher.

Write the Paper in Class.   A great deal of the writing is done in the classroom. As this experience is new to many students, it is usually begun by the time of the second class meeting. The students select one of the topics that they plan to include in their autobiographies and write about it during one class period. They discuss their topics with each other in order to identify similarities in experience and goals and to plan how they might best organize their papers. During this phase, the teacher serves as a guide and motivator by walking around the room, putting students in contact with each other and talking with various individuals. At the end of the period, students are told to finish their essays at home and to be prepared to read them out loud at the next class meeting.

Read the Paper Aloud in Class.   On the first day that papers are to be read, the teacher sets the stage by reminding the students that each one will "perform" and that all members of the class, including the teacher, are to give each performer their total attention. At the start, many students express "shyness" or some other reluctance about reading the papers out loud, so the teacher either asks for a volunteer or makes arrangement in advance to assure that someone will start. Almost without fail, after the first essay is read, most students relax and seem to look forward to their turn. Usually these essays contain common themes such as getting a second start at schooling, improving personal conditions and serving as positive models for younger children. At the end of these readings, it is much easier to use the group participation approach.

Assess the Writing Strengths and Weaknesses of the Class As a Whole and of Individual Students.   The teacher makes an immediate assessment of all the papers, considering content, organization and mechanics, and whether and if so, how, referencing is used. The teacher makes up folders for each member of the class and comments on individual strengths and weaknesses. The teacher is careful to write out comments and to avoid such notations as "Awk," "Sp," or "!", since many students know that such abbreviations and symbols are in *some way* negative but do not understand what they actually mean. The use of such symbols, therefore, serves to inhibit that very spirit that the teacher hopes to generate in the class. The teacher does eventually acquaint the students with these and many other symbols of academic life but this activity is reserved for later in the course.

Analyze the Papers in Class. At the next class period, the teacher gives an overview of the strengths and weaknesses of the class as a whole. The teacher begins by complimenting all students on the content of their papers and for their willingness to share their experiences with the class. Next, the teacher describes the essential features of a composition. For example, all compositions require planning, including selecting a topic, deciding on the main points and assembling supportive materials. This material may be collected from the library, as is the case for research papers, or it may be gathered by assembling a set of known facts, as is the case with autobiographies. However it is acquired, the supportive data must be organized so that it has an introduction, a body and a conclusion.

The introduction is defined as doing for the paper just what an introduction does for a person, namely, telling in some fashion why the topic of a paper is important or interesting. The thesis sentence is described as the vehicle through which the introduction is made. Students are given examples of essays containing easily identifiable thesis and topic sentences, and they practice describing how and why they fit together.

The body of the paper is described as the section wherein the significant points of the thesis statement are developed. One way of organizing the body is to go from the general to the specific by developing the thesis statement through a series of paragraphs, each of which is introduced by its own topic sentence.

The conclusion is described as that part of the paper which ties up all of the loose ends. The teacher points out that this can be done either through summarizing what has gone on before, or by making a concluding statement of the importance or significance of what has been covered in the paper. This activity is identified as a restatement of the thesis sentence through the use of other words.

Coherence and unity are described as making sure that all the points being covered fit together both in sub-categories and as major topics. The class works on exercises requiring reorganization for unity and rewriting for coherence.

The teacher states that most classroom compositions require the use of standard English grammatical patterns. It is reemphasized that written standard English is a part of the students' culture, and examples may be reintroduced at this time. Vernacular Black English grammar is described again as a form of communication which is logical, systematic and meaningful, but the teacher also points out that it is not usually used as a written form in the classroom. VBE-SE contrasts are used to identify points of possible conflict.

A common grammatical difficulty for these students is SE-VBE verb treatment, especially as it pertains to copula deletion, subject-verb agreement, present-past tense differentiation and use of the participle as a regular past tense form. The teacher uses paradigm practice as a way of strengthening problem areas. Special attention is given to helping the students recognize their particular points of conflict so that they can begin early to double check their papers for individual problems.

The teacher points out to students that some spelling problems may be the result of speech variety differences while others may not. Regular spelling pattern drills (Hoover and Fabian, 1975) are introduced to the students and contrastive exercises based on Standard English-Vernacular Black English contrasts (Lewis and Hoover, 1973) are individually assigned. Students are assigned to rewrite their compositions utilizing the teacher's comments as well as those made by the group.

Repeat the Process.   The various steps involved in putting the paper together are practiced throughout the remainder of the course, both in the class itself and in the various supplementary language laboratories. These include exercises on thesis and topic sentences, specifics and generalization, and spelling, grammar and punctuation. Individual teacher conferences are held and special assignments are made by the teacher and peer instructors where such is deemed necessary and advisable.

Provide the Research.   The research paper receives the focus of attention for the rest of the course. It is pointed out that this form causes many students problems not because it is necessarily difficult, but because students either do not understand the research paper format or do not know how to go about locating the necessary documentation. In order to overcome these difficulties, the teacher provides students with the research material and concentrates on teaching them what to do with it.

Topics are assigned which concern community conditions, educational goals, the arts and other subjects whose interest factor has been corroborated by students and faculty members. The teacher provides the students with a set of research documents related to the assigned topics. Students read the research materials, make cursory outlines and start on the task of turning the research documents into a research paper.

Explain Documentation Procedures.   Footnoting is explained as using information which supports the paper and which shows that actual research has been done. Ways of using the direct quote, the paraphrase and summarization are explained, and students examine samples of various documentation styles. The teacher explains the differnce between documentation and plagiarism. The purposes of the bibliographic source card versus the information note card are explained and illustrated. The teacher then gives the students sets of note cards to use and students practice taking notes in class which are then reviwed by the teacher and other students.

The teacher explains several methods of footnoting and provides the students with style sheet references to use as guides. The Nairobi Method of footnoting involves giving the source and its bibliographic listing number. Students are then asked to use their research data to turn their outlines into first drafts.

Make Revisions.   The teacher stresses the point that students should not be ashamed or discouraged by their rough drafts even if it appears that some ideas are not clearly expressed or if other problems are apparent. The teacher suggests that proofreading be done in three stages: once for general flow, once for grammar and spelling and again for punctuation. Students check their work against a "Proofing Sheet" which categorizes specific points in areas of organization, style and mechanics. They also refer to a Standard English— Vernacular Black English guide sheet which contrasts some grammatical features which cause problems. Students are encouraged to use teacher and peer assistance as well as these proofing materials.

The teacher makes the point that factors such as neatness, use of headings, and completing assignments on time sometimes affect evaluations of students' papers and provides information on how to prepare for these details. The teacher informs the students that this information concerns academic survival skills rather than intellectual ones.

Prepare A Paper on One's Own.   The last assignment requires that students select topics and do the research on their own. The group paraticipational approach is still utilized to some degree in that students consult with their teacher and peers and may exchange actual research materials or give sources. They make progress reports, bring outlines and rough drafts to class for review and revision, but they complete the final copy including proof reading independently.

Serve as A Model for the Future.   Assessment of the final paper is made by the teacher (See Hoover and Politzer, this volume) and by the class as a whole if time permits. Those papers which have been successfully completed are duplicated and kept in the department files to be used as models in future courses. The overall result of this activity is that through the Nairobi Method, many bidialectal students have made significant progress in writing compositions in Standard English in acceptable college level form. The instructional method may differ from that of more traditional or mainstream schools, but the ultimate goal of proficiency in composition is the same. Learning through the group participational method has produced a number of confident, good writers who are writing and encouraging others to write successfully in the schools, on the job, and on behalf of the local community.

REFERENCES

Brooks, C. The English language of the south. In J. Williamson & V. Burke (Eds.), *A various language: Perspectives on American dialects.* New York: Holt, Rinehart and Winston, 1971.

Dalby, D. Black through white: Patterns of communication in Africa and the new world. In Wolfram, W. & Clarke, N. (Eds.), *Black-White Speech Relationships.* Washington, D.C.: Center for Applied Linguistics, 1971.

Dalby, D. The African element in American English. In Kochman, T. (Ed.), *Rappin' and Stylin' Out: Communication in Urban Black America.* Urbana, Ill.: University of Illinois Press, 1972.

Holt, G. Inversion in black communication. In Kochman, T. (Ed.) *Rappin' and Stylin' out: Communication in Urban Black America.* Urbana, Ill.: University of Illinois Press, 1972.

Hoover, M., & Fabian, M. *Patterns for reading.* Dubuque, Iowa: Kendall-Hunt Publishing Co., 1975.

Hoover, M., & Politzer, R. (this volume).

Hoover, M., Lewis, S., Daniels, S., Croft, J., & Randall, D. *The Nairobi handbook.* East Palo Alto, Cal.: Nairobi College Press, 1974.

Johnson, G. *Folk Culture on St. Helena Island, South Carolina.* Chapel Hill N.C.: University of North Carolina Press, 1930.

Lewis, S. A., & Hoover, M. R. *Teacher training workshops on Black English and Language arts teaching.* Center for Educational Research at Stanford, Stanford University, 1979.

Lewis, S., & Hoover, M. Vernacular Black English-standard Black English contrasts. Paper prepared for Nairobi college staff training session. East Palo Alto, California, 1973.

Taylor, O. Black English: What is it? In R. Williams & O. Taylor (Eds.), *Nine black writers on communication.* Bloomington: Indiana University Press 1974.

Taylor, O. Response to social dialects and the field of speech. In R. Shuy (Ed.), *Sociolinguistic theory: Materials and Practice.* Washington, D.C.: Center for Applied Linguistics, 1971, 13-20.

Traugott, E. Principles in the history of American English. *The Florida FL Reporter,* Spring/Fall 1972, Vol. 10, No. 1, 2.

Turner, L. *Africanisms in the Gullah dialect.* New York: Arno Press, 1969.

Welmers, W. *African language structures.* Berkeley, Cal.: University of California Press, 1973.

13

Bias in Composition Tests with Suggestions for a Culturally Appropriate Assessment Technique

Mary Rhodes Hoover
Robert L. Politzer

INTRODUCTION

The decline of composition skills at the college level has become an increasingly popular topic in recent years. Thirty percent of freshmen at Ohio State College were found unprepared for college writing; 70% of University of Texas freshmen must take basic English courses; the University of California at Berkeley has 50% of its freshmen in remedial courses, a 20% increase since 1968; and 75% of its freshmen failed the College Entrance Examination Board's English Composition Test. A professor at Cornell has alleged that current freshmen are "illiterate on the third grade level instead of the eighth grade level" (Fiske 1977).

Writing skills at levels other than college level are equally low and declining. Students in high schools rarely have above "minimal" writing skills; teen-agers' essay-writing is "more awkward" than it was in 1969, according to the National Assessment of Educational Progress; elementary school children are not even taught adequate reading skills, much less composition skills (Shiels 1975).

Reasons given for the decline in composition skills are many and varied. Some blame the influence of television; some point to open admissions programs which result in the existence of larger numbers of low-income students in colleges. Others place the blame on the entire "progressive education" movement which has permeated American education during the last 30 to 40 years (Fiske 1977).

More specifically, some scholars have blamed various subject matter specialists, e.g., structural linguists, who allegedly give priority to speech as opposed to writing; or composition teachers who themselves are untrained in writing skills and ignore the "process" of writing, concentrating instead on "creativity" in such genres as journal writing and "free" writing (Shiels 1975; Eley 1965).

Students who are bidialectal and whose dominant speech variety is quite different from "mainstream" or "network" American English appear to represent a disproportionate share of the low performance in composition and literacy skills; a 1975 U.S. Office of Education study shows the illiteracy rate among Blacks to be 42% as opposed to 8% for Whites (Gadway, 1976).

Various reasons can be given to account for the above-mentioned statistics. Perhaps the most general reason is simply that some students have been disadvantaged by an educational system which does not provide access to effective instruction (Van Geel 1974) and which has emphasized ineffective "innovations" at the expense of basic skills (Cassidy 1977).

Bidialectal speakers are also victimized by negative attitudes toward their speech and culture on the part of teachers (Politzer and Hoover 1977; Shuy and Fasold, 1973). The varying grammatical and spelling patterns of these students based on rule-governed influences from West African languages, Spanish, and other sources which show up in their written work (Wolfram and Whiteman 1971; Crystal 1972) are often misunderstood and resented by English teachers whose training emphasizes analysis of standard literary works (Shiels 1977).

The teacher's negative attitude toward the bidialectal student's mode of communication will of course affect the teacher's assessment of the student's communication skills. It is also likely to interfere with the student's ability to communicate effectively, because students are quick to sense the teacher's rejection of their speech styles. To quote a student from St. Mary's College in the Bay Area of California:

"The papers you write in class—their whole attitude toward them is bad. They say the structure is not too good and the style is bad, when you are writing from your heart... it's like they are rejecting your whole culture." (Moskowitz 1974)

There can be little doubt that a sense of rejection of one's own culture will put anyone under psychological pressure and interfere with effective communication.

Various "solutions" to the problem of decline of composition skills have been proposed. Some advocate a beefing up of elementary and high school curricula and requirements, e.g., the Bay Area Writing Project (Bader 1977; Maeroff 1977) and teaching of Standard English as a second dialect (Shiels

1977; Hoover, Lewis, et al. 1974; Lewis, this volume; Reed 1972). Some advocate more intensive college programs (Fiske 1977).

Part of the proposed remedy for the decline of communication skills is also a more rigorous composition testing program designed to screen out students with low performance (Shiels 1975). Within the general context of the new educational emphasis on "back to basics" ("Back to Basics" 1974), new composition assessment measures will undoubtedly assume an ever increasing importance.

The purpose of this paper will be to examine the problem of linguistic and cultural bias inherent in the assessment of composition skills, to deal briefly with the consequences of such bias and to suggest some ways to arrive at culturally appropriate assessment techniques.

Before giving some detailed examples concerning bias in composition tests, we would like to spell out some of the principles that have guided our discussion.

We view writing similarly to reading (see Hoover, Politzer and Taylor, 1975), as an act of communication. This view has several important implications: 1) The effectiveness of the composition should be judged *primarily* on the basis of whether the communicative intent of the writer has been transmitted to the reader; 2) Written communication involves at least two individuals, namely the reader as well as the writer, and communicative breakdown cannot necessarily be ascribed to the *writer alone;* 3) The *greater* the linguistic and cultural gap between the reader and writer, the more *likely* is the occurrence of communicative breakdown between the two.

We would also like to stress that the above principles should not be interpreted as leading to an "anything goes" approach and absolute permissiveness in the judging of composition. While we advocate effectiveness of communication as the primary standard, we also recognize that it is in the nature of written communication that, in most situations at least, standard speech and standard conventions of writing should be utilized. We do question, however, the insistence on a theoretical superstandard, especially if it is applied at the expense of communicative effectiveness. As far as the linguistic and cultural communication gap between a bidialectal vernacular speech dominant student and a middle class standard speech dominant teacher is concerned, we do not advocate nor do we believe that the problem can be solved by "accepting" the vernacular speech (especially in contexts in which its use is judged to be sociolinguistically inappropriate by bidialectal speakers as well as by the middle class teachers). But we do believe that the narrowing of a communication gap should be at least as much the teacher's responsibility as the student's and that the teacher has some obligation to know and to accept communicative styles characteristic of working class and minority cultures.

BIAS IN COMPOSITION TESTS

The format for standardized testing in composition consists either of multiple choice questions (testing the ability of the student to recognize problems in spelling, grammar, punctuation, sentence structure, logic and diction) or the actual writing of an essay. The following comments on these two types of assessments refer to the brochure on English Composition Test with Essay (ECT), published by the College Entrance Examination Board, and the ACT assessment (ACT) published by the American College Testing Program (Form 15A, 1973). These tests and test samples are used as representatives of typical composition assessment measures.

In the multiple choice format, most of the bias is found in the grammar, sentence structure, diction and style sections. It consists primarily of an emphasis on "superstandard" English (Fasold 1972) to the detriment of the a simple standard which would be more natural and familiar to bidialectal speakers. For example, a sentence structure item based on "superstandard" expectations involve the "correct" placement of clauses: "What it is about *from its title* seems clear" (ACT #49) instead of the expected "What it is about seems clear *from its title.*"

So-called "diction" or choice of words is probably the aspect of the tests most subject to bias. As Humpty Dumpty said in *Alice in Wonderland,* "When I use a word, it means just what I choose it to mean, neither more nor less." When questioned as to whether one can make words mean many different things, Humpty replied, "The question is, which is to be Master— that's all." As far as the tests are concerned, the master is evidently the "superstandard" which has decreed that multisyllabic words are more "correct" and "logical" than more simple expressions. For example, in the ACT, "pioneered" is preferred to "started up by"; "reach my destination" to "get there" (ACT #39); and "prove to be" to "come out to be" (ACT #55).

Cliches, proverbial usage, and overused figurative language are also generally considered as "incorrect" yet the communicative style of many minority cultures often utilizes proverbial usage and a great deal of "unusual" metaphor (Daniel, 1972). Item 42 of the ACT asks the student to decide whether the underlined portion of "my thoughts were *irresistibly sucked* toward the moment when..." should remain or be replaced by *pulled helplessly, uncontrollably drawn* (the "correct" answer), or *propelled mercilessly.* The correct answer puts a premium on using the expected rather than the unexpected metaphor which may be more highly valued in non-conventional, non-middle class rhetoric.

For the first time since 1971 the College Entrance Examination Board is now using an essay writing section. From the brochure describing the instrument, it appears that the bias in this assessment is likely to be in the scoring process. The authors propose that twenty minute essays be scored by a group of high school and college English teachers. It has been established that many teachers overreact against spelling and grammatical patterns associated with the speech of minority groups. Yet no mention is made of involving black or other bidialectal judges, nor does there seem to be any plan to instruct the judges in characteristics of these vernacular languages so that they at least understand that these varieties are rule-governed.

It has been stated that "there is no objective standard by which students' writing can be measured " (Fiske 1977). However, the decision to score the compositions on a holistic basis (read for the total impression they make upon a reader) will undoubtedly contribute even further to biasing the raters' judgments. Though most of the "subskills" of composition—diction, grammar, sentence structure, style, logic—are subject to bias within themselves, they do constitute an attempt toward a more objective approach to scoring. The use of specific subskills is designed to guard against the possibility that an error in one, perhaps relatively less important subskill (e.g., punctuation or grammar) should obscure the fact that other important goals of the essay (e.g., effective communication) have been achieved. Since bidialectal students are more likely than others not to live up to standard norms in areas like grammar, punctuation, etc., there is little doubt that they more than others will become victims of biases created by holistic scoring procedures. We would therefore suggest that objective scoring procedures which are not holistic but which break down scoring into specific rating scales (Carroll, 1974) should be used in order to minimize bias effects prejudicial to students from minority groups.

Whether the scoring is holistic or based on subskills, categories like "logic" or "style" will undoubtedly be used in the evaluation process. As far as "logic" is concerned, we should guard against confusing logic with the use of certain connectives (e.g., see ACT #17, which prefers "however" to "furthermore"). As Labov (Labov 1969) has pointed out, transitional phases of the type "moreover," "on the other hand," "as aforementioned," have a certain prestige in certain types of "educated" prose style but little if any relation to the logical presentation of an argument. Moreover, what is considered good "style" varies greatly across cultures, and is therefore highly subject to bias. The ECT brochure states that style includes the use of rhythm, rhyme, metaphor and use of grammar for effect, e.g., use of noun clauses to qualify main statements. Black rhetorical models such as Malcolm X, Martin Luther King and Stokely Carmichael (Kwame Ture) use stylistic devices particular to Black culture. Though these individuals have made their impact primarily through the oral language channel, the written counterpart of their speeches has created an important written genre. In fact, were one to do an ethnography of conposition (Hymes 1972), i.e., an examination of the uses of writing in the black community, one would probably find the written version of speeches of very high popularity, perhaps surpassed only by the newspaper, the political pamphlet and the autobiography.

To give an example of black rhetoric: Malcolm X's style (Illo 1972) is characterized by the use of chiasmus, i.e., use of two opposing forces as in the "house Negro vs. the field Negro" (Breitman 1966); parallelisms, e.g., "John knows it, Stokely knows it, you know it"; analogies, e.g., the wolf and the sheep (Breitman 1966); lists of direct and forceful verbs, e.g., "We've been colonized, enslaved, lynched, exploited..."; and proverbs and rhymes for emphasis and introduction to a topic, e.g., "It's time to stop acting and start facting" (Breitman 1966). Short, direct sentences are often used for effect. Many of these rhetorical devices may often not be recognized as acceptable by English teachers influenced by traditional notions of "good style" (Shiels 1975). Many English teachers seem to disdain short sentences, although sentence length is not an indication of complexity of thought (Botel 1975). The home-spun example/analogy greatly valued in black speech is looked down upon and not valued as highly as a condensed metaphor. Parallelism and use of a series of nearly synonymous words are likely to be found "redundant," and redundancy as a stylistic device has probably little prestige in the thinking of traditional English teachers.

RESULTS OF COMPOSITION TESTING

The new composition assessment instruments, standardized and local, at the college level, will undoubtedly be used to screen out minorities and those whose speech is farthest away from the "superstandard" requirements for written composition in much the same way that reading tests are used (Hoover, Politzer, and Taylor 1975; Wolfram 1976). In fact, it is alleged that the tests have already been used for this purpose (Minton 1976; "Brooklyn College," 1977).

The most pernicious aspect of the screening-out procedure is the "blame the victim" mentality accompanying it. The fact is that many students, but particularly those in low income areas, are not provided with critical organized writing assignments in the elementary and senior high schools. They are, in fact, encouraged to ignore mechanics and write "creatively" and with "flow" (Macrorie 1970). Then they are given composition tests which reveal their lack of skill in the mechanics of writing. The tests become, then, measures used to screen out working class students and effectively battle affirmative action guidelines, truly a "Catch 22" state of affairs!

Not only will working class students be screened out through the testing process, but those already admitted will be increasingly forced to take "exit" composition assessments which often result in their being ousted from school or forced to take remedial classes which are not designed for their needs. San

Francisco State University and Brooklyn College are among the schools now requiring exit tests. The use of tests as screening out devices will result in less affirmative action and less minority access to institutions. As Flighter says (in Fiske 1977), "The subjective nature of the scoring of these tests will contribute to the screening out process, introducing one more obstacle in the path of social mobility."

TOWARD CULTURALLY FAIR ASSESSMENT
AND TEACHING TECHNIQUES

At Nairobi College in East Palo Alto, California, founded because of the problems inherent in White institutions' attempts to absorb large numbers of Black, Chicano, and other minority students, a number of devices were used to appropriately assess the reading, composition and other language arts skills of predominantly bidialectal adults who had been deprived of adequate instruction in literacy in the lower schools. The assessment was tied to an instructional program—the Nairobi Method—which had demonstrated its effectiveness (Coombs 1973).

The Nairobi Method, described in more detail elsewhere (Lewis, this volume; Hoover, Lewis, et al. 1973), uses group participational learning style and places an emphasis on high expectations as the model for teaching composition and other language arts skills.

As part of this emphasis on competence and high expectations, students are encouraged to use Black Standard English (Taylor 1971) as a goal. Black Standard English follows the same grammatical rules as any other standard variety of American English, but is characterized by the occasional use of Black lexical items, proverbs, and certain features of Black pronunciation. Students are also exposed to the logic and rule-governed nature of Vernacular Black English. However, it is explained to the students that those who recommend only an emphasis on the vernacular variety of Black English are aware neither of the value placed in Black culture on mastering many skills (as seen in the trickster figure so characteristic of African-American folklore, c.f., Brown 1973), nor of the fact that within Black language itself there are many varieties.

The assessment process is directly connected to the method. The research paper is stressed as the model in the composition class. Therefore, emphasis is placed on assessing the ability to read, analyze and paraphrase research accurately. In other words, assessment is based on reading as well as on composition skill.

Reading skill is assessed by measuring the students' ability to analyze English spelling patterns and to show that they understand what they have read. Students are first given a paragraph to read which contains most of the spelling patterns of English. The oral reading of this paragraph gives a diagnostic picture of the students' "decoding" ability and indicates the spelling patterns which they need to practice reading in order to achieve fluency in reading.

Students' ability to comprehend is tested by having them answer a series of questions based on the paragraph which they orally read for assessment of decoding skills. Students are then asked to utilize the material in the paragraph used for reading in the writing of a short composition in which materials from the paragraph are quoted as research evidence. The written composition gives, therefore, an indication of the student's level of skill in regards to grammar, spelling, punctuation, and ability to paraphrase.

This method of assessing comprehension has been chosen because answering recall type questions following the reading of a short paragraph seems to be a relatively bias-free method of assessing reading comprehension.

Papers are graded on three levels—content, mechanics (grammar, spelling, punctuation, footnote format), and organization. Two grades are given in the grammar section—one for vernacular competence, another for Standard Black English competence. The student may be placed, on the basis of these measures, in one or more of three language arts laboratories (word analysis, grammar, vocabulary and comprehension) and/or a composition class.

RECOMMENDATIONS

Those who are in positions to influence policy in education—professors, teachers, researchers, government officials—must assume the burden of past errors in education and become advocates of those who have consistently been disadvantaged from the beginning of our education system (Coontz 1974). We have allowed tests to play a major role in channeling students into mentally retarded classes, and in screening out minorities and other working class people from progress in the educational system. We have allowed instruction in schools to become so watered-down as to constitute "educational malpractice" ("Education: the Illiteracy Problem," 1977). If we continue to maintain a liberal, bemused ivory tower attitude toward literacy, the new "back to basics" movement concerning literacy will undoubtedly "swing to the right" and erase all of the effects of the civil rights movement in the area of affirmative action and attention to cultural pluralism in the classroom, in much the same way that progressive education made a "swing to the left," often endorsing innovation and the "affective domain" at the expense of basic skills and literacy (Mathews 1966).

We would, therefore, like to make the following recommendations: Objective or normed tests of composition should not be used—at least not until a great deal more work is done concerning their reliability, validity and freedom from cultural bias. Reading and writing instruction in the lower schools must receive much greater emphasis. In judging compositions a simple standard rather than a superstandard style should become our guideline.

We particularly endorse the elimination of composition tests at the college level until such time as the lower schools have had time to institute the teaching of the process of composition, and until stringent measures are taken to assure that the tests are scored objectively by judges trained in the diversity of rhetorical styles in various cultures and the characteristics and rule-governed nature of vernacular language varieties. The purpose of the latter recommendation is *not* necessarily to pave the way toward accepting vernacular as standard, but to bring about an improvement of the general negative attitude toward the competence of writers who use vernacular grammatical patterns. Furthermore, representatives of various cultures should also be included among the teams called up to judge the quality of compositions.

Improving instruction in reading and in the process of writing for the working class student is a longer range goal, but it can be accomplished. There is a burgeoning literature on schools across the country where inner-city children are achieving (Weber 1970; Thomas 1976; Hoover, 1978a) because of greater emphasis on such factors as time spent on reading, the involvement of a competent skills-oriented administrator, and the use of teaching techniques appropriate to minority learning styles.

Encouraging teachers to accept a standard rather than a superstandard variety in composition may be difficult. Although our approaches to teaching composition have become increasingly unstructured, our books concerning usage have remained relatively unchanged, emphasizing "diction" which allows for no cultural differences, and sentence structure so ornate that even editors must keep several guides to usage at hand.

Teacher training programs could be of great assistance in implementing our recommendations concerning the abandoning of a "superstandard" norm and the use of teaching techniques appropriate for minority students. Some universities offer programs focusing on the needs of bidialectal/bilingual students and their learning styles and language characteristics (University of California at Berkeley; Stanford University; University of Pennsylvania). Other universities are developing programs specifically geared to teaching the process of composition to future teachers (University of Pennsylvania; University of Iowa). Research institutions can also assist with the implementation of our recommendations by engaging in research supportive of working class students' competence and working class communities' expectations that schools will provide literacy for their children (Hoover 1978b). As Don L. Lee, poet and founder of the Institute for Positive Education and the Third World Press in Chicago has stated, "In the 1970's it is not a luxury to be able to read and write, it is a requirement." (Lee 1974).

REFERENCES

Bader, L. "High School Graduation Standards to be Stiffened by New York City." *New York Times,* April 25, 1977, pp. 1, 34.

"Back to Basics in the Schools." *Newsweek,* Oct. 21, 1974, pp. 87–95.

Botel, M. "A Syntactic Complexity Formula." *Assessment Problems in Reading.* Ed. by W. MacGinitie, 1975.

Breitman, G. *Malcolm X Speaks.* New York: Grove Press, 1966.

"Brooklyn College Gives Disputed English Test." *New York Times,* Jan 1, 1977, p. 49.

Brown S. "Backgrounds of Folklore in Negro Literature. *Mother Wit from the Laughing Barrel,* ed. by A. Dundes, 1973.

Carroll, J. "Defining Language Comprehension." *Language Comprehension and the Acquisition of Knowledge.* Ed. by Carroll and Freedle. New York: John Wiley, 1974.

Cassidy, J. "Innovations . . . Don't Help Children Learn Better." *National Enquirer,* Mar. 8, 1977, p. 3.

Coombs, O. "Nairobi College," *Change,* Vol. 5, No. 3 (April, 1973), pp. 38–45.

Coontz, S. "The Failure of American Education," *International Socialist Review,* Vol. 35, No. 7 (July-August, 1974), pp. 7–42.

Crystal, D. "Dialect Mixture and Sorting Out the Concept of Freshman English Remediation." *Florida FL Reporter.* Spring/Fall 1972, pp. 43–46.

Daniel, J. *Toward an Ethnography of Afro-American "Proverbial Usage,"* Black Lines V$_2$, 2 (Winter 1972), 3–12.

"Education: The Illiteracy Problem." New York: *Guardian,* Mar. 23, 1977, p. 2.

Eley, E. "English Programs for Terminal Students." *Research and Development of English Programs in Jr. College.* Ed. by J. Archer, W. Ferrell. Champaign, Ill.: NCTE, 1965.

Fasold, R. "Sloppy Speech in Standard English." Paper read at the Fourth Triennial Conference on Symbolic Processes. Washington, D.C., April 27, 1972.

Fiske, E. "City University—a Remedial-Writing Leader." *New York Times,* April 4, 1977, pp. 1, 51.

Fiske, E. "Study Finds Prestigious Colleges Worth Added Costs." *New York Times,* April 6, 1977, p. B4.

Fiske, E. "Colleges are Bolstering Courses Designed to Improve Writing Ability." *New York Times,* February 7, 1977, p. 1.

Gadway, C. "Functional Literacy Basic Reading Performance." Denver, Colorado: National Assessment of Educational Progress, 1976.

Hoover, M. "Characteristics of Black Schools at Grade Level: A Description." *Reading Teacher,* April 1978a, Vol. 31, No. 7.

Hoover, M. "Community Attitudes toward Black English." *Language in Society,* April 1978b. Vol. 7.

Hoover, M., Lewis, S., *et al. Nairobi Writing Handbook.* San Francisco: Julian Richardson, 1973.

Hoover, M., Politzer, R. and Taylor, O. "Bias in Achievement and Diagnostic Reading Tests: A Linguistically Oriented View," Paper presented at NIE Conference on Test Bias, Annapolis, December, 1975.

Hymes, D. "Toward Ethnographies of Communication: The Analysis of Communicative Events." *Language and Social Context,* ed. by P. Giglioli. Baltimore, Md.: Penguin Books, 1972.

Illo, J. "The Rhetoric of Malcolm X." *Language Communication and Rhetoric in Black America.* Ed. by A. Smith. New York: Harper & Row, 1972.

Labov, W. "The Logic of Nonstandard English," in G. Alatis, ed. Monograph Series in Languages and Linguistics. *20th Annual Round Table.* Washington, D.C.: Georgetown University Press, 1969.

Lee, Don L. *Plan to Planet.* Chicago, Ill.: Third World Press, 1974.

Macrorie, K. *Uptaught.* New York: Hayden Book Co., 1970.

Maeroff, G. "California Project Spurs Teachers to Improve Methods With the Objective of Better Writing in High Schools." *New York Times,* February 8, 1977, p. 16.

Mathews, M. *Teaching to Read Historically Considered.* Chicago, Illinois: University of Chicago Press, 1966.

Minton, T. "Getting into College: What Counts at Cornell." *New York Times,* May 10, 1976.

Moskowitz, R. "UC Toughens its English Requirements." *San Francisco Chronicle,* May 1974.

Politzer, R. and Hoover, M. *Attitudes Toward Black English Speech Varieties and Black Pupils' Achievement.* Stanford, Ca.: Stanford Center for Research and Development in Teaching, 1977.

Reed, C. E. "Adopting TESOL Approaches to the Teaching of Written Standard English as a Second Dialect to Speakers of American Black English Vernacular." Washington, D.C., TESOL Convention, 1972.

Sheils, M. "Why Johnny Can't Write." *Newsweek,* December 8, 1975, pp. 58-65.

Shuy, R. and Fasold, R. *Language Attitudes: Current Trends and Prospects.* Washington, D.C.: Georgetown University Press, 1973.

Taylor, O. "Response to Social Dialects and the Field of Speech." *Sociolinguistics: A cross Disciplinary Perspective.* Washington, D.C.: Center for Applied Linguistics, 1971.

Thomas, J. "Administration of a Program Where Bidialectal Children Read at Grade Level." Paper presented at International Reading Association conference, Anaheim, Cal: 1976.

Van Geel, T. "The Right to be Taught Standard English: Exploring the Implications of Lau v. Nichols for Black Americans." *Syracuse Law Review.* Vol. 25: 863, 1974.

Weber, G. *Inner City Children Can Learn to Read.* Washington, D.C.: Council for Basic Education, 1970.

Wolfram, W. "Levels of Sociolinguistic Bias in Testing." *Black English: A Seminar.* Ed. by Harrison and Trabasso. New York: John Wiley, 1976.

Wolfram, W. and Whiteman, M. "The role of Dialect Interference in Composition." Florida *FL Reporter,* Fall 1971, Vol. 9, No. 2.

Author Index

Numbers in *italics* indicate pages with complete bibliographic information.

Subject Index